MCSE Exam Notes™:
Proxy Server 2

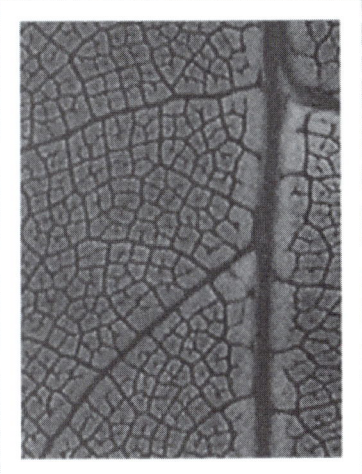

Scott Richardson
Todd Lammle

NETWORK PRESS®
SYBEX

Associate Publisher: Guy Hart-Davis
Contracts and Licensing Manager: Kristine Plachy
Acquisitions & Developmental Editor: Neil Edde
Editor: Jane Ross
Project Editor: Raquel Baker
Technical Editor: Donald Fuller
Book Designer: Bill Gibson
Graphic Illustrator: Tony Jonick
Desktop Publisher: Franz Baumhackl
Production Coordinator: Susan Berge
Indexer: Nancy Guenther
Cover Designer: Archer Design
Cover Illustrator/Photographer: FPG International

Screen reproductions produced with Collage Complete.
Collage Complete is a trademark of Inner Media Inc.
SYBEX, Network Press, and the Network Press logo are registered trademarks of SYBEX Inc.
Exam Notes is a trademark of SYBEX Inc.

Library of Congress Card Number: 98-87585
ISBN: 0-7821-2304-X

Manufactured in the United States of America

10 9 8 7 6 5 4 3 2 1

November 1, 1997

Dear SYBEX Customer:

Microsoft is pleased to inform you that SYBEX is a participant in the Microsoft® Independent Courseware Vendor (ICV) program. Microsoft ICVs design, develop, and market self-paced courseware, books, and other products that support Microsoft software and the Microsoft Certified Professional (MCP) program.

To be accepted into the Microsoft ICV program, an ICV must meet set criteria. In addition, Microsoft reviews and approves each ICV training product before permission is granted to use the Microsoft Certified Professional Approved Study Guide logo on that product. This logo assures the consumer that the product has passed the following Microsoft standards:

- The course contains accurate product information.
- The course includes labs and activities during which the student can apply knowledge and skills learned from the course.
- The course teaches skills that help prepare the student to take corresponding MCP exams.

Microsoft ICVs continually develop and release new MCP Approved Study Guides. To prepare for a particular Microsoft certification exam, a student may choose one or more single, self-paced training courses or a series of training courses.

You will be pleased with the quality and effectiveness of the MCP Approved Study Guides available from SYBEX.

Sincerely,

Holly Heath
ICV Account Manager
Microsoft Training & Certification

MICROSOFT INDEPENDENT COURSEWARE VENDOR PROGRAM

For my father.
I guess I'm following
in your footsteps after all.
—Scott Richardson

Acknowledgments

First of all, I need to thank all of the people at Sybex who helped mold this book into a finished product. Thanks to Jane Ross for all your help. Thanks to Raquel Baker for all your patience and understanding. Thanks to Don Fuller for catching my technical goofs. Thanks to the production folks Susan Berge, Franz Baumhackl, and Bill Gibson. And thanks to Neil Edde for getting me started.

I would like to thank Todd Lammle for giving me a chance to work on this project, and for all his help.

I also need to thank Don Porter for being my "proxy" author when I hurt my wrist and couldn't type, and for being, now and forever, the wearer of the "blue robe." And lastly, thanks to Nadeem for being my Amiga buddy way back when (Stunt Car Racer rules!)

Table of Contents

Introduction

If you've purchased this book, you are probably chasing one of the Microsoft professional certifications: MCP, MCSE, or MCT. All of these are great goals, and they are also great career builders. Glance through any newspaper and you'll find employment opportunities for people with these certifications—these ads are there because finding qualified employees is a challenge in today's market. The certification means you know something about the product, but more importantly, it means you have the ability, determination, and focus to learn—the greatest skill any employee can have!

You've probably also heard all the rumors about how hard the Microsoft tests are—believe us, the rumors are true! Microsoft has designed a series of exams that truly test your knowledge of their products. Each test not only covers the materials presented in a particular class, it also covers the prerequisite knowledge for that course. This means two things for you—that first test can be a real hurdle and each test *should* get easier since you've studied the basics over and over.

This book has been developed in alliance with the Microsoft Corporation to give you the knowledge and skills you need to prepare for one of the key exams of the MCSE certification program: Implementing and Supporting Microsoft Proxy Server 2.0 (Exam 70-088). Reviewed and approved by Microsoft, this book provides a solid introduction to Microsoft networking technologies and will help you on your way to MCSE certification.

Is This Book for You?

The MCSE Exam Notes books were designed to be succinct, portable exam review guides that can be used either in conjunction with a more complete study program (book, CBT courseware, classroom/lab environment) or as an exam review for those who don't feel the need for more extensive test preparation. It isn't our goal to "give the answers away," but rather to identify those topics on which you can expect to be tested and to provide sufficient coverage of these topics.

Perhaps you've been working with Microsoft networking technologies for years now. The thought of paying lots of money for a specialized

MCSE exam preparation course probably doesn't sound too appealing. What can they teach you that you don't already know, right? Be careful, though. Many experienced network administrators have walked confidently into test centers only to walk sheepishly out of them after failing an MCSE exam. As they discovered, there's the Microsoft of the real world and the Microsoft of the MCSE exams. It's our goal with these Exam Notes books to show you where the two converge and where they diverge. After you've finished reading through this book, you should have a clear idea of how your understanding of the technologies involved matches up with the expectations of the MCSE test makers in Redmond.

Or perhaps you're relatively new to the world of Microsoft networking, drawn to it by the promise of challenging work and higher salaries. You've just waded through an 800-page MCSE study guide or taken a class at a local training center. Lots of information to keep track of, isn't it? Well, by organizing the Exam Notes books according to the Microsoft exam objectives, and by breaking up the information into concise manageable pieces, we've created what we think is the handiest exam review guide available. Throw it in your briefcase and carry it to work with you. As you read through the book, you'll be able to identify quickly those areas you know best and those that require more in-depth review.

NOTE The goal of the Exam Notes series is to help MCSE candidates familiarize themselves with the subjects on which they can expect to be tested in the MCSE exams. For complete, in-depth coverage of the technologies and topics involved, we recommend the MCSE Study Guide series from Sybex.

How Is This Book Organized?

As mentioned above, this book is organized according to the official exam objectives list prepared by Microsoft for the Implementing and Supporting Microsoft Proxy Server 2.0 exam. The chapters correspond to the broad objectives groupings, such as Planning, Installation, and Setting Up and Managing Resource Access. These groupings are also reflected in the organization of the MCSE exams themselves.

Within each chapter, the individual exam objectives are addressed in turn. And in turn, the objectives sections are further divided according to the type of information presented.

Critical Information

This section presents the greatest level of detail on information that is relevant to the objective. This is the place to start if you're unfamiliar with or uncertain about the technical issues related to the objective.

Necessary Procedures

Here you'll find instructions for procedures that require a lab computer to be completed. From installing operating systems to modifying configuration defaults, the information in these sections addresses the hands-on requirements for the MCSE exams.

NOTE Not every objective has procedures associated with it. For such objectives, the Necessary Procedures section has been left out.

Exam Essentials

In this section, we've put together a concise list of the most crucial topics that you'll need to comprehend fully prior to taking the MCSE exam. This section can help you identify those topics that might require more study on your part.

Key Terms and Concepts

Here we've compiled a mini-glossary of the most important terms and concepts related to the specific objective. You'll understand what all those technical words mean within the context of the related subject matter.

Sample Questions

For each objective, we've included a selection of questions similar to those you'll encounter on the actual MCSE exam. Answers and explanations are provided so you can gain some insight into the test-taking process.

NOTE For a more comprehensive collection of exam review questions, check out the MCSE Test Success series, also published by Sybex.

How Do You Become an MCSE?

Attaining Microsoft Certified Systems Engineer (MCSE) status is a challenge. The exams cover a wide range of topics and require dedicated study and expertise. This is, however, why the MCSE certificate is so valuable. If achieving the MCSE were too easy, the market would be quickly flooded by MCSEs and the certification would become meaningless. Microsoft, keenly aware of this fact, has taken steps to ensure that the certification means its holder is truly knowledgeable and skilled.

To become an MCSE, you must pass four core requirements and two electives. Most people select the following exam combination for the MCSE core requirements for the most current track:

Client Requirement

70-073: Implementing and Supporting Windows NT Workstation 4.0

or

70-064: Implementing and Supporting Microsoft® Windows 95®

or

70-098: Implementing and Supporting Microsoft Windows 98

Networking Requirement

70-058: Networking Essentials

Windows NT Server 4.0 Requirement

70-067: Implementing and Supporting Windows NT Server 4.0

Windows NT Server 4.0 in the Enterprise Requirement

70-068: Implementing and Supporting Windows NT Server 4.0 in the Enterprise

Electives

Some of the more popular electives include:

70-059: Internetworking Microsoft TCP/IP on Microsoft Windows NT 4.0

70-087: Implementing and Supporting Microsoft Internet Information Server 4.0

70-081: Implementing and Supporting Microsoft Exchange Server 5.5

70-026: System Administration for Microsoft SQL Server 6.5

70-027: Implementing a Database Design on Microsoft SQL Server 6.5

70-088: Implementing and Supporting Microsoft Proxy Server 2.0

70-079: Implementing and Supporting Microsoft Internet Explorer 4.0 by Using the Internet Explorer Administration Kit

---

TIP This book is a part of a series of MCSE Exam Notes books, published by Network Press (Sybex), that covers four core requirements and your choice of several electives—the entire MCSE track!

Where Do You Take the Exams?

You may take the exams at any one of more than 800 Sylvan Prometric Authorized Testing Centers around the world or through Virtual University Enterprises (VUE).

For the location of a Sylvan testing center near you, call (800) 755-EXAM (755-3926). Outside the United States and Canada, contact your local Sylvan Prometric Registration Center. You can also register for an exam with Sylvan Prometric via the Internet. The Sylvan site can be reached through the Microsoft Training and Certification site or at: http://www.slspro.com/msreg/microsoft.asp.

To register for an exam through VUE, call 888-837-8616 (North America only) or visit their Web site at http://www.vue.com/ms/.

NOTE At the time of writing, the exams are $100 each.

When you schedule the exam, you'll be provided with instructions regarding appointment and cancellation procedures, ID requirements, and information about the testing center location.

What Does the Proxy Server 2.0 Exam Measure?

Microsoft has done an excellent job of creating a mix of questions that measure all of the topics associated with the Proxy Server 2.0 exam objectives. Although some objectives such as caching, arrays, and security are emphasized more heavily than others, you cannot afford to ignore the other objectives. The one question you miss because you didn't study that particular topic might be the difference between passing and failing. That said, passing and even doing well on the Proxy Server 2.0 exam is certainly possible if you are thoroughly prepared.

Microsoft lists a number of recommended prerequisites for the Proxy Server 2.0 Exam, and with good reason. Your knowledge of Windows NT Server, Internet Information Server (IIS), TCP/IP, and topics covered on the Networking Essentials exam will establish a foundation that will make understanding the issues associated with Proxy Server much easier. Your understanding of issues such as security, client configuration, optimization, and troubleshooting will all be affected by your knowledge of these subjects.

If you are choosing to take the Proxy Server exam as one of your two electives for your MCSE certification, you probably should take it last after taking all of the core exams and the TCP/IP exam as your other elective.

How Does Microsoft Develop the Exam Questions?

Microsoft's exam development process consists of eight mandatory phases. The process takes an average of seven months and contains more than 150 specific steps. The phases of Microsoft Certified Professional exam development are listed here.

Phase 1: Job Analysis
Phase 1 is an analysis of all the tasks that make up the specific job function based on tasks performed by people who are currently performing

the job function. This phase also identifies the knowledge, skills, and abilities that relate specifically to the certification for that performance area.

Phase 2: Objective Domain Definition

The results of the job analysis provide the framework used to develop exam objectives. The development of objectives involves translating the job function tasks into a comprehensive set of more specific and measurable knowledge, skills, and abilities. The resulting list of objectives, or the objective domain, is the basis for the development of both the certification exams and the training materials.

NOTE The outline of all Exam Notes books is based upon the official exam objectives lists published by Microsoft. Objectives are subject to change without notification. We advise that you check the Microsoft Training and Certification Web site (www.microsoft.com\train_cert\) for the most current objectives list.

Phase 3: Blueprint Survey

The final objective domain is transformed into a blueprint survey in which contributors—technology professionals who are performing the applicable job function—are asked to rate each objective. Based on the contributors' input, the objectives are prioritized and weighted. The actual exam items are written according to the prioritized objectives. The blueprint survey phase helps determine which objectives to measure, as well as the appropriate number and types of items to include on the exam.

Phase 4: Item Development

A pool of items is developed to measure the blueprinted objective domain. The number and types of items to be written are based on the results of the blueprint survey. During this phase, items are reviewed and revised to ensure that they are:

- Technically accurate

- Clear, unambiguous, and plausible

- Not biased toward any population, subgroup, or culture

- Not misleading or tricky

- Testing at the correct level of Bloom's Taxonomy

- Testing for useful knowledge, not obscure or trivial facts

Items that meet these criteria are included in the initial item pool.

Phase 5: Alpha Review and Item Revision

During this phase, a panel of technical and job function experts reviews each item for technical accuracy, then answers each item, reaching consensus on all technical issues. Once the items have been verified as technically accurate, they are edited to ensure that they are expressed in the clearest language possible.

Phase 6: Beta Exam

The reviewed and edited items are collected into a beta exam pool. During the beta exam, each participant has the opportunity to respond to all the items in this beta exam pool. Based on the responses of all beta participants, Microsoft performs a statistical analysis to verify the validity of the exam items and to determine which items will be used in the certification exam. Once the analysis has been completed, the items are distributed into multiple parallel forms, or versions, of the final certification exam.

Phase 7: Item Selection and Cut-Score Setting

The results of the beta exam are analyzed to determine which items should be included in the certification exam based on many factors, including item difficulty and relevance. Generally, the desired items are answered correctly by 25 percent to 90 percent of the beta exam candidates. This helps ensure that the exam consists of a variety of difficulty levels, from somewhat easy to extremely difficult.

Also during this phase, a panel of job function experts determines the cut score (minimum passing score) for the exam. The cut score differs from exam to exam because it is based on an item-by-item determination of the percentage of candidates who would be expected to answer the item correctly. The experts determine the cut score in a group session to increase the reliability.

Phase 8: Live Exam

Once all the other phases are complete, the exam is ready. Microsoft Certified Professional exams are administered by Sylvan Prometric.

Tips for Taking Your Proxy 2.0 Exam

Here are some general tips for taking your exam successfully:

- Arrive early at the exam center so you can relax and review your study materials, particularly tables and lists of exam-related information.

- Read the questions carefully. Don't be tempted to jump to an early conclusion. Make sure you know *exactly* what the question is asking.

- Don't leave any unanswered questions. They count against you.

- When answering multiple-choice questions you're not sure about, use a process of elimination to get rid of the obviously incorrect questions first. This will improve your odds if you need to make an educated guess.

- Because the hard questions will eat up the most time, save them for last. You can move forward and backward through the exam.

- This test has many exhibits (pictures). It can be difficult, if not impossible, to view both the questions and the exhibit simulation on 14- and 15-inch screens usually found at the testing centers. Call around to each center and see if they have 17-inch monitors available. If they don't, perhaps you can arrange to bring in your own. Failing this, some have found it useful to quickly draw the diagram on the scratch paper provided by the testing center and use the monitor to view just the question.

- Many participants run out of time before they are able to complete the test. If you are unsure of the answer to a question, you may want to choose one of the answers, mark the question, and go on—an unanswered question does not help you. Once your time is up, you cannot go on to another question. However, you can remain on the question you are on indefinitely when the time runs out. Therefore, when you are almost out of time, go to a question you feel you can figure out—given enough time—and work until you have got it (or the night security guard boots you out!).

- You are allowed to use the Windows calculator during your test. However, it may be better to memorize a table of the subnet addresses and to write it down on the scratch paper supplied by the testing center before you start the test.

Once you have completed an exam, you will be given immediate, online notification of your pass or fail status. You will also receive a printed Examination Score Report indicating your pass or fail status and your exam results by section. (The test administrator will give you the printed score report.) Test scores are automatically forwarded to Microsoft within five working days after you take the test. You do not need to send your score to Microsoft. If you pass the exam, you will receive confirmation from Microsoft, typically within two to four weeks.

Contact Information

To find out more about Microsoft Education and Certification materials and programs, to register with Sylvan Prometric, or to get other useful information, check the following resources. Outside the United States or Canada, contact your local Microsoft office or Sylvan Prometric testing center.

Microsoft Certified Professional Program—(800) 636-7544
Call the MCPP number for information about the Microsoft Certified Professional Program and exams, and to order the latest Microsoft Roadmap to Education and Certification.

Sylvan Prometric Testing Centers—(800) 755-EXAM
Contact Sylvan to register to take a Microsoft Certified Professional exam at any of more than 800 Sylvan Prometric testing centers around the world.

Microsoft Certification Development Team—Web: http://www .microsoft.com/Train_Cert/mcp/examinfo/certsd.htm
Contact the Microsoft Certification Development Team through their Web site to volunteer for participation in one or more exam

development phases or to report a problem with an exam. Address written correspondence to:

Certification Development Team

Microsoft Education and Certification

One Microsoft Way

Redmond, WA 98052

Microsoft TechNet Technical Information Network—(800) 344-2121
This is an excellent resource for support professionals and system administrators. Outside the United States and Canada, call your local Microsoft subsidiary for information.

How to Contact the Authors

You may contact the author of this book through the publisher:

Sybex Inc.

Customer Service Department

1151 Marina Village Parkway

Alameda, CA 94501

Phone: (510) 523-8233

Fax: (510) 523-2373

E-mail: info@sybex.com

How to Contact the Publisher

Sybex welcomes reader feedback on all of their titles. Visit the Sybex Web site at www.sybex.com for book updates and additional certification information. You'll also find online forms to submit comments or suggestions regarding this or any other Sybex book.

CHAPTER

1

Planning

Microsoft Exam Objectives Covered in This Chapter:

▶ **Choose a secure access strategy for various situations. Access includes outbound access by users to the Internet and inbound access to your Web site. Considerations include:** *(pages 4 – 17)*

- Translating addresses from the internal network to the Local Address Table (LAT)
- Controlling anonymous access
- Controlling access by known users and groups
- Setting protocol permissions
- Auditing protocol access
- Setting Microsoft Windows NT security parameters

▶ **Plan an Internet site or an intranet site for stand-alone servers, single-domain environments, and multiple-domain environments. Tasks include:** *(pages 18 – 30)*

- Choosing appropriate connectivity methods
- Choosing services
- Using Microsoft Proxy Server in an intranet that has no access to the Internet
- Choosing hardware

▶ **Choose a strategy to balance Internet access across multiple Proxy Server computers. Strategies include:** *(pages 31 – 36)*

- Using DNS
- Using arrays
- Using Cache Array Routing Protocol (CARP)

▶ **Choose a rollout plan for integrating a Proxy Server with an existing corporate environment.** *(pages 37 – 42)*

▶ **Choose a fault tolerance strategy. Strategies include:** *(pages 43 – 49)*

- Using arrays
- Using routing

T he objectives covered in this chapter are concerned with planning your Proxy Server environment. Before you begin to install Proxy Server 2, you need to gather information, to establish security strategies, and to consider other planning issues such as load balancing and fault tolerance. There are usually several different methods of implementing each of these. What you choose will depend on the needs and means of your organization.

Before you begin installing Microsoft Proxy Server, you should examine your existing network with the following questions in mind:

- Are you using TCP/IP as your network protocol?

- Are you using IPX/SPX?

- Do you wish to create an intranet with no access to the Internet, or do you want your users to be able to access Internet resources?

- Do you wish to allow external Internet users to access resources on your intranet?

- How important is uninterrupted access to and from your network?

- How will the number of users on your network affect your deployment of proxy servers?

- How will your existing equipment affect your strategy?

The material covered in this chapter shows you how each of these questions relates to your Proxy Server environment and how your answers affect your planning decisions. This information is important not only in the testing room but also in real life. Just as you wouldn't set off on a camping trip without first considering what you need to take and where you are going, so you should not install Microsoft Proxy Server without first doing the planning.

Choose a secure access strategy for various situations. Access includes outbound access by users to the Internet and inbound access to your Web site. Considerations include:

- Translating addresses from the internal network to the Local Address Table (LAT)
- Controlling anonymous access
- Controlling access by known users and groups
- Setting protocol permissions
- Auditing protocol access
- Setting Microsoft Windows NT security parameters

Security is an extremely important part of Microsoft Proxy Server and therefore of the Proxy Server exam. Developing a secure access strategy ensures that you can control inbound access to your network from the Internet and can also control outbound access from your internal network to the Internet. You can accomplish this by the following methods:

- Configuring the Local Address Table (LAT) properly
- Controlling client's access according to user or group in your internal network
- Setting permissions on protocols such as HTTP, FTP, etc.
- Optimizing the security settings on your NT Server

You can expect to see questions about all of these topics on the Proxy Server exam. In particular, expect questions on the LAT and on controlling access, both anonymous access and user- or group-based access. These concepts and procedures also apply to real-world situations, where a breach of security can often be financially damaging (especially if the result is **you** losing your job).

Critical Information

Security considerations can be divided into two categories: outbound access and inbound access. Most of the information presented in this chapter concerns both of these. The Local Address Table and the authentication method used both affect internal and external users. Protocol permissions, depending on the proxy service being used, can apply to both inbound and outbound traffic. Even Windows NT server configuration settings can affect both inbound and outbound traffic.

Translating Addresses from the Internal Network to the Local Address Table (LAT)

If you are using TCP/IP as your internal protocol, then IP addressing becomes an issue. During installation of Proxy Server, you will be asked to construct a Local Address Table (LAT). The purpose of the LAT is twofold. First, when you define internal IP address ranges, any local client requesting an object from an internal server will bypass the proxy server and obtain that object directly from the internal server. Second, by excluding external addresses from the LAT, you can filter processing of external client requests to internal servers.

It is important that no IP addresses external to your network be included in the LAT. This applies also to the IP address of the external network card on your proxy server. Otherwise, access to internal resources would be granted to external addresses. Also, internal requests for those addresses would bypass the proxy server.

Controlling Anonymous Access

Your next consideration is to decide how you want to control anonymous access to your network. When Internet Information Server (IIS) is installed, a default user account is created, named IUSR_ *computername*.

SEE ALSO For more information on IIS, see the *MCSE: Internet Information Server 4 Study Guide* (Sybex, 1998).

You will need to configure the authentication method that you will use in the WWW services properties pages in Internet Service Manager. Allow Anonymous is one of your choices. If you select this option, anonymous users will be able to access whatever resources for which the IUSR_*computername* account has permissions.

WARNING If anonymous logon is allowed, all client applications will use it. You must disable anonymous logon to force users to log on with an account and a password.

You can control anonymous user access to specific directories or files on your Web site. Use NTFS permissions to assign No Access rights for the IUSR_*computername* account to the directory or file you wish to restrict.

WARNING Permissions to the IUSR_*computername* account are not replicated correctly across an array.

You will need to manually configure these permissions. In the following situations, you should grant permissions to the Everyone group instead of granting them directly to the IUSR_*computername* account:

- You have multiple proxy servers configured as an array.

- You want to allow anonymous access to Web publishing from the local IIS computers.

- You want to authenticate users that pass through the Web proxy server for client requests.

Controlling Access by Known Users and Groups

There are two methods available to control access by users and groups: basic authentication and Windows NT Challenge/Response authentication.

Basic authentication is sent across the wire in clear text, although the user credentials are encoded.

WARNING   Even though the user credentials are encoded, someone using a program such as UUdecode who has access to a packet-sniffing device can easily decode them.

Basic authentication offers very weak security, and should not be used unless necessary. If, for instance, you have Unix-based Web browsers in your network, these browsers can only use basic authentication for Web documents requiring password access. When you configure basic authentication, you can apply it either to all users or to a subset of users.

Windows NT Challenge/Response authentication does not transmit the user password across the network. Instead, it performs a series of complex calculations on both the server and the client. The user is not prompted for the account name or password. The client software uses established logon information from the current user. Like Basic authentication, Challenge/Response authentication can be applied to all users or to a subset of users. This type of authentication is more secure, but there are some limitations:

- The client browser must be Microsoft Internet Explorer. In fact, Microsoft states that browsers other than Microsoft Internet Explorer 4 may experience problems with client configuration scripts (JavaScripts) or pages using Secure Sockets Layer (SSL).

- The client and the server must be in the same or a trusted domain.

- Platforms other than Windows cannot use it.

Setting Protocol Permissions

The types of protocols for which you can define permissions depend on the proxy service you are configuring—Web Proxy, WinSock Proxy, or Socks Proxy. The Web Proxy service allows four options:

- FTP Read
- Gopher
- Secure
- WWW

In order to access these options, access control must be enabled. You can then select one of the options listed above and assign either of the following: Read access for FTP Read or Gopher; or Full access for Secure or WWW.

TIP For administration purposes, you should create groups and assign various permissions to them, and then add or remove users to and from the groups as needed.

The WinSock Proxy service presents numerous protocol options for which permissions can be assigned. In addition, unlike the Web Proxy service, you can define new protocols as needed. If you need to assign protocol permissions for the HTTP protocol, go to the Permissions tab of the WinSock Proxy service properties pages. Again, access control must be enabled. Select HTTP from the pop-up Protocol menu, and then click on Edit. You can then choose a group or user to give access to this protocol. Any user not given access or not belonging to a group given access will be denied use of the HTTP protocol.

The Socks Proxy service is somewhat different in its application of permissions. By default, all Socks requests are denied. You can permit or deny requests to or from a Domain/Zone, an IP subnet, or All. You select a port number or a range of port numbers to apply this permission to. When you select the port number, you can define the permission as applying to a number Equal To the port number listed (EQ), Not Equal To (NEQ), Greater Than (GT), Less Than (LT), Greater Than Or Equal To (GE), or Less Than Or Equal To (LE). Although not as advanced as the WinSock Proxy service, the Socks Proxy service has the advantage of wide support on both Windows and non-Windows platforms.

Auditing Protocol Access

Microsoft Proxy Server has three service logs, one each for Web Proxy service, WinSock Proxy service, and Socks Proxy service. These logs help you to determine what protocols are being used, to track protocols used by a specific user, to track what time the requests occur, and to determine if the request was successful. Logging is enabled by default for each service when you install Microsoft Proxy Server. The default location for the log files is *drive*:\root\SYSTEM32\MSPLOGS. The logging function is discussed in greater detail in Chapter 5: Monitoring and Optimization.

Setting Microsoft Windows NT Security Parameters

Using Microsoft Windows NT in combination with Microsoft Proxy Server 2 provides a powerful tool to access the Internet for internal users, and to provide access to your internal resources for external users. However, because of the potential for misuse from both sets of users, care must be taken to provide a secure environment.

Microsoft recommends several Windows NT Server configuration changes when installing Proxy Server:

- Disable IP forwarding. This will prevent unauthorized packets from entering your network.

- Enable access control. Not using access control with proxy server is considered an insecure environment. You must enable access control in order to assign permissions to users and groups and to set any password authentication settings.

- Make sure only internal addresses are contained in the Local Address Table (LAT). Not doing so can expose your entire network to external users.

- Use a secure password policy. Use long, difficult-to-guess passwords. In particular, make sure that the administrator password contains uppercase and lowercase characters and numbers and that it is not too short.

- Limit the number of accounts you add to the Administrator group. Avoid giving any account any rights that it doesn't need.

- Use account policies. Regulate such policies as forcing periodic changes of passwords and limiting the number of logon attempts before locking out the account.

- Check permissions on network shares. Set default access on shared directories to read-only access.

- Avoid using network drive mappings, particularly if you use the same computer for Proxy Server and for Web publishing with Internet Information Server.

- Use NTFS volumes instead of FAT volumes. Only then can you take advantage of NTFS file security.

- Do not run applications or services that you are not using. If you are not using Gopher or FTP, disable them in the Services Control Panel, or don't install them. This lessens the chances that a mistake on your part will result in a security hole.

- On your external adapters, unbind services that are not necessary. Disable the Server service on external network adapters. Also, unbind the WINS client.

- Do not include DNS or gateway information in your client configurations. Users with this information about your network could possibly manage to get around the proxy server.

- Ports 1024 through 1029 are used for listening by Remote Procedure Calls (RPCs) and should be disabled. This ensures that RPC listening occurs only on the internal network.

SEE ALSO   Microsoft's white paper on Proxy Server security at `http://www.microsoft.com/proxy` also contains valuable security advice.

Necessary Procedures

Necessary procedures for this exam objective include creating a Local Address Table (LAT), setting authentication types, setting protocol permissions for the WinSock Proxy service, setting protocol permissions for the Socks Proxy service, and disabling IP forwarding. All of these deal with the security of your network.

Constructing a Local Address Table (LAT)

During the installation process for Microsoft Proxy Server 2 you will be presented with the Local Address Table Configuration screen.

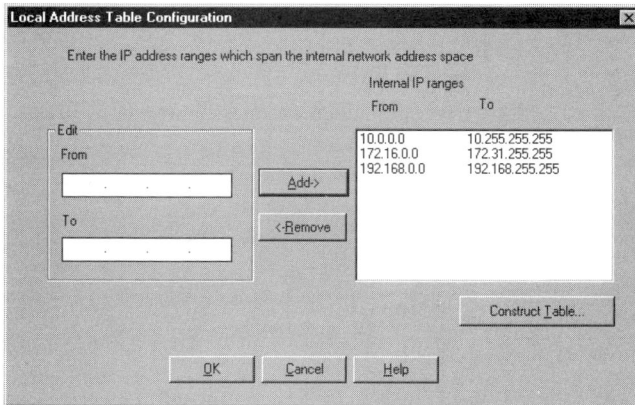

1. Click on Construct Table and you will see the Construct Local Address Table screen.

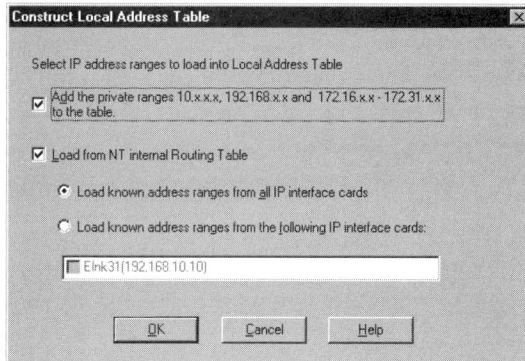

2. If you are using the IP address ranges reserved for private addresses in your network, then select the Add The Private Ranges checkbox. You can also have the installation process construct the correct IP address ranges according to the internal NT routing table.

3. Once you have selected to load from the internal NT routing table, you have the option to Load Known Address Ranges From All IP

Interface Cards, or Load Known Address Ranges From the Following IP Interface Cards. If you choose the first option, you may need to remove any entries for external interfaces. By choosing the second option you can exclude external interfaces yourself.

4. Once you have selected the correct options for your installation, click OK. You will receive a message warning you that external IP addresses may have been included in the IP address ranges selected.

WARNING   Once you are finished constructing the LAT, you should double check to make sure that no external addresses are included. This includes the address of the external IP interface in the proxy server. Failure to do so could create security openings.

---

5. Click OK on the message and you will be returned to the Local Address Table Configuration screen. At this point, you may need to add single IP addresses or address ranges that are part of your internal network but were not included in the internal NT routing table. You can do this by typing the first address in the range in the From field, and the last address in the To field. If you are adding a single address, type the same address in the From and To fields. If you need to remove addresses, select them in the Internal IP Ranges field and click Remove.

TIP   If you find that any private subnets on your network are not listed in the internal NT routing table, you should review your server or network configuration to make sure that the subnet will be accessible to TCP/IP connections.

---

6. Once you are done editing the LAT, click OK. The LAT will then be created and stored in a file called MSPLAT.TXT. The default location for this file to be stored is C:\MSP\CLIENTS. If you install Proxy Server to a different location, the default location will change accordingly. Proxy Server clients will regularly download this file from this shared directory in order to keep the client configuration current.

After installation, changes to the LAT can be accomplished by loading the Microsoft Internet Service Manager, viewing the properties pages for the Socks Proxy service, the WinSock Proxy service, or the Web Proxy service, and clicking on Local Address Table in the Configuration field.

Setting Authentication Type in Internet Service Manager

1. Start Internet Service Manager by selecting Start ➤ Programs ➤ Microsoft Proxy Server ➤ Internet Service Manager.

2. Select Properties for the WWW service, and you will see the following screen:

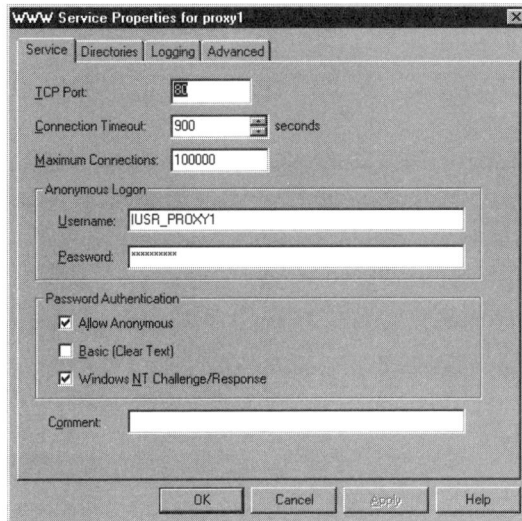

3. In the Password Authentication section, the three choices presented are Allow Anonymous, Basic (Clear Text), and Windows NT Challenge/Response. Select the authentication type that you require and make sure there is not a check by the ones you do not wish to use. Click OK.

4. If you have chosen Basic or Windows NT Challenge/Response, then select Properties for the Web Proxy service.

5. Click on the Permissions tab.

6. If you wish to allow access to all users, clear the Enable Access Control checkbox.

7. If you wish to allow a subset of users, check the Enable Access Control checkbox and add the user permissions for access rights to each service (FTP, Gopher, WWW, and Secure).

Setting Protocol Permissions for the WinSock Proxy Service

1. Start Internet Service Manager and select Properties for the WinSock Proxy service.

2. Click on the Permissions tab.

3. Select the protocol for which you need to assign permissions and click Edit.

4. Assign access to the appropriate groups or users. Click OK twice to return to the Internet Service Manager.

Setting Protocol Permissions for the Socks Proxy Service

1. Start Internet Service Manager and select Properties for the Socks Proxy service.

2. Click on the Permissions tab.

3. Click Add. You will see the screen labeled Socks Permission.

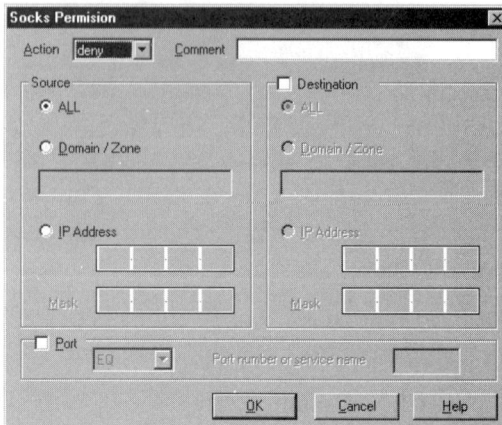

4. Select an action: Deny or Permit. Select Source or Destination.

5. Enter a short comment in the Comment field for easy recognition later.

6. Select All, Domain/Zone, or IP Address depending on your needs.

   A. If you select Domain/Zone, type in the name of the Domain.

   B. If you select IP Address, enter an IP address and the subnet mask to create a range.

7. Click on the Port checkbox to activate it.

8. Type in the port number or service name.

9. Select the qualifier, e.g., ports EQ (equal) or GT (greater than).

10. Click OK.

Disabling IP Forwarding

1. Start Network in Control Panel.

2. Select the Protocols tab and then select Properties for TCP/IP Protocol.

3. Select the Routing tab.

4. Clear the Enable IP Forwarding checkbox and click OK.

5. Click Close.

6. Restart the server.

Exam Essentials

Know how to determine if an IP address range should be included in the Local Address Table (LAT).   Internal address ranges should be included in the LAT. External addresses should not.

Know the different types of authentication.   There are three types of authentication: Allow Anonymous, Basic (Clear Text), and Windows NT Challenge/Response. Basic authentication transmits encoded user credentials across the network and provides weak security. Windows NT

Challenge/Response does not transmit user credentials across the network, but it is only supported by Internet Explorer on Windows platforms.

Know where to modify protocol permissions, and the differences in these permissions between Web Proxy, WinSock Proxy, and Socks Proxy services.   Web Proxy services can only apply permissions to FTP, Gopher, Secure, and WWW. WinSock Proxy services can apply permissions to a wide range of protocols, and more can be added. Socks Proxy services apply permissions to the TCP/IP port numbers.

Know how Windows NT security parameters can affect the security of your network with Proxy Server.   Review Windows NT security parameters, and be aware of the implications of enabling IP Forwarding, not enabling Access Control, administrative user rights, shares, network drives, etc., on Proxy Server security.

Key Terms and Concepts

Basic (Clear Text) authentication: Transmits clear-text-encoded user credentials across the network. Supported by a wide variety of browsers and platforms

CERN: This refers to an industry standard established by a European council for application-aware proxy services over HTTP-based client/server communications.

Local Address Table (LAT):   A Proxy Server configuration file defining the IP address ranges that are internal to the network. All addresses external to the network should be excluded from this file.

Socks Proxy service: This service provides transparent redirection of client requests for a wide variety of platforms. Microsoft Proxy Server 2 supports Socks version 4.3a.

Web Proxy service: This service supports CERN-compliant Web browsers running on any platform.

Windows NT Challenge/Response authentication: Does not transmit user credentials across the network, using instead a series of complex calculations on both the client and server to authenticate the user. Available only to Internet Explorer clients using Windows

WinSock Proxy service: This service provides transparent support through the use of APIs for redirection of Windows-based client requests.

Sample Questions

1. Your proxy server has the following configuration:

	Start address	Subnet mask
Internal network card:	192.168.20.2	255.255.255.0
External network card:	172.16.31.2	255.255.0.0
Router:	172.16.31.1	255.255.0.0

What addresses should you include in the LAT?

A. 172.16.31.0 through 172.16.31.255

B. 192.168.20.0 through 192.168.20.255 and 172.16.31.1

C. 192.168.20.2 and 172.16.31.0 through 172.16.31.255

D. 192.168.20.0 through 192.168.20.255

Answer: D. You should add all of the addresses on your internal network. None of the external addresses should be added.

2. What changes should you make to your proxy server to increase network security?

A. Enable IP forwarding.

B. Disable the Server service on the external network card.

C. Use only NTFS volumes.

D. Include DNS and gateway references on your client configurations.

Answer: B and C. You should disable IP forwarding, so answer A is incorrect. Disabling the Server service on the external network card prevents external users from accessing that service. Using NTFS volumes allows you to take advantage of NTFS file security.

You should not include DNS and gateway references on your client configurations, since internal users could use that information to bypass the proxy server.

3. You administer a proxy network servicing Windows, Macintosh, and Unix clients, many of them using Netscape browsers. What is the most secure authentication type that all clients can use?

   A. Allow Anonymous

   B. Basic (Clear Text)

   C. Windows NT Challenge/Response

Answer: B. Basic authentication is the most secure type you could use in this situation. Windows NT Challenge/Response can only be used with Internet Explorer clients on Windows platforms. Allow anonymous, of course, allows everyone and is therefore less secure.

Plan an Internet site or an intranet site for stand-alone servers, single-domain environments, and multiple-domain environments. Tasks include:

- Choosing appropriate connectivity methods
- Choosing services
- Using Microsoft Proxy Server in an intranet that has no access to the Internet
- Choosing hardware

Now that you have considered how security will be implemented in your network, it is time to look at the network itself.

- What protocols will you use?

- How will the proxy server fit into that network?

- What type of hardware do you need in your computer in order to successfully install Proxy Server and have it function properly?

The decisions you make at this point are crucial, since purchasing decisions, deployment strategies, and the deployment schedule will all be affected. Being able to answer the above questions is not only necessary for you to pass the Proxy Server exam, but it is also important when it comes to successfully deploying Microsoft Proxy Server. If it seems like there is a lot of preparation to go through before you ever run the Setup program for Proxy Server, that's because there is! But careful planning now can save you many headaches (and late nights) later on.

Critical Information

The issues that are relevant to this objective can be divided into three categories:

- The connectivity method the proxy server will use to communicate with the clients

- The services the proxy server will offer to the clients

- The type of hardware the proxy server needs to have in order to provide these services

On the exam, expect to encounter multiple questions concerning the first two items: connectivity methods and proxy services. The third item will also be tested although less heavily than the first two.

Choosing Appropriate Connectivity Methods

How will the clients in your network communicate with the proxy server? The connectivity method referred to in this objective does not refer to the type of cabling used or whether you will be using Ethernet or Token Ring. The connectivity method as used in this objective is defined as the protocol that the client and server use to communicate with each other across the network.

So, what protocol should you use for your proxy server network? What protocols **can** you use? With Proxy Server, you can choose between IPX/SPX and TCP/IP. Both protocols have advantages and disadvantages.

SEE ALSO To learn more about TCP/IP and IPX/SPX protocols, see the MCSE: *TCP/IP for NT Server 4 Study Guide*, 3rd ed. (Sybex, 1998).

IPX/SPX—Advantages and Disadvantages

Let's start with IPX/SPX, which, under Microsoft's implementation, is called NWLink IPX/SPX Compatible Transport. IPX/SPX is a protocol used primarily in Novell NetWare networks. Some of the advantages of IPX/SPX are as follows:

Speed: Generally speaking, IPX/SPX is a faster network protocol than TCP/IP.

Dynamic addressing: Unlike TCP/IP, with IPX/SPX manual administration of network addresses is unnecessary. In a large network, this can be quite a time saver.

Existing NetWare network: If you are already using this protocol in your network, you might want to avoid using up more bandwidth with multiple protocols.

Security: Having a different protocol on your internal network than the Internet (TCP/IP) makes it harder for a potential hacker to access internal resources.

The disadvantages of IPX/SPX include:

Protocol conversion: If you are using your proxy server as an IPX gateway to the Internet, every client request and response received will need to be converted twice—from TCP/IP to IPX/SPX and back. This protocol conversion creates overhead that could possibly bog down your network. This protocol conversion will also take place when retrieving items from cache if the Web browser is configured to use the Web Proxy service on a network using only IPX/SPX.

NOTE   Caching is discussed in detail in Chapter 3: "Setting Up and Managing Resource Access."

Windows 95 or Windows NT: Proxy Server's IPX Gateway only supports Windows 95 or Windows NT. Windows 3.*x* clients, DOS clients, and Macintosh clients are out in the cold.

TCP/IP—Advantages and Disadvantages

TCP/IP has rather different advantages and disadvantages. First, the advantages:

Caching: Clients using TCP/IP can use the Web Proxy service, with the full benefits of caching without protocol conversion.

No protocol conversion: No protocol conversion is necessary between the client and the proxy server.

Supports all clients: Virtually every platform including (especially) Unix, along with Windows 3.*x*, DOS, and Macintosh can use TCP/IP.

Scalability: TCP/IP is well suited to large, segmented networks.

Jump on the bandwagon: TCP/IP will be much more of a default protocol in the next releases of both Windows NT and NetWare. You can get a head start by using TCP/IP as your network protocol now.

Disadvantages of TCP/IP:

Address administration: Each TCP/IP client must be assigned a unique network address, either manually or using DHCP. In a large network, this can become time consuming.

Security: While it is possible for TCP/IP to be just as secure as IPX/SPX, it may require more careful administration to accomplish this.

So which protocol should you choose? Again, the answer depends on your needs. However, generally speaking, IPX/SPX is recommended if you have an existing NetWare network. TCP/IP is recommended in most other situations, and will soon be the default network protocol for both Windows NT and NetWare.

Choosing Services

Next in line for your consideration is the type of proxy services that you will use. Microsoft Proxy Server offers three proxy services: Web Proxy service, WinSock Proxy service, and Socks Proxy service. Again, as with the protocols discussed in the previous pages, each service has its advantages and disadvantages. Or, it might be more accurate to say that each proxy service has its own individual purpose, which may or may not suit your needs.

Web Proxy Service

The following list summarizes the features of the Web Proxy service:

Compliance with CERN-Proxy protocol: The Web Proxy service supports any browser on any platform that is compatible with the standard CERN-Proxy protocol. Examples of such operating systems are:

Windows 3.*x*

Windows 95

Windows NT

Macintosh

Unix

NOTE   CERN refers to an industry standard established by a European council for application-aware proxy services over HTTP-based client/server communications.

HTTP and FTP caching: Caching refers to the process of storing frequently requested objects locally so that subsequent requests for them are served locally instead of being retrieved from the remote site.

Reverse proxying and reverse hosting in conjunction with Web publishing: Reverse proxying refers to the process of the proxy server listening for HTTP requests for an internal Web server, and forwarding those requests to that server. This allows for the internal Web server to exist in a more secure environment behind the proxy server. Reverse hosting extends this a step further by allowing the proxy server to maintain a list of internal Web servers allowed to publish to the Internet. The proxy server then allows secure access to multiple Web servers sitting behind it.

NOTE   Reverse proxying and reverse hosting are discussed in detail in Chapter 3: "Setting Up and Managing Resource Access."

User-level–defined permissions for each protocol: Protocols for which you can define permissions with the Web Proxy service include FTP, Gopher, WWW, and Secure.

SEE ALSO   Secure refers to Secure Sockets Layer (SSL). For more information on SSL, see the MCSE: *Proxy Server 2 Study Guide*, 1st ed. (Sybex, 1998).

Restricted access to the Internet: You can implement restrictions (filters) for your internal users by domain, by IP address, or by an IP address and subnet mask for a range of IP addresses.

IP address aggregation: This is a fancy way of saying that all requests to the Internet through the Web Proxy service will use the proxy server IP address as the source address. By hiding the IP addresses of the internal network, security is increased and the use of unregistered or private addresses is possible.

Logged information: Client requests can be logged and monitored.

WinSock Proxy Service

The WinSock Proxy service differs in its approach. Applications that are compatible with Windows Sockets operate as if they had a direct Internet connection.

TIP   It is important to note that the WinSock Proxy service does not support caching.

The following is a list of the WinSock Proxy service features:

Supports using either TCP/IP or IPX/SPX on the internal network: IPX/SPX requires that the proxy server act as an IPX gateway and, along with the client computer, that it perform protocol conversion.

Windows NT Challenge/Response authentication: The WinSock Proxy service allows any client application to use this type of authentication. This authentication only takes place the first time the application links to Windows Sockets.

Compatibility: Compatible with almost all Windows Sockets 1.1-compatible applications.

Control of both inbound and outbound access: Permissions can be applied by protocol, port number, user, or group. Permissions for inbound connections for a port number can be different from the permissions for outbound connections on the same port number.

Restricted access to the Internet: You can implement restrictions (filters) for your internal users by domain, IP address, or an IP address and subnet mask for a range of IP addresses. These permissions apply globally to all users.

Restricted access to your intranet: External users are blocked from accessing the internal network.

IP address aggregation: As with the Web Proxy service, all requests to the Internet through the WinSock Proxy service use the proxy server IP address as the source address. By hiding the IP addresses of the internal network, security is increased and the use of unregistered or private addresses is possible.

Logged information: Client requests can be logged and monitored.

Client compatibility: Compatibility with Windows-based client computers

Socks Proxy Service

Microsoft Proxy Server also offers the Socks Proxy service. The Socks Proxy service provides secure communications between the client and the server. The Socks Proxy service is similar to the WinSock Proxy service in that it provides transparent redirection of TCP/IP requests to the proxy server. However, the Socks Proxy service can provide this redirection to non-Windows platforms.

WARNING   The Socks Proxy service does not support the UDP protocol. Only the WinSock Proxy service provides this support. For detailed information on the UDP protocol, see the *MCSE: TCP/IP for NT Server 4 Study Guide*, 3rd ed. (Sybex, 1998).

The following is a list of the features of the Socks Proxy service:

- Supports using the TCP/IP protocol on the internal network

- Supports the Identification Protocol (the Identd Simulation service)

- Compatibility with all popular operating systems

- Supports the Socks standard configuration file

- Logs information about Socks requests

Using Microsoft Proxy Server in an Intranet without Internet Access

Microsoft Proxy Server can still have a place in your network even if your intranet will not have access to the Internet. There are two important benefits that can be realized: caching and security. Caching helps lower network traffic, and security allows you to keep documents secure from various groups of users in your domain.

The following are some examples of possible benefits of using Microsoft Proxy Server in your intranet:

- Cache documents stored on a Web server on the other side of a slow link.

- Post company-wide announcements or policies, which are then cached.

- Keep secure information, such as accounting or payroll documents, available only to the users who should have access to them.

- Use FTP caching on an FTP site storing standard applications.

Many more examples could be listed, but you probably get the idea by now. Deciding now, in the planning stage, what features you want will assist you with other planning issues such as choosing a protocol, choosing services, etc.

Choosing Hardware

Now it's time to examine the computer on which you will be installing Microsoft Proxy Server. Microsoft lists the absolute minimum hardware requirements as follows:

- Intel 486 DX/33 or faster, or Alpha AXP

- At least 10MB of disk space for installation of the Proxy Server, and 100MB + 0.5MB for each user for caching. Caching cannot be configured unless there is an NTFS partition of at least 5MB.

- At least 24MB of RAM, 32MB for RISC-based systems

You're probably thinking that these requirements seem awfully low and you're right! You will definitely want to increase your requirements from those listed above. In fact, you could probably double or triple them and just begin approaching the optimum configuration for your network. Microsoft also has recommended configurations for small businesses, medium businesses, large businesses, and ISPs. Depending on the number of users in your network, the following recommendations might apply:

- At least a Pentium 133MHz; 166MHz for larger networks

- Between 250MB and 4GB of disk space for caching

- 32MB of RAM; 64MB for larger networks

When choosing your hardware remember that more is better (within reason). This is particularly true of the amount of RAM in the computer. A reasonable amount of RAM for an NT Server that is not yet running any services would be 64MB, and this should really be increased as the services running on it are increased. The disk space you need for caching is something you can define more precisely after your proxy server has been in use. The hardware on which you are running your proxy server should not run out of space under typical usage. The CPU typically is not the bottleneck for performance with the proxy server but, if you are buying new hardware, choose a CPU that you think will be sufficient for at least two years.

As this book goes to press, a Pentium 166MHz configuration is not available from most vendors. By the time this book comes out, you may not even be able to find Pentium 200s. And anything new would be either a Pentium Pro or Pentium II, neither of which come in 166MHz. So, in a real-world situation, you should choose from the available configurations the one that best fits your needs, rather than trying to follow the Microsoft recommended configuration to the letter.

Necessary Procedures

The issues covered in this objective have more to do with planning than with manipulating or configuring your proxy server. However, you should grab a pencil and paper and go through the following steps, to come up with a list of your needs:

1. Write down the needs of your network with regards to network protocols. Include existing configurations, caching needs, computer platforms used, and anything else you think is relevant.

2. Write down what you hope to accomplish by installing Microsoft Proxy Server. Do you need to increase security, decrease latency in Web requests, support a variety of computer platforms, etc.?

3. Write down the structure of your network. Will you have an intranet? Will you allow access to the Internet? Does the topology of your network present unique problems?

4. How much hardware will you need to accomplish the goals you wrote down for the previous three items? Write out the hardware configuration for your proxy server.

Exam Essentials

Know the protocols that can be used with Microsoft Proxy Server, and the advantages and disadvantages of using each one. The protocols that can be used with Microsoft Proxy Server are TCP/IP and IPX/SPX. TCP/IP is a widely-used, scalable protocol that is supported by virtually all computer platforms. IPX/SPX is a protocol typically used in NetWare environments. It can only be used with the WinSock Proxy service and requires protocol conversion to take place when used with Microsoft Proxy Server.

Know what services Microsoft Proxy Server provides, and know what each service has to offer. Web Proxy service supports CERN-compliant Web browsers running on any platform. It provides user-defined security for FTP, Gopher, Secure, and WWW protocols. It is the only proxy service that provides caching. WinSock Proxy service supports both TCP/IP and IPX/SPX on the internal network. WinSock-compliant applications perform as though connected directly to the Internet. It does not support caching. It supports extensive application of permissions by port, protocol, user, or group. It supports only Windows-based client computers. Socks Proxy service supports all platforms. It supports TCP/IP in the internal network by providing transparent redirects to the proxy server. Permissions can be applied globally by IP Address, by Domain/Zone, and by port number.

Know the minimum and recommended hardware requirements for Microsoft Proxy Server. Keep in mind that the hardware requirements you decide on and what Microsoft recommends may be different. Go with Microsoft's recommendations when taking the exam.

Key Terms and Concepts

Caching: The process of storing any requested object in disk space on a local server

DHCP: Dynamic Host Configuration Protocol. DHCP is used to dynamically assign IP address and related TCP/IP configuration information to network hosts.

IPX/SPX: Internetwork Packet Exchange/Sequenced Package Exchange. A routable network protocol used primarily in NetWare-based networks

SSL: Secure Sockets Layer. A protocol that uses data encryption and decryption to provide secure communication

TCP/IP: Transmission Control Protocol/Internet Protocol. A suite of protocols used on the Internet that allows cross communication between diverse hardware configurations and operating systems

Windows Sockets: A networking API used to create TCP/IP-based sockets applications

Sample Questions

1. You launch a Web browser from a Windows NT Workstation in a network using Microsoft Proxy Server. The Web browser is not configured to connect to the Internet through a proxy server. Which proxy service will be used?

   A. Web Proxy service

   B. WWW service

   C. WinSock Proxy service

   D. Socks Proxy service

   Answer: C. When using Windows-based TCP/IP applications, all requests will be redirected by WINSOCK.DLL to the WinSock Proxy service. If the Web browser were configured to access the Internet through a proxy server, the Web Proxy service would be used.

2. You have been asked to design your corporation's new proxy server network. Which of the following are reasons you would choose TCP/IP as your network protocol?

   A. Dynamic addressing

   B. Caching without protocol conversion

   C. Existing NetWare servers

   D. Support for all platforms

Answer: B and D. TCP/IP requires that the network administrator either address each machine manually or configure each machine to obtain the information from a DHCP server. Existing NetWare servers would be a reason to use IPX/SPX as your network protocol. Caching without protocol conversion and support for all platforms are both benefits of TCP/IP.

3. You administer a proxy server network with 500 client computers. What is the minimum amount of disk space you should reserve for caching?

   A. 500MB

   B. 100MB

   C. 250MB

   D. 350MB

   Answer: D. To determine the minimum recommended amount of disk cache, start with 100MB and add 0.5MB for each client computer.

Choose a strategy to balance Internet access across multiple Proxy Server computers. Strategies include:

- Using DNS
- Using arrays
- Using Cache Array Routing Protocol (CARP)

Larger networks may require the use of multiple proxy servers. Once you determine that you will need multiple proxy servers, you are then confronted with the need for load balancing. Load balancing refers to the process of distributing the workload equally among multiple servers. This is an important objective both in the Proxy Server exam and in real world implementation. Installing multiple proxy servers provides no benefit to a network if all client traffic still goes through one proxy server. Understanding how to use DNS, arrays, and Cache Array Routing Protocol (CARP) to achieve load balance will help you on the exam. It will also help you to get your network optimized.

Critical Information

Load balancing can be achieved by using DNS, arrays, and the Cache Array Routing Protocol (CARP). DNS stands for Domain Name System and is used to map domain names to IP addresses.

Using DNS

One method of achieving load balance is through the use of DNS round robin. This means that you take the individual IP address for each proxy server and map it to the same domain name, e.g., `msproxy.mynetwork` `.com`. As the DNS server receives lookup requests it cycles through the list of IP addresses mapped to that domain name.

WARNING   This method by itself does not provide fault tolerance. When a proxy server goes down, DNS will continue to give out its IP address each time it cycles through the list. Requests from clients that receive that IP address will fail because the proxy server will be unreachable.

Using Arrays

Multiple proxy servers configured in an array act as a single system. An array provides load balancing and, unlike using only DNS for load balancing, it provides fault tolerance as well. This is accomplished by having each proxy server maintain a list of servers that are currently up and a list of those that are currently down. Using an array also provides enhanced performance, particularly for the Web Proxy service, which can then take advantage of distributed caching. Another benefit of using an array is automatic synchronous administration of all array members, which applies to all proxy services.

There are some things you should take into account before implementing an array:

- Before you can create or join an array, you must have an account with administrative privileges on each array member.

- Administer only one member of an array at a time. Administering more than one at a time could cause problems with array synchronization.

- Have client computers use the automatic configuration when possible. The client computers will then be configured to access a particular proxy server in the array, which will reduce the routing decisions the array must perform.

- If you are configuring the WinSock Proxy service for an array, you must manually edit the MSPCLNT.INI file on the proxy server to specify the array's DNS name in the [Servers IP Addresses] section.

- You still need to create a domain name in DNS and map it to the IP addresses of all the proxy servers in the array.

NOTE Array configuration is discussed in detail in Chapter 2: Installation and Configuration.

Using Cache Array Routing Protocol (CARP)

An array will use the Cache Array Routing Protocol (CARP) to achieve load balancing and fault tolerance with caching. CARP achieves this by using multiple proxy servers arrayed as a single logical cache. The request resolution path is determined by calculations based on the proxy array member identities and the Uniform Resource Locator (URL). These calculations can take place at the proxy server level or at the browser, if the browser is Internet Explorer. What this means is that any object requested from cache is at most only two hops away.

The cache object will either be retrieved directly by the browser from the proxy server that has the object in cache, or it will be retrieved from the correct proxy server by the first array member accessed by the browser. This is called *queryless distributed caching*. Either the browser or the first proxy server in the array contacted will know the exact location of the object in cache. This reduces network traffic by eliminating the need for a proxy server to query other member servers in the array to see if they have that object in cache, thereby increasing the speed with which the request is served. Also, it means that cache objects will not be duplicated between member servers in the array, which lowers the total amount of disk space needed for caching. Another benefit of CARP is that it automatically adjusts to the subtraction or addition of proxy servers in the array.

Necessary Procedures

There is only one actual procedure associated with this objective, and that is editing the MSPCLNT.INI file to support a DNS name for an array. To accomplish this, use the following procedure:

1. Start the Internet Services Manager and select Properties for one of the proxy services.

2. Click on Client Configuration.

3. Change the value for "Client Connects To Microsoft WinSock Proxy Server By" to Manual.

4. Click OK and then click Apply.

5. Now load the MSPCLNT.INI file into a text editor. The default location for this file is C:\MSP\CLIENTS.

6. In the [Servers IP Addresses] section, insert the array's domain name in the Name entry.

Exam Essentials

Know the advantages and disadvantages of load balancing using DNS. Map the IP addresses from each proxy server to the same domain name. Configure clients to use that domain name to access proxy services.

Know the advantages of load balancing using arrays. Using an array provides load balancing and fault tolerance, since the array automatically reconfigures itself to the loss of individual proxy servers.

Know the effects of the Cache Array Routing Protocol (CARP) on load balancing. CARP provides load balancing through the use of distributed caching. Cache objects are not duplicated between servers, and objects retrieved from the Internet are distributed equally among the caches of array members.

Key Terms and Concepts

Cache Array Routing Protocol (CARP): A hash-based routing protocol that provides a deterministic request resolution path through an array of proxies

DNS: Domain Naming System. DNS is used to map domain names to IP addresses.

DNS round robin: If multiple IP addresses are mapped to the same domain name, DNS servers will cycle through the lists of IP addresses each time a request for that domain name is received.

Distributed caching: The process of distributing caching duties across multiple proxy servers acting as a single logical unit

Fault tolerance: Refers to the ability to continue services in the event that an individual proxy server goes down

Proxy array: Multiple proxy servers configured to work together provide load balancing, fault tolerance, and distributed caching.

Queryless distributed caching: Calculations performed either by the browser or by the first proxy server to receive the request are used to determine the exact location of the cached object. Querying proxy servers to discover the location of a cached object is unnecessary.

Sample Questions

1. Your network has multiple proxy servers configured as an array. A user opens Internet Explorer configured to access the Internet through the proxy server. An object that exists in cache is requested. How many hops will the request take before arriving at the proxy server containing the requested object in cache?

   A. Two

   B. One

   C. Three

   D. It depends on the Internet path required to reach the requested object.

   Answer: B. Internet Explorer is capable of performing the necessary calculations to determine the exact location of the object in cache. Therefore, the request goes directly to the proxy server containing the object in its cache. An external path through the Internet would only be involved if the object requested were not in cache.

2. You wish to create an array. What group or groups must you be a member of in order to be able to do this?

   A. The Domain Admins group in the proxy server's domain

   B. The Backup Operators group

   C. The Administrators group on the Primary Domain controller of the proxy server domain

   D. The local Administrators group for each proxy server to be added to the array

   Answer: A and D. You must have administrative rights on each proxy server you wish to have join the array. Being a member of the local Administrators group on each server will accomplish this. Being a member of the Domain Admins group will also accomplish this, since by default this group is made a member of each server's local Administrators group in the domain.

3. You are configuring a proxy array on your network. You use only TCP/IP as your network protocol. What is the best way to achieve load balancing?

    A. Divide client configurations into several groups, each pointing at a different proxy server.

    B. Map one IP address to multiple domain names. Configure each client to use that IP address for proxy services.

    C. Map one domain name to multiple IP addresses. Configure each client to use that domain name for proxy services.

    D. Use DHCP to handle load balancing proxy assignments.

Answer: C. Map one domain name to all array member's IP address. DNS round robin will then distribute requests equally. Dividing client configurations would work, but it is not as efficient and would require significantly more administration. DHCP does not provide functionality to accomplish load balancing.

Choose a rollout plan for integrating a Proxy Server with an existing corporate environment.

Deciding how to implement proxy servers in an existing network combines many of the design aspects that have been discussed up to this point. Microsoft has made recommendations for various sizes of network. These recommendations will not give you specific answers for your network, but they will give you a general idea of how Microsoft Proxy Server should be implemented, and what types of strategies Microsoft recommends. They will also help you with scenario-based questions on the exam. Another issue you may need to consider is workstation configuration. Will you need to have the proxy client installed? Will this involve any additional training for the end user? Will Help Desk staff need additional training to support these newly configured desktop machines?

Critical Information

Microsoft recommends different proxy server configurations for small, medium, and large networks.

Small Network

A small network typically has the following characteristics:

- Single LAN segment

- Uses either IPX or NetBEUI

- Dial-up connectivity to an Internet Service Provider (ISP)

- Up to 250 clients

In a small network such as this, a single proxy server should be used. The proxy server should be set up to use the Auto Dial feature. Caching should be enabled and active caching should be used to populate the cache during off-hours.

TIP Active caching refers to the process of pre-downloading frequently requested sites during off-hours and is discussed in detail in Chapter 3: "Setting Up and Managing Resource Access."

In a small network, the following methods can be used to enhance network security:

- Password authentication

- User permissions

- Protocol definitions

- Domain filtering. This is a feature provided by Microsoft Proxy Server by which you can filter access to specific sites. Domain filtering is discussed in detail in Chapter 3: "Setting Up and Managing Resource Access."

- Cache filtering. Caching can be configured to always cache or to never cache particular Web sites.

- Dynamic packet filtering. This feature is enabled by default and gives the proxy server the ability to open and close TCP/IP ports as needed for transmission.

Of course, your "small network" may not conform to these specifications. Specific decisions about your network will need to be made with this in mind.

Medium Network

A medium network will typically have the following characteristics:

- A central office with more than one LAN segment
- A branch office with only one LAN segment
- IPX or IP protocol
- Dial-up connectivity from the branch office
- Dial-up or dedicated connectivity to an ISP from the central office
- Up to 2000 clients

With this type of network you should employ multiple proxy servers. The branch office should have a proxy server on its LAN segment to provide local caching. Active caching, however, should only be enabled at the central office. Multiple proxy servers at the central office should be configured as an array, which will provide global security, distributed caching, and dedicated connectivity. Each server in the array should be dual-homed, which means that it will have two network cards. One card is internal, the second has a connection to the external network or the Internet. One server will be configured as a RAS (Remote Access Service) server to provide on-demand access to the branch network.

SEE ALSO   For more information about RAS, see the *MCSE: NT Server 4 Study Guide*, 2nd ed. (Sybex, 1998).

The following methods can be used to provide security in a medium-sized network:

- Password authentication

- User permissions

- Protocol definitions

- Domain filtering

- Cache filtering

- Static (manual) packet filtering. This serves the same function as dynamic packet filtering except that the filtered ports are administered manually by the administrator.

Once again this specific configuration may not match your network exactly. Your decisions should be based on your needs and your network.

Large Network

A large network typically has the following characteristics:

- A central office with multiple LAN segments and a backbone LAN

- Multiple branch offices with single LAN segments

- IPX and IP protocols

- Dial-up connectivity from branch offices

- Dedicated link connectivity from the central office to an ISP

- Over 2000 clients

In this configuration, each departmental LAN should have a proxy server. Each branch office should have a proxy server. The backbone LAN should have a proxy server array. Active caching should be enabled at the proxy server array. Departmental proxy servers and branch offices should be configured to look upstream to the proxy array for caching if the object requested is not in their own cache. As with the medium network configuration, servers in the proxy array can be dual homed, with an internal connection and an external connection. For truly large networks, proxy arrays can be cascaded. Security methods for the large network are the same as for the medium-sized network.

If you decide to use the WinSock Proxy service on your Windows clients, then you will need to install the Microsoft Proxy client. In a large network you will need to account for this in your rollout schedule. If you are providing Internet access for the first time to your users, another issue to consider is bandwidth. How will increased network usage affect this bandwidth? If the effect is significant, you may need to take steps to increase available bandwidth, either by limiting Internet usage or by implementing hardware solutions.

Necessary Procedures

Using the information outlined in this objective, make a sketch of your network. If you don't administer or work with a network, sketch out what you think would be a reasonable network. Place proxy servers into your network and define the function of each one. List the outbound security procedures you would use, caching strategies, and strategies for secure external access.

Exam Essentials

Know how the size and topology of a network affects proxy server implementation. This is a rather general exam objective, but important. You should understand when and where to use single proxy servers and arrays. You should know what can be done to enhance network security.

Understand what effect your implementation of Proxy Server will have on your network. You should understand how client computers will be affected. Will the Microsoft Proxy client need to be installed on each computer? What effect will increased network utilization have on available bandwidth?

Key Terms and Concepts

Active caching: The process of downloading frequently requested sites in advance during periods of low network utilization

Cache filtering: You can specify sites to be either always cached or never cached.

Domain filtering: Refers to denying access to specific Internet sites by domain name or by IP address

Dynamic packet filtering: When dynamic packet filtering is enabled, Proxy Server opens and closes TCP/IP ports as needed for transmission.

NetBEUI: A small, very fast, non-routable protocol suitable for use in small networks

Static packet filtering: TCP/IP ports are manually enabled or disabled by the administrator.

Sample Questions

1. You administer a geographically diverse network with 3000 users. What type of proxy server implementation should you use?

   A. A single proxy server for each LAN segment

   B. Three layers of proxy servers chained together

   C. Departmental and branch office proxy servers configured to look upstream to a proxy server array

   D. Use only a proxy server array provided by your ISP.

   Answer: C. A proxy server for each LAN segment would be overkill. Layers of proxy servers chained together would not provide the same caching and fault tolerance benefits of an array. Using only a proxy array provided by the ISP would move caching benefits farther away from the user and would prevent you from being able to administrate security policies.

2. Which of the following may be used to provide security in a medium-sized network?

   A. Domain filtering

   B. Protocol definitions

C. User permissions

D. Cache filtering

Answer: A, B, C, D. All of these can be used to provide security, along with password authentication and static packet filtering.

Choose a fault tolerance strategy. Strategies include:

- Using arrays
- Using routing

Fault tolerance built into your network can save you many headaches. Nothing will have your phone ringing quicker than having people on your network be unable to retrieve e-mail or to reach their favorite Web sites (although we all know that no one surfs the Web during work hours, right?). You are likely to encounter multiple questions about arrays on the exam and one of the principal functions of an array is fault tolerance. Although you may not see as many questions concerning routing, expect to see at least one or two.

Critical Information

Fortunately, Microsoft has provided a couple of different ways to achieve fault tolerance. In this context, fault tolerance is defined as the ability to provide uninterrupted access to the Internet or to other segments of the network even if a proxy server or a dedicated connection goes down. Although Microsoft has grouped arrays and routing together in this objective, they each provide a different type of fault tolerance.

Using Arrays

An array is a group of proxy servers acting as a single logical unit. This means that an array will cause multiple proxy servers to cooperate with each other to avoid interruptions in service. In order to achieve fault tolerance in providing services, each proxy server in an array maintains a list of servers that are available and a list of servers that are unavailable or down. When a proxy server receives a request, it uses a mathematical procedure called a hash to determine the correct route to an object in cache. Because each proxy server maintains a list of which servers are up or down, the request will not be routed to a server that is currently down.

Arrays are appropriate to medium and large networks. It would be appropriate to place an array at an ISP or at a central office. Figure 1.1 illustrates a simple proxy array.

FIGURE 1.1: Simple proxy array

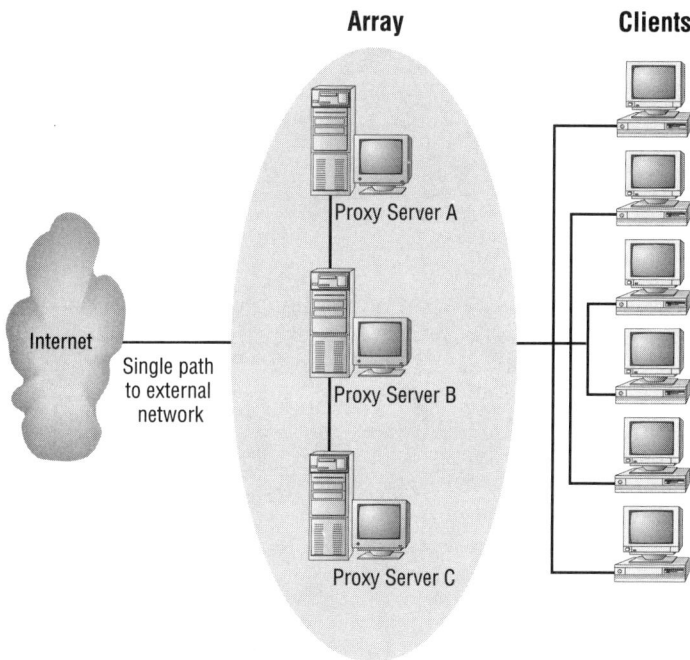

If Proxy Server A goes down, there will be no interruption in service to the clients. Proxy Servers B and C will detect that A is down and will not route any requests there. When Proxy Server A comes back up, Proxy Servers B and C will detect that as well, and will resume routing requests to A.

Using Routing

Routing is a proxy server function that provides fault tolerance in upstream paths, either to other portions of your network or to the Internet. Referring back to Figure 1.1, notice that, in this network design, there is still only one connection to the external network. What happens if that connection goes down? Any requests for Internet objects that are not already contained in cache will fail. There is no fault tolerance built into the network. This is where routing comes in. By configuring routing you can provide a backup network path either to the Internet or to the central office from a branch office. Figure 1.2 illustrates a network using routing for fault tolerance.

FIGURE 1.2: Using routing for fault tolerance on a network

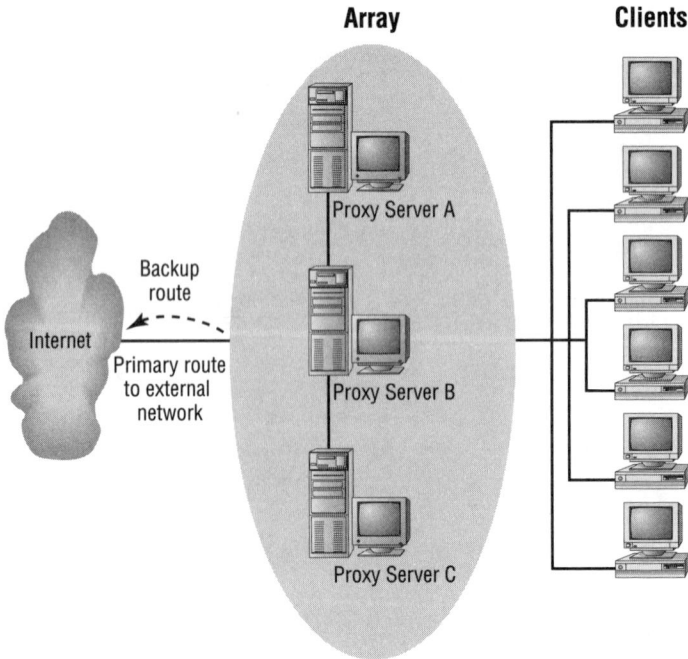

Routing is only supported by the Web Proxy service. When configuring routing, you have two options. You can configure a proxy server to route client requests to a proxy server upstream. This is called upstream routing. You can also configure it to route client requests directly to the Internet. Of course, this takes place only if the object requested does not reside in cache. Now, by enabling a backup route you can provide fault tolerance. Again, you have two choices: routing to a proxy server or array upstream or routing directly to the Internet. This route can be a slower dedicated connection, an ISDN line, or even a modem connection.

Suppose you have a branch office with a T1 dedicated connection to the central office. This would be the route you would normally use in your network. However, being a well-prepared network administrator, you have configured a backup route using a modem connected to the proxy server. This proxy server can then use the Auto Dial feature to connect to a RAS server at the central office. When the branch office proxy server senses that its upstream partner is unreachable, the backup route is automatically activated. So when the T1 connection goes down, and it will go down periodically, the users at the branch office still have access, even if it is significantly slower.

Necessary Procedures

Once more, this objective emphasizes planning, and so does not have a lot of procedures associated with it. Configuration of proxy arrays is discussed in detail in Chapter 2. Configuration of upstream routes and backup routes is the only procedure to be discussed at this time.

Configuring a Backup Route for the Web Proxy Service

1. Load the Internet Services Manager and select Properties for the Web Proxy service.

2. Click on the Routing tab. You will see the following screen:

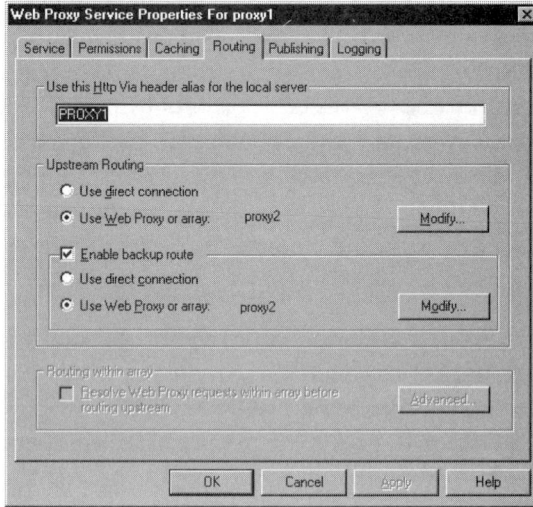

3. For upstream routing, select either Use Direct Connection or Use Web Proxy Or Array.

4. If you choose Use Direct Connection, you are done.

5. If you choose Use Web Proxy Or Array, click on Modify. You will see the screen labeled Advanced Routing Options.

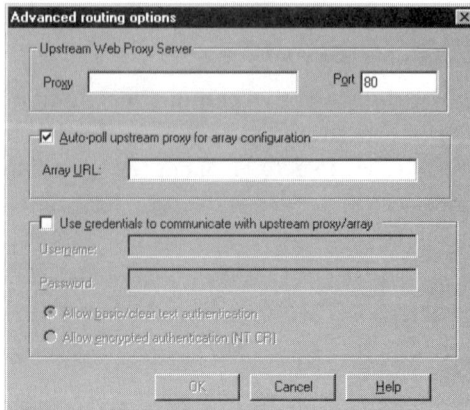

6. Type in the name of the upstream proxy server. Click OK. You will be returned to the Routing Properties screen.

7. Select the Enable Backup Route checkbox. Choose either Direct Connection or Use Web Proxy Or Array, in the area below the Enable Backup Route checkbox.

8. If you choose Direct Connection, you are finished. Click Apply.

9. If you choose Use Web Proxy Or Array, click on Modify.

10. Type in the name of the proxy server you wish to use as a backup route.

11. Click OK, and then click Apply.

Exam Essentials

Know how proxy arrays can be used to enhance fault tolerance. An array is a group of proxy servers acting as a single logical unit. An array will cause multiple proxy servers to cooperate with each other to avoid interruptions in service. Expect questions about proxy arrays on the exam. Be sure you understand how arrays, distributed caching, and CARP affect fault tolerance.

Know how routing with the Web Proxy Service can be used to create fault tolerance. By enabling a backup route you can provide fault tolerance. You should understand how routing can provide fault tolerance for multi-site networks, or networks with more than one connection out to the Internet. This is another topic on which you are likely to encounter at least one or two questions on the Proxy Server exam.

Key Terms and Concepts

Backup route: An alternate route configured to provide access to the rest of the network or to the Internet in the event that the primary route fails

Proxy array: Refers to multiple proxy servers configured to work together to provide load balancing, fault tolerance, and distributed caching

Routing: In the context of Microsoft Proxy Server, this is the process of having a proxy server route its requests to an upstream proxy or array. The proxy server is then able to switch to a backup network connection in the event of a failure on the primary route.

Upstream routing: Refers to configuring a proxy server to point upstream to another proxy server or a proxy array

Sample Questions

1. Which of the following does an array use to provide fault tolerance?

   A. A list of array members currently up and currently down on each array member

   B. DNS round robin

   C. CARP

   D. Active caching

   Answer: A and C. An array maintains a list of available and unavailable servers and uses CARP to provide fault tolerance. DNS round robin provides load balancing, not fault tolerance. Active caching downloads frequently requested Web sites in advance—it does nothing for fault tolerance.

2. You have a branch office connected to a central office by a 56K frame relay circuit. You want to configure fault tolerance in the network connection for this branch office. Which of the following is the best solution?

   A. Configure a single proxy server at the branch office to point upstream to an array at the central office. The array will provide fault tolerance.

   B. Install a separate T1 line to the Internet from the branch office and configure it as a backup route.

   C. Configure a single proxy server at the branch office to point upstream to a proxy array at the central office. Configure a backup route using a modem connection to a RAS server at the central office.

D. Configure a single proxy server at the branch office to point upstream to a proxy array at the central office. Configure a backup route to use a direct connection.

Answer: C. Of the alternatives presented, configuring a single proxy server at the branch office to point upstream to a proxy array and configuring a modem connection as a backup route is the best. Pointing to an array upstream alone does not provide fault tolerance in the network path, as there is still a single point of failure. Installing a T1 line to the branch office would be nice, but is probably not the cost-effective solution that management would appreciate. Also, the backup route should not bypass the rest of the network and connect directly to the Internet. The last answer is wrong because you still only have one connection from the branch office to the central office.

3. Of the following proxy services, which support routing?

A. FTP service

B. Web Proxy service

C. Socks Proxy service

D. WinSock Proxy service

Answer: B. The Web Proxy service is the only service to support routing. Neither the Socks Proxy Service nor the WinSock Proxy service offers this support. The FTP service is not a proxy service.

CHAPTER

2

Installation and Configuration

Microsoft Exam Objectives Covered in This Chapter:

▶ **Create a LAT.**(pages 53 – 58)

▶ **Configure server authentication. Authentication options include:**
(pages 58 – 64)
- Anonymous logon
- Basic authentication
- Microsoft Windows NT Challenge/Response authentication

▶ **Configure Windows NT to support Microsoft Proxy Server.**
(pages 64 – 71)

▶ **Configure the various Proxy Server services.**(pages 72 – 90)

▶ **Configure Microsoft Proxy Server for Internet access. Situations
include:**(pages 90 – 100)
- Configuring Proxy Server to provide Internet access through a dial-up connection to an ISP.
- Configuring Proxy Server to act as an IPX gateway.
- Configuring multiple Microsoft Proxy Servers for Internet access.
- Configuring multiple Proxy Servers spread across several different geographic locations.

▶ **Select and use software configuration management tools (for
example, Control Panel, Windows NT Setup, Regedt32).**
(pages 100 – 108)

▶ **Configure auditing.**(pages 108 – 111)

▶ **Given a scenario, decide which user interface to use to perform
administrative tasks.**(pages 111 – 117)

▶ **Identify the licensing requirements for a given Proxy Server site.**
(pages 117 – 118)

▶ **Configure Proxy Server arrays.**(pages 118 – 122)

▶ **Configure arrays to provide fault-tolerance for Web Proxy client
requests.**(pages 123 – 128)

Use packet filtering to prevent unauthorized access. Tasks include: *(pages 128 – 138)*

- Using packet filtering to enable a specific protocol.
- Configuring packet filter alerting and logging.

Configure hierarchical caching. *(pages 138 – 142)*

Now that you have planned out every facet of your Proxy Server installation, you are ready for a completely trouble-free, surprise-free installation, right? Well, maybe not, but, having done the planning, you'll certainly have fewer problems and surprises. In Chapter 1, you considered various planning options and made specific decisions about your installation. The objectives covered in this chapter are concerned with implementing those decisions.

Create a LAT.

The Local Address Table (LAT) serves two purposes. It tells the Proxy Server which addresses are part of the internal network by storing a list of those addresses. Any local client requesting an object from an internal server will then bypass the proxy server and obtain the object directly from that server. Also, by excluding external addresses from the LAT, the processing of external client requests to internal servers is blocked. For this reason, it is important that no IP addresses external to your network, including the IP address of the external network card on your proxy server, be included in the LAT. Otherwise, access to internal resources would be granted to external addresses. Also, internal requests for those addresses will bypass the proxy.

Critical Information

As you begin the Proxy Server installation, one of the first screens you'll see asks you to construct a LAT. You have several ways of going about this. You can add the correct address ranges manually by entering the starting and ending IP addresses of the range in the From and To boxes, and clicking Add. Or you can click on Construct Table, and the installation process will perform this function for you. If you click on Construct Table, you will be presented with the Construct Local Address Table screen. Here you have the option of automatically adding the IP address ranges reserved for private networks and of loading address ranges from the internal NT routing table. If you decide that you want to load address ranges from the internal NT routing table, you can either load ranges from all known IP interface cards or you can select the internal IP interface cards yourself.

This brings up an important point. If you add all known IP interface cards, you will need to manually remove any address ranges that were added from external interface cards (cards that are used for the connection out to the Internet). Once you are finished here, click OK. You will then be warned that any external address added to the LAT should be manually removed.

WARNING Depending how large your network is, it can be somewhat confusing to keep straight which address ranges are internal and which are external. Double check to make sure no external addresses are included, or you could have a security hole.

Necessary Procedures

Constructing a Local Address Table (LAT) is the only procedure associated with this objective.

Constructing a Local Address Table (LAT)

1. As part of the installation process for Microsoft Proxy Server 2, you will be presented with the Local Address Table Configuration screen.

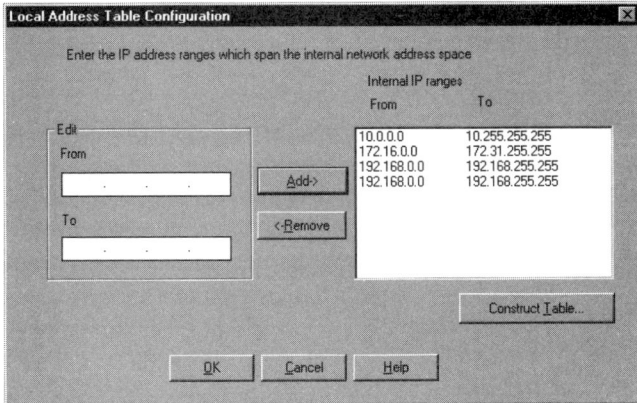

2. Click on Construct Table and you will see the Construct Local Address Table screen.

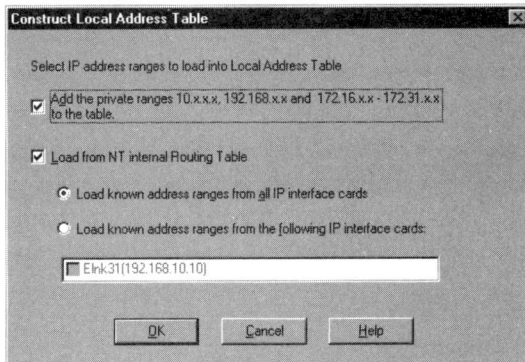

3. If you are using the IP address ranges reserved for private networks in your network, then select the Add the Private Ranges checkbox. You can also have the installation process construct the correct IP address ranges according to the internal NT routing table.

4. Once you have selected Load From The Internal NT Routing Table, you have the option to Load Known Address Ranges From All IP Interface Cards, or Load Known Address Ranges From The Following IP Interface Cards. If you choose the first option, you will need to remove any entries for external interfaces. By choosing the second option you can exclude external interfaces yourself.

5. Once you have selected the correct options for your installation, click OK. You will receive a message warning you that external IP addresses may have been included in the IP address ranges selected.

WARNING   Once you are finished constructing the LAT, you should double check to make sure that no external addresses are included. This includes the address of the external IP interface in the proxy server. Failure to do so would create security openings.

---

6. Click OK to return to the Local Address Table Configuration screen. At this point, you may need to add single IP addresses or address ranges that are part of your internal network but were not included in the internal NT routing table. You can do this by typing the first address of the range in the From field, and the last address in the To field. If you are adding a single address, type the same address in the From and To field. If you need to remove addresses, select them in the Internal IP Ranges field and click Remove.

TIP   If you do find that any private subnets on your network are not listed in the internal NT routing table, you should review your server or network configuration to make sure that the subnet will be accessible to TCP/IP connections.

---

7. Once you are done editing the LAT, click OK. The LAT will then be created and stored in a file called MSPLAT.TXT. The default location for this file to be stored is C:\MSP\CLIENTS. Proxy Server clients will regularly download this file from this shared directory in order to keep the client configuration current.

After installation, changes to the LAT can be accomplished by loading the Microsoft Internet Service Manager, viewing the properties pages for the Socks Proxy, the WinSock Proxy, or the Web Proxy service, and clicking on Local Address Table in the Configuration section.

Exam Essentials

Know how to determine if an IP address range should be included in the Local Address Table (LAT). Internal address ranges should be included in the LAT. External addresses should not.

Know how to construct a LAT, including manually adding and removing IP address ranges, adding private IP address ranges, and loading address ranges from the internal NT routing table. Given a network scenario, you should be able to identify which IP addresses should be included in the LAT. You should know all the different methods you can use when creating the LAT.

Key Terms and Concepts

Internal network: A privately operated network usually with controlled access to and from the Internet.

IP address range: A group of IP addresses, usually defined by a network address and a subnet mask.

Local Address Table (LAT): A Proxy Server configuration file defining the IP address ranges that are internal to the network. All addresses external to network should be excluded from this file.

MSPLAT.TXT: The file containing the LAT.

Sample Questions

1. What is the purpose of the Local Address Table (LAT)?

   A. To store Proxy Server caching configuration information

   B. To define internal and external networks

   C. To assign IP addresses to Proxy Server clients

   D. To store protocol permissions configuration

Answer: B. Internal networks are defined in the LAT. Any network not included in the LAT is considered to be an external network. The LAT does not store caching or protocol configuration. The proxy server does not assign IP addresses to clients.

2. What is the default location for the file containing the LAT?

    A. C:\MSP\MSPLAT.TXT

    B. C:\MSP\CLIENTS\MSPLAT.TXT

    C. C:\MSP\SETUPBIN\MSPLAT.TXT

    D. C:\MSP\CLIENTS\I386\MSPLAT.TXT

Answer: B.

Configure server authentication. Authentication options include:

- Anonymous logon
- Basic authentication
- Microsoft Windows NT Challenge/Response authentication

Once again we find ourselves dealing with a security issue in this objective. The three types of authentication are very different in their functionality and purpose, and a thorough understanding of each is essential.

Critical Information

There are three types of authentication available with Internet Information Server (IIS): Allow Anonymous Logon, Basic (Clear Text), and Windows NT Challenge/Response. Each of these provides a different level of security. When used in conjunction with the other security features provided by Microsoft Proxy Server 2, a very secure network can be accomplished.

Anonymous Logon

When Internet Information Server (IIS) is installed, a default user account is created named IUSR_*computername*.

SEE ALSO For more information on IIS, see the *MCSE: Internet Information Server 4 Study Guide*, 2nd ed. (Sybex, 1998).

You will need to configure the authentication method in the WWW service's properties pages in Internet Service Manager. Figure 2.1 shows the Internet Services Manager screen. To choose a service and view its properties pages, click once to select the service. Then choose Properties from the File menu. You can also double click on the service in Internet Service Manager to go directly to its properties pages.

FIGURE 2.1: The Internet Service Manager screen

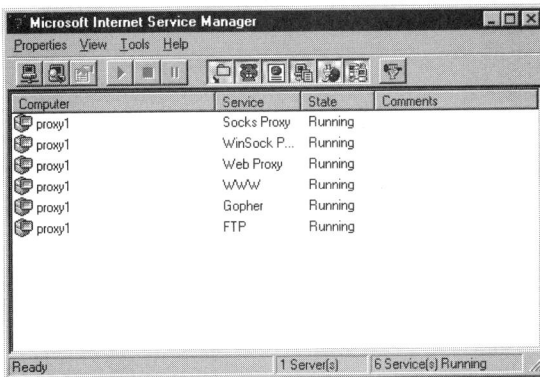

In the Password Authentication section of the WWW service properties pages, Allow Anonymous is one of your choices. If you select this option, anonymous users will be able to access whatever resources for which the IUSR_*computername* account has permissions.

WARNING   If Anonymous Logon is allowed, all client applications will use it. You must disable Anonymous Logon to force users to logon with an account and a password.

You can control anonymous user access to specific directories or files on your Web site. Use NTFS permissions to assign No Access rights for the IUSR_*computername* account to the directory or file you wish to restrict.

WARNING   Permissions to the IUSR_*computername* account are not replicated correctly across an array.

You need to manually configure these permissions. In the following situations, you should grant permissions to the Everyone group instead of granting them directly to the IUSR_*computername* account:

- You have multiple proxy servers configured as an array.

- You want to allow anonymous access to Web publishing from the local IIS computer.

- You want to authenticate users that pass through the Web proxy for client requests.

Basic Authentication

Most browsers on most platforms support Basic authentication. User credentials (username and password) are encoded and then sent across the wire.

WARNING   Even though the user credentials are encoded, someone using a program such as UUdecode who has access to a packet-sniffing device can easily decode them.

Basic authentication offers very weak security and should not be used unless necessary. If, for instance, you have Unix-based Web browsers in your network, they can only use Basic authentication for Web documents requiring password access. When you configure Basic authentication, you can apply it either to all users, or to a subset of users.

Microsoft Windows NT Challenge/Response Authentication

Windows NT Challenge/Response authentication does not transmit the user credentials across the network. Instead, it performs a series of complex calculations on both the client and the server. The user is not prompted for the account name or password. The client software uses established logon information from the current user. Like Basic authentication, Challenge /Response authentication can be applied to all users or to a subset of users. This type of authentication is more secure, but there are some limitations:

- The client browser must be Microsoft Internet Explorer. In fact, Microsoft states, in the Proxy Server documentation, that browsers other than Microsoft Internet Explorer 4 may experience problems with client configuration scripts (JavaScripts) or pages using Secure Sockets Layer (SSL).

- The client and the server must be in the same or a trusted domain.

- Platforms other than Windows cannot use it.

Necessary Procedures

Necessary procedures for this objective include configuring the WWW service for Anonymous Logon, Basic authentication, and Microsoft Windows NT Challenge/Response authentication.

Setting Authentication Type in Internet Service Manager

1. Start Internet Service Manager by selecting Start ➤ Programs ➤ Microsoft Proxy Server ➤ Internet Service Manager.

2. Select Properties for the WWW service, and you will see the following screen:

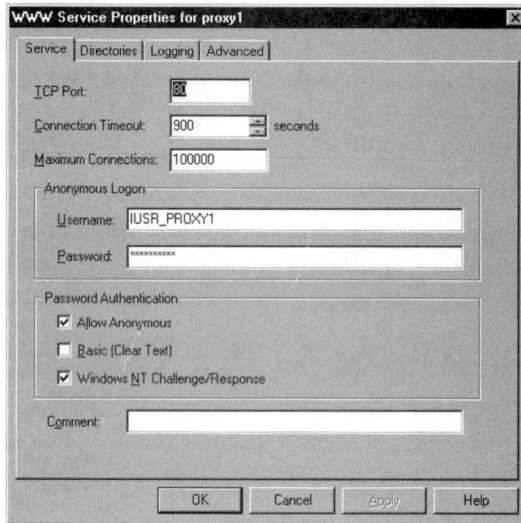

3. In the Password Authentication section, the three choices presented are Allow Anonymous, Basic (Clear Text), and Windows NT Challenge/Response. Select the authentication type that you have chosen and make sure there is not a check by the ones you will not use. Click OK.

4. If you have chosen Basic or Windows NT Challenge/Response, then select the properties page for the Web Proxy service.

5. Click on the Permissions tab.

6. If you wish to allow access to all users, clear the Enable Access Control box.

7. If you wish to allow a subset of users, check the Enable Access Control box and add the user permissions for access rights to each service (FTP, Gopher, WWW, and Secure).

Exam Essentials

Know the different types of authentication. There are three types of authentication: Allow Anonymous Logon, Basic (Clear Text), and

Windows NT Challenge/Response. Basic authentication transmits encoded user credentials across the network, and provides weak security. Windows NT Challenge/Response does not transmit user credentials across the network, but is only supported by Internet Explorer on Windows platforms.

Know how to configure the WWW service for each type of authentication. Review the procedures on how to configure the WWW service for Anonymous Logon, Basic authentication, and Windows NT Challenge/Response authentication.

Know how to apply authentication methods to a subset of users. Understand how to apply these authentication methods to a subset of users using access control.

Key Terms and Concepts

Basic (Clear Text) authentication: Transmits clear-text-encoded user credentials across the network. Supported by a wide variety of browsers and platforms.

UUdecode: A program that decodes UUencoded files from ASCII format back to binary.

Windows NT Challenge/Response authentication: Does not transmit user credentials across the network, using instead a series of complex calculations on both the client and server to authenticate the user. Available only to Internet Explorer clients using Windows.

Sample Questions

1. Which of the following platforms can use Windows NT Challenge/Response authentication?

   A. Unix

   B. Windows 95

   C. Macintosh

   D. Windows NT

Answer: B and D. Of the operating systems listed, only Windows 95 and Windows NT can use Windows NT Challenge/Response authentication.

2. Encoded user credentials, weak security, and compatibility with most operating systems and browsers are features of what authentication method?

   A. Windows NT Challenge/Response authentication

   B. Basic authentication

   C. Anonymous Logon

   D. Packet filtering

Answer: B. Windows NT Challenge/Response authentication features enhanced security and can only be used by Windows platforms. Anonymous access does not require authentication. Packet filtering is not an authentication method. Basic authentication is the correct answer.

3. What service must be configured to set the authentication type?

   A. Web Proxy service

   B. WWW service

   C. WinSock Proxy service

   D. Socks Proxy service

Answer: B. Authentication is configured in the properties pages of the WWW service.

Configure Windows NT to support Microsoft Proxy Server.

This objective is concerned with configuring Windows NT to support Microsoft Proxy Server. Logically, this topic should be the first item in the installation section of the Microsoft objectives, since it concerns settings and configurations that need to be taken care of before you begin the installation of Proxy Server. Important considerations here include: the disk file system used, service packs, and issues concerning TCP/IP and IPX/SPX.

Critical Information

One of the first things you need to do before installing Proxy Server is to make sure that you have installed the correct service pack on your NT Server. Proxy Server requires at least Service Pack 3. Proxy Server also requires at least Internet Information Server (IIS) 3. Version 2 of IIS is installed with Windows NT 4.0. It is automatically upgraded to IIS 3 when Service Pack 3 is applied. If IIS is upgraded to version 4 after Proxy Server 2 is installed, then Proxy Server must be reinstalled.

WARNING   If you install IIS after you have applied Service Pack 3, you must reapply the service pack in order for it to be upgraded to IIS 3. For more information about IIS, see the *MCSE: Internet Information Server 4 Study Guide*, 2nd ed. (Sybex, 1998).

Your disk configuration should also be resolved before installation. If you wish to take advantage of caching, you must have at least one NTFS partition greater than 5MB in size. The use of multiple drives for the cache is recommended, as this will increase cache access speed. The caching process is the only part of Proxy Server that requires an NTFS partition. You can install Proxy Server itself on a FAT partition.

SEE ALSO   For more information on FAT and NTFS, see the *MCSE: NT Server 4 Study Guide*, 2nd ed. (Sybex, 1998).

The domain and all necessary users and groups should be set up before you begin installation. You can install Proxy Server on a primary domain controller, a backup domain controller, or a stand-alone server.

Optimum security is achieved by installing Proxy Server as a stand-alone server in its own domain.

You will also need to configure your internal network adapter. Your proxy server should only have one default gateway, and that should be configured on the external adapter. Leave the default gateway blank for the internal adapter. By this time, you will have decided on your network protocol. You should make sure that this protocol, either IPX/SPX or TCP/IP, is enabled in the bindings for the internal adapter, and that all protocols you are not using are disabled. Also, specify a static IP address and disable DHCP. One more important thing: make sure that IP forwarding is disabled.

WARNING   Installing RAS will cause IP Forwarding to automatically be enabled. You will need to disable it again.

The external network adapter should have only TCP/IP enabled, and should have all TCP/IP settings configured, including: IP address, subnet mask, default gateway, DNS server, and Domain Name. Again, the external card should be the only one that has a default gateway set. If you are using IPX/SPX on your internal network, make sure that this protocol is disabled on the external card.

If IPX/SPX is being used on the internal network, there are some further configurations to take into account. If your network has Novell servers or IPX routers, you should change the frame type detection to Auto. If your network does not have either of these, change the frame type detection to Manual and choose the correct frame type. And since Novell uses the Service Advertising Protocol (SAP) to advertise services, you will need to install the SAP agent. Once installed, this service starts automatically.

SEE ALSO   For more information on IPX/SPX and SAP, see the *MCSE: Proxy Server 2 Study Guide*, 1st ed. (Sybex, 1998).

Necessary Procedures

Necessary procedures for this objective include converting partitions from FAT to NTFS, enabling and disabling a specific protocol on a network card, disabling IP forwarding, configuring frame type detection, and installing the SAP agent. All of these should be done before you begin installation of Proxy Server.

Converting a Partition from FAT to NTFS

If you did not create an NTFS partition when you installed Windows NT Server, you will need to do so before you install Proxy Server. If you have a partition that does not contain data that you need to retain, you can simply reformat the partition as NTFS. If the partition contains data you must keep, you can use CONVERT.EXE to convert the existing partition to NTFS without losing any data. Use the following procedure:

1. From a Command Prompt, type **CONVERT /?**. This will give you the syntax of the command.

2. If the partition to convert were assigned the drive letter D, then you would type at the Command Prompt **CONVERT D: /FS:NTFS**. If the drive you have specified is the current drive, you will see a message stating that and asking if you want to perform the conversion at the next restart. Answer **Yes**, and the next time you restart the server the partition will be converted to NTFS.

Enabling or Disabling a Protocol on a Network Adapter

1. Start Network in Control Panel.

2. Select the Bindings tab, and use the "Show Bindings For" pull-down menu to select All Adapters. You will see the following

screen. The bindings for all network adapters will be displayed here.

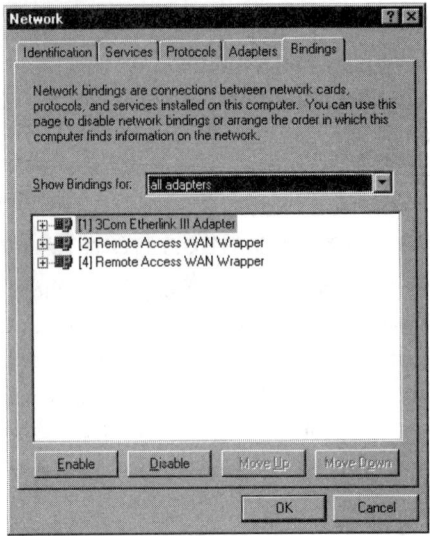

3. Click on the plus sign next to the network adapter you wish to configure.

4. Protocols that are disabled will have a red circle with a line through it next to them. If you need to enable that protocol, click on it and click Enable. To disable a protocol, click on it and click Disable.

5. Click OK, and restart the computer when prompted.

Disabling IP Forwarding

1. Start Network in Control Panel.

2. Select the Protocols tab and then select Properties for TCP/IP Protocol.

3. Select the Routing tab.

4. Clear the Enable IP Forwarding checkbox and click OK.

5. Click Close.

6. Restart the server.

Configuring Frame Type Detection

1. Start Network in Control Panel and select the Protocols tab.

2. Select Properties for NWLink IPX/SPX Compatible Transport, and you will see the screen labeled NWLink IPX/SPX Properties.

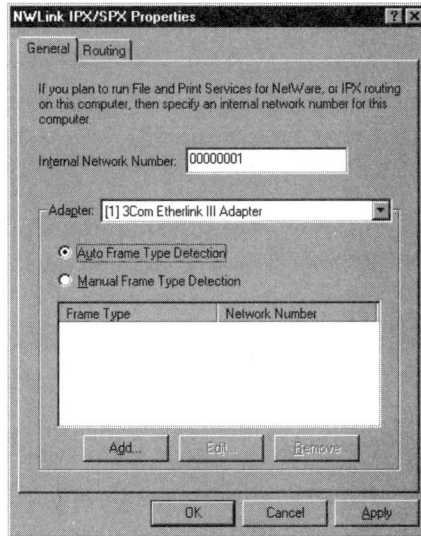

3. From here, depending on your needs, you can select either Auto Frame Type Detection or Manual Frame Type Detection. If you select manual, you can click on Add and then select the correct frame type from the pull-down menu. Type in the correct network number (do not use all zeros), then click Add.

4. Click OK, and then click Close. Restart the computer when prompted.

Installing the SAP agent

1. Start Network in Control Panel.

2. Select the Services tab.

3. Click Add.

4. Select SAP Agent and click OK.

5. Insert the Windows NT CD-ROM if necessary.

6. Click Close and restart the computer when prompted.

Exam Essentials

Know the disk configuration requirements to install Proxy Server.
Proxy Server can be installed on a FAT partition but, in order to use
caching, you must have at least one NTFS partition available.

Know how to set up internal and external network adapters.
Disable unnecessary protocols. Configure a default gateway only on
the external adapter. Make sure IPX/SPX is disabled on the external
card. Disable IP Forwarding.

Know how to configure IPX/SPX frame type detection. If there
are existing NetWare servers, you should set the frame detection type
to Auto. Otherwise, choose Manual and select the correct frame type
and network number.

TIP If you have different versions of NetWare on the same network,
e.g., 3.12 or lower with 4.11 servers, only the 802.2 frame type will be
detected automatically, which means that the 3.12 or lower servers
will not be detected. In this situation, manual frame detection type
should be used.

Key Terms and Concepts

Backup domain controller: An NT server that receives a copy of
the master database and security policies from the primary domain
controller.

Default gateway: The IP address that requests are sent to when
the destination is unknown.

FAT: A file system, supported by all Windows operating systems,
that uses a table to keep track of segments of disk space used for
file storage.

NTFS: A file system supported by Windows NT that offers
enhanced security, file system recovery, object-oriented applications, and support for very large storage media.

Primary domain controller: An NT server used to authenticate client logons and to maintain security policies for an NT domain. It contains the master database for all user security information.

Service Advertising Protocol: A broadcast protocol used in NetWare networks to advertise services.

Sample Questions

1. Your corporate network consists of both NetWare and Windows NT servers. Which method of frame type detection should you configure?

   A. Manual

   B. Auto

   C. Manual, with 802.3 frame type added

   D. Auto, with Ethernet_II frame type added

   Answer: B. When you have existing NetWare servers, Auto frame type detection should be selected.

2. Microsoft Proxy Server can be installed on the following computers:

   A. Primary domain controller

   B. Member server

   C. Windows NT workstation

   D. Backup domain controller

   Answer: A, B, and D. Proxy Server cannot be installed on a Windows NT workstation.

3. SAP stands for:

   A. Service Algorithm Protocol

   B. Standard Advertising Protocol

   C. Simple Advertising Package

   D. Service Advertising Protocol

   Answer: D. SAP stands for Service Advertising Protocol.

Configure the various Proxy Server services.

Understanding the features of each proxy service and how to configure those services is crucial to successfully taking the exam and also to successfully installing Proxy Server. In this objective you will review how to configure the services that Proxy Server will offer to clients.

Critical Information

Proxy Server offers three services: the Web Proxy service, the WinSock Proxy service, and the Socks Proxy service.

Web Proxy Service

As discussed in Chapter 1, the Web Proxy service supports all CERN-compliant Web browsers without regard to the operating system. After Proxy Server is installed, you can access the Web Proxy service properties pages from the Internet Service Manager. There are six tabs available to choose from: Service, Permissions, Caching, Routing, Publishing, and Logging.

Service

The Service tab allows you to make configuration changes that are common to all services. This tab includes a Shared Services section that you will use to configure Security, Array, Auto Dial, and Plug-in settings that are common to all the proxy services. Figure 2.2 shows the Web Proxy service properties pages with the Service tab selected. Note the Shared Services section on the left side of the screen. The settings that are configured in this section are discussed in greater detail later in this chapter.

F I G U R E 2.2: The Service tab of the proxy service properties pages is used to configure shared services.

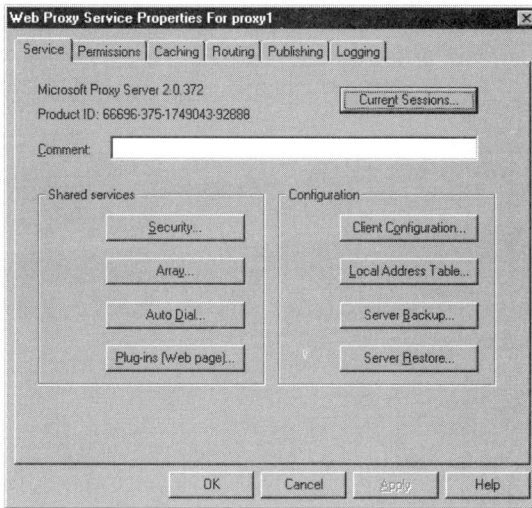

Permissions

Selecting the Permissions tab allows you to configure permissions for the Web Proxy service. The Web Proxy service allows four options for which you can configure permissions:

- FTP Read
- Gopher
- Secure
- WWW

In order to access these options, access control must be enabled. You can then select one of the options listed above and assign either read access for FTP Read or Gopher, or full access for Secure or WWW. Clicking on Edit will then allow you to add users or groups to whom you wish to allow access to that protocol.

Caching

The Caching tab allows you to configure how Proxy Server will cache objects. Once Enable Caching has been selected, Proxy Server will perform what is called passive caching. This means that any object requested from the Internet will be stored in the proxy server's cache. You can also enable active caching. Active caching is the process of downloading frequently requested sites in advance during periods of low network utilization. Proxy Server uses three factors to determine which objects it will refresh with active caching and when that caching will take place:

The Time-to-Live (TTL) of the object: As the TTL nears expiration, active caching automatically updates the object from the Internet.

The object's popularity relative to its rate of change: Proxy Server gives priority in active caching to the most frequently requested objects.

Current server load: Proxy Server determines times when server load is low and performs active caching at these times. This does not mean that active caching will not retrieve any objects during times of high server load. But the bulk of active caching is done during times of low server load.

Both passive and active caching use a Time-to-Live (TTL) in determining how long it will keep a particular object in cache. A longer TTL causes the object to remain in cache longer, therefore the external network is not accessed as often. For some sites this works well. However, some sites change their content daily or even from minute to minute. For these sites, having a long TTL could result in receiving false or outdated data. For passive caching, there are three different settings available:

Updates are more important (more update checks): When this option is selected, the TTL for all objects is set to 0 minutes, unless the object has its own TTL specified. This is useful for sites with highly volatile information such as stock quotes, search pages, etc.

Equal importance: When this option is selected, the TTL for all objects without a TTL specified will be set to 20% of the object's age, assuming the object provides Proxy Server with a time last modified. It also specifies a minimum TTL of 15 minutes, and a maximum of 1440 minutes.

Fewer network accesses are more important (more cache hits): When this option is selected, the TTL is set to 40% of the object's age, again assuming that the object does not have its own TTL and the object provides Proxy Server with a time last modified. It specifies a minimum TTL of 30 minutes, a maximum of 2880 minutes.

For all of these options, if FTP caching is enabled, the default TTL is 1440 minutes. By clicking on the Advanced button, you can specify all of these settings yourself. You can also specify a limit to the size of an object in cache. By default, no limit is set. In the Advanced Cache Policy screen, you can also determine how long Proxy Server will serve an object from cache if the object cannot be updated from the source Web site. Default is 50% of the TTL. From this screen, you can also create cache filters. You can create a filter specifying that all or part of a particular site either always be cached or never be cached.

Active caching also has three settings:

- Faster user response is more important (more prefetching)
- Equal importance
- Fewer network accesses are more important (less prefetching)

Finally, the Web Proxy service properties pages allow you to specify the cache size. Microsoft recommends at least 100MB + 0.5MB for each client computer.

Routing

Routing is a Proxy Server function that provides fault tolerance in upstream paths, either to other portions of your network or to the Internet. By configuring routing you can provide a backup network path either to the Internet or to the central office from a branch office. Routing is only supported by the Web Proxy service.

When configuring routing, you have two options. You can configure a proxy server to route client requests to a proxy server upstream (this is called upstream routing), or you can configure it to route client requests directly to the Internet. Of course, this takes place only if the object requested does not reside in cache. Now by enabling a backup route you can provide fault tolerance. Again, you have two choices: routing to a proxy server or array upstream, or routing directly to the Internet. This route can be a slower dedicated connection, an ISDN line, or even a modem connection. You can also tell Proxy Server to resolve requests within an array before looking upstream.

Publishing

Publishing enables you to provide secure access from external users to an internal Web site. When Web publishing is enabled, there are three ways you can configure Proxy Server to deal with incoming Web requests. They can be discarded, sent to the local Web server, or sent to another Web server. This means that the external user will not actually see the Web server they are accessing. Mappings can also be configured to route specific URLs to specific Web servers. Some older browsers do not provide the full publishing server name in their request. For these browsers, you should configure a default mapping to which all requests of these types can be sent.

Logging

The Web Proxy service can be configured to log in regular format or in verbose format. It can be configured to log to a text file or to a SQL/OBDC database. If logging to a text file is selected, the Web Proxy service can be configured to create a new log file daily, weekly, or monthly. The number of old log files can be limited, and the Web Proxy service can be stopped if the disk becomes full. By default the log files are stored in *drive*:\root\SYSTEM32\MSPLOGS, although this location can be changed. Log files for the Web Proxy service are named in the following format: W3*yymmdd*.LOG. If you choose to log to a SQL/OBDC database, you must provide the following information: the OBDC Data Source Name (DSN), the table, and the username and password for the database.

WinSock Proxy Service

Applications using the WinSock Proxy service operate as if they had a direct connection to the Internet. In order to use the WinSock Proxy service, the client must be using a Windows operating system. After installation, there are three configuration tabs that are specific to WinSock Proxy service: Protocols, Permissions, and Logging.

Protocols

The WinSock Proxy service has many protocols already defined. Examples include HTTP, FTP, RealAudio, and POP3, to list just a few.

New protocols can be added as needed. To add a protocol, simply click on Add and type in a protocol name. Type the port number used by the protocol, and indicate if it will use TCP or UDP. Define if the protocol definition will be used for outbound or inbound traffic. You can also identify a range of ports to be used for subsequent connections. The protocol definitions can also be saved to or loaded from a file.

Permissions

The WinSock Proxy service presents numerous protocol options for which permissions can be assigned. If, for example, you need to assign protocol permissions for the HTTP protocol, go to the Permissions tab of the WinSock Proxy Service properties pages. Access control must be enabled. Select HTTP from the pop-up Protocol menu, and then click on Edit. You can then choose a group or user to give access to this protocol. Any user not given access or not belonging to a group given access will be denied use of the HTTP protocol. You can assign permissions to any protocol defined under the Protocols tab.

Logging

The WinSock Proxy service can be configured to log in regular format or in verbose format. It can be configured to log to a text file or to a SQL/OBDC database. If logging to a text file is selected, the WinSock Proxy service can be configured to create a new log file daily, weekly, or monthly. The number of old log files can be limited, and the WinSock Proxy service can be stopped if the disk becomes full. By default the log files are stored in *drive*:*root*\SYSTEM32\MSPLOGS, although this location can be changed. Log files for the Web Proxy service are named in the following format: WS*yymmdd*.LOG. If you choose to log to a SQL/OBDC database, you must provide the following information: the OBDC Data Source Name (DSN), the table name, and the username and password for the database.

Socks Proxy Service

The Socks Proxy service is similar to the WinSock Proxy service in that it provides transparent redirection of TCP/IP requests to the proxy server. However, it can be used by most popular client operating systems. There are two configuration tabs that are specific to the Socks Proxy service: Permissions and Logging.

Permissions

The Socks Proxy service is somewhat different in its application of permissions. By default, all Socks requests are denied. You can permit or deny requests to or from a Domain/Zone, an IP subnet, or All. You select a port number or a range of port numbers to apply this permission to. When you select the port number, you need to define the permission as applying to a number Equal To the port number listed (EQ), Not Equal To (NEQ), Greater Than (GT), Less Than (LT), Greater Than or Equal To (GE), or Less Than or Equal To (LE). Although not as advanced as the WinSock Proxy service, the Socks Proxy service has the advantage of wide support on both Windows and non-Windows platforms.

Logging

The Socks Proxy service can be configured to log in regular format or in verbose format. It can be configured to log to a text file or to a SQL/OBDC database. If logging to a text file is selected, the Socks Proxy service can be configured to create a new log file daily, weekly, or monthly. The number of old log files can be limited, and the Socks Proxy service can be stopped if the disk becomes full. By default the log files are stored in *drive*:\root\SYSTEM32\MSPLOGS, although this location can be changed. Log files for the Web Proxy service are named in the following format: SP*yymmdd*.LOG. If you choose to log to a SQL/OBDC database, you must provide the following information: the OBDC Data Source Name (DSN), the table name, and the username and password for the database.

Necessary Procedures

There are several procedures associated with this important objective and they all have to do with configuring proxy services. Knowing how to configure these services properly is essential to proper implementation of Proxy Server, and to being successful on the Proxy Server exam.

Assigning Permissions in the Web Proxy Service

1. Start Internet Service Manager by selecting Start ➤ Programs ➤ Microsoft Proxy Server ➤ Internet Service Manager. Select Properties for the Web Proxy service.

2. Click on the Permissions tab. You will see the following screen:

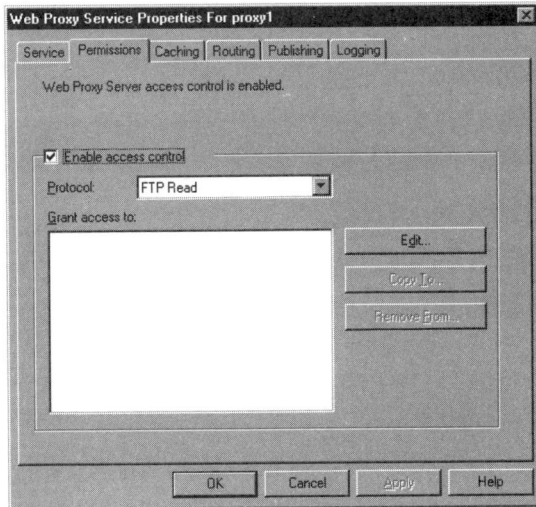

3. Make sure Enable Access Control is checked.

4. In the Protocol pull-down menu, select the protocol for which you need to assign permissions.

5. Click Edit.

6. Click Add.

7. Select the user or group to whom you need to give access for this protocol.

8. Click OK, then click OK again.

Configuring Passive Caching and Active Caching

1. Start Internet Service Manager by selecting Start ➤ Programs ➤ Microsoft Proxy Server ➤ Internet Service Manager.

2. Select Properties for the Web Proxy service.

3. Click on the Caching tab. You will see the following screen:

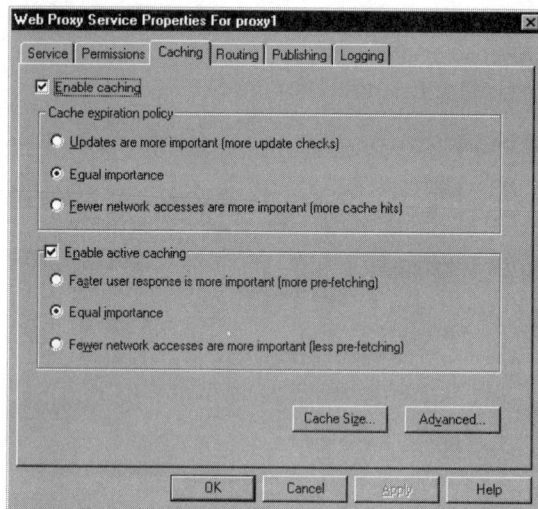

4. To enable passive caching, check the Enable Caching box.

5. Under Cache expiration policy, select one of the three options:

   A. Updates Are More Important (More Update Checks)

   B. Equal Importance

   C. Fewer Network Accesses Are More Important (More Cache Hits)

6. If you wish to change the default settings for caching, click on the Advanced button.

7. To configure active caching, make sure the Enable Active Caching box is checked. Then select one of the three options:

   A. Faster User Response Is More Important (More Pre-Fetching)

   B. Equal Importance

   C. Fewer Network Accesses Are More Important (Less Pre-Fetching)

8. Click on OK.

Configuring a Cache Filter

1. Start Internet Service Manager by selecting Start ➤ Programs ➤ Microsoft Proxy Server ➤ Internet Service Manager.

2. Select Properties for the Web Proxy service.

3. Click on the Caching tab.

4. Click on the Advanced button.

5. Click on the Cache Filters button. You will see the screen labeled Cache Filters:

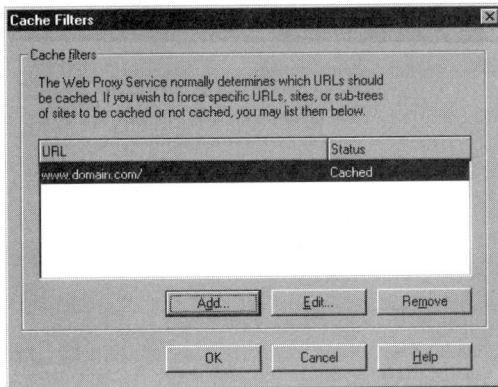

6. Click Add.

7. Type the URL you wish to block. Asterisks may be used as wild cards, e.g., `*.adomain.com/` or `www.adomain.com/somepath/*`

8. Under Filtering Status, select Always Cache or Never Cache.

9. Click OK twice.

Configuring Routing

1. Start Internet Service Manager by selecting Start ➤ Programs ➤ Microsoft Proxy Server ➤ Internet Service Manager. Select Properties for the Web Proxy service.

2. Click on the Routing tab. You will see the following screen:

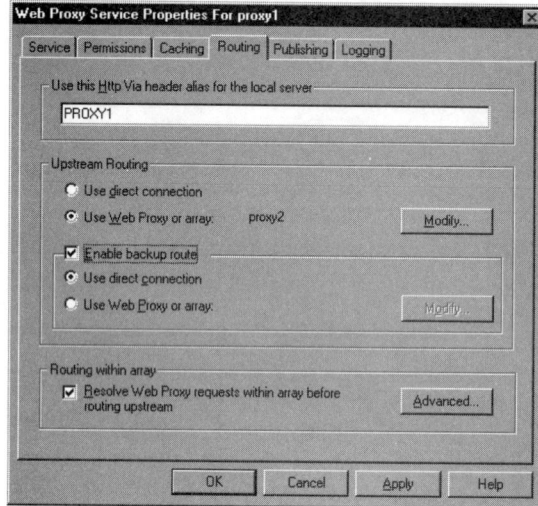

Web Proxy Service Properties For proxy1

Service | Permissions | Caching | Routing | Publishing | Logging

Use this Http Via header alias for the local server

PROXY1

Upstream Routing

○ Use direct connection
● Use Web Proxy or array: proxy2   [Modify...]

☑ Enable backup route
  ● Use direct connection
  ○ Use Web Proxy or array: [Modify...]

Routing within array

☑ Resolve Web Proxy requests within array before routing upstream   [Advanced...]

[OK] [Cancel] [Apply] [Help]

3. For upstream routing, select either Use Direct Connection or Use Web Proxy Or Array.

4. If you choose Use Direct Connection, you are done.

5. If you choose Use Web Proxy Or Array, click on Modify. You will see the screen labeled Advanced Routing Options:

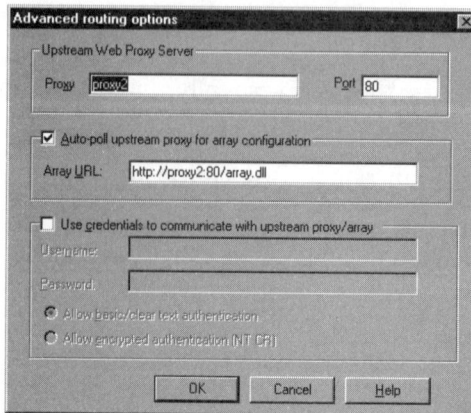

Advanced routing options

Upstream Web Proxy Server

Proxy [proxy2]   Port [80]

☑ Auto-poll upstream proxy for array configuration

Array URL: [http://proxy2:80/array.dll]

☐ Use credentials to communicate with upstream proxy/array

Username: [ ]

Password: [ ]

○ Allow basic/clear text authentication
○ Allow encrypted authentication (NT CR)

[OK] [Cancel] [Help]

6. Type in the name of the upstream proxy server. Click OK. You will be returned to the Routing properties screen.

7. Select the Enable Backup Route checkbox. Choose either Use Direct Connection or Use Web Proxy Or Array in the area below the Enable Backup Route checkbox.

8. If you choose Direct Connection, you are finished. Click Apply.

9. If you choose Use Web Proxy Or Array, click on Modify.

10. Type in the name of the proxy server you wish to use as a backup route.

11. Click OK, and then click Apply.

Configuring Web Publishing

1. Start Internet Service Manager by selecting Start ≻ Programs ≻ Microsoft Proxy Server ≻ Internet Service Manager.

2. Select Properties for the Web Proxy service.

3. Click on the Publishing tab. You will see the following screen:

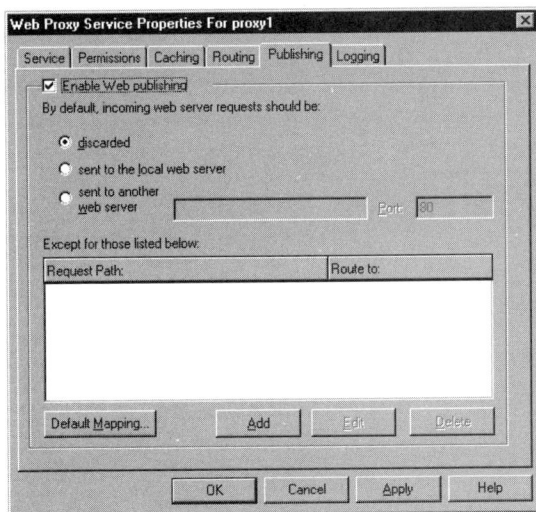

4. Put a check in the Enable Web Publishing checkbox.

5. Choose what you wish to do with incoming Web requests: discard, send to the local Web server, or send to another Web server.

6. If you wish, create a default mapping for older Web browsers by clicking on Default Mapping and typing in the default server name.

7. Create mappings for specific paths to multiple Web servers by clicking on Add.

8. Type in both the incoming path to listen for, and the URL to send the request to. Note that both paths must be typed out in full, e.g., http://www.mydomain.com.

9. Click OK twice.

Configuring Logging

Configuring logging is actually the same for all three proxy services. Logging is enabled by default.

1. Start Internet Service Manager by selecting Start ➤ Programs ➤ Microsoft Proxy Server ➤ Internet Service Manager.

2. Select Properties for the service for which you wish to configure logging. Select the Logging tab. You will see a screen similar to the following, depending on which service you selected:

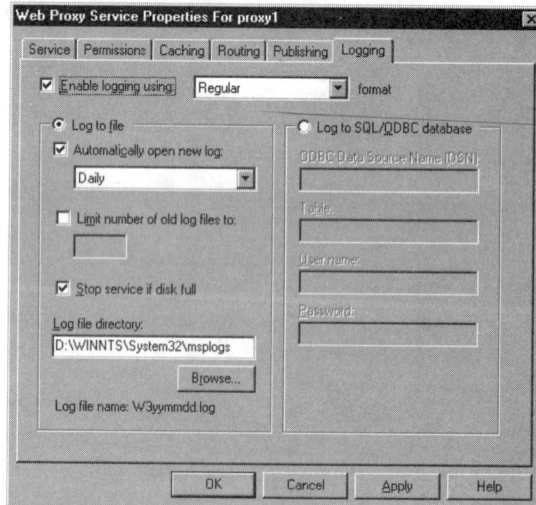

3. Logging should be enabled already. Select Regular or Verbose from the pull-down Format menu.

4. By default, Log To File will be selected. If you leave this enabled, you have the option to automatically open new log files either daily (the default), weekly, or monthly.

5. You can limit the number of old log files by putting a check in this box, and entering a number.

6. "Stop Service If Disk Full" is checked by default; uncheck it if you wish.

7. You can also change the directory the log files are stored in by clicking Browse.

8. You can also select Log To SQL/OBDC Database. If you select this, Log To File is automatically deselected.

9. Once selected, you enter an OBDC Data Source Name (DSN), a Table, a Username, and a Password.

10. Click OK and you are done.

Adding Protocol Definitions to the WinSock Proxy Service

1. Start Internet Service Manager by selecting Start ➤ Programs ➤ Microsoft Proxy Server ➤ Internet Service Manager.

2. Select Properties for the WinSock Proxy service.

3. Click on the Protocols tab.

4. Click Add. You will see the screen labeled Protocol Definition:

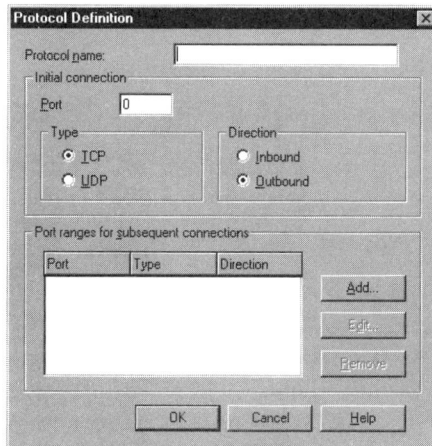

5. Type in the protocol name.

6. Enter the initial connection port.

7. Select TCP or UDP, and Inbound or Outbound.

8. If port ranges for subsequent connections are needed, click Add.

9. Define the port range.

10. Select TCP or UDP, Inbound or Outbound.

11. Click OK twice.

Configuring Protocol Permissions in the WinSock Proxy Service

1. Start Internet Service Manager by selecting Start ➤ Programs ➤ Microsoft Proxy Server ➤ Internet Service Manager.

2. Select Properties for the WinSock Proxy service.

3. Click on the Permissions tab.

4. Select the protocol for which you need to assign permissions and click Edit.

5. Assign access to the appropriate groups or users.

6. Click OK twice to return to the Internet Service Manager.

Configuring Permissions in the Socks Proxy Service

1. Start Internet Service Manager by selecting Start ➤ Programs ➤ Microsoft Proxy Server ➤ Internet Service Manager.

2. Select Properties for the Socks Proxy service.

3. Click on the Permissions tab.

4. Click Add. You will see the following screen labeled Socks Permission:

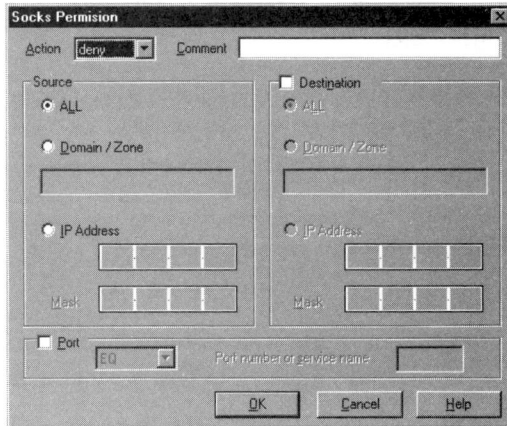

5. Select Action: Deny or Permit. Select Source or Destination.

6. Enter a short comment in the Comment field for easy recognition later.

7. Select All, Domain/Zone, or IP Address depending on your needs.

   A. If you select Domain/Zone, type in the name of the Domain.

   B. If you select IP Address, enter the IP address and the subnet mask to create a range.

8. Click on the Port checkbox to activate it.

9. Type in the port number or service name.

10. Select the qualifier, i.e., EQ (equal), GT (greater than), etc.

11. Click OK.

Exam Essentials

Know what functions the Web Proxy service can provide and how to configure those functions.   The Web Proxy service offers functionality in the areas of permissions, caching, routing, Web publishing, and logging.

Know what functions the WinSock Proxy service can provide and how to configure those functions. The WinSock Proxy service offers predefined and custom protocol definitions, protocol permissions, and logging.

Know what functions the Socks Proxy service offers and how to configure those functions. The Socks Proxy service offers permissions based on IP addresses and port numbers, and logging.

Key Terms and Concepts

Active caching: The process of downloading frequently requested sites in advance during periods of low network utilization.

Backup route: An alternate route configured to provide access to the rest of the network or to the Internet in the event that the primary route fails.

Caching: The process of storing requested objects in disk space on a local server.

Cache filtering: Specifying sites either to always be cached or to never be cached.

Passive caching: The process of caching objects as they are requested.

Permissions: Rules associated with an object that determine the amount and type of access users will have to that object.

Proxy array: Multiple proxy servers configured to work together provide load balancing, fault tolerance, and distributed caching.

Routing: In the context of Microsoft Proxy Server, this is the process of having a proxy server route its requests to an upstream proxy or array, and of a proxy server being able to switch to a backup network connection in the event of a failure on the primary route.

Socks Proxy service: This service provides transparent redirection of client requests for a wide variety of platforms. Microsoft Proxy Server 2 supports Socks version 4.3a.

TCP: Part of the TCP/IP protocol suite, TCP provides reliable, full duplex, connection-oriented transport.

Time-to-Live (TTL): The amount of time an object will be stored in cache before it must be updated from the original site.

Upstream routing: Configuring a proxy server to point upstream to another proxy server or a proxy array.

User Datagram Protocol (UDP): Part of the TCP/IP protocol suite, UDP provides connectionless-oriented transport.

Web Proxy service: This service supports CERN-compliant Web browsers running on any platform.

WinSock Proxy service: This service provides transparent support through the use of APIs for redirection of Windows-based client requests.

Sample Questions

1. You administer a corporate network and wish to configure active caching. You will need to configure the properties for which service?

   A. Web Proxy service

   B. Socks Proxy service

   C. Gopher service

   D. WinSock Proxy service

   Answer: A. Only the Web Proxy service offers caching. Neither the Socks nor the WinSock Proxy service support caching. Gopher is not a Proxy Server service.

2. Logging is enabled for all of your proxy services. They are configured to log to a text file. By default, what directory will the log files be stored in?

   A. C:\WINNT\SYSTEM\MSPLOGS

   B. C:\WINNT\MSPLOGS

   C. C:\WINNT\SYSTEM32\MSPLOGS

   D. C:\WINNT\SYSTEM34\LOGS

   Answer: C. The default location for log files is C:\WINNT\SYSTEM32\MSPLOGS.

3. Which proxy service includes many predefined protocols including HTTP, FTP, RealAudio, and HTTPS?

 A. WinSock Proxy service

 B. Socks Proxy service

 C. WWW Proxy service

 D. Web Proxy service

Answer: A. The WinSock Proxy service contains many predefined protocols for which permissions can be assigned. The Socks Service has no predefined protocols. There is no such thing as a WWW Proxy service. The Web Proxy service only has four protocols to assign permissions to: FTP Read, Gopher, HTTP, and Secure.

Configure Microsoft Proxy Server for Internet access. Situations include:

- Configuring Proxy Server to provide Internet access through a dial-up connection to an ISP.
- Configuring Proxy Server to act as an IPX gateway.
- Configuring multiple Microsoft Proxy Servers for Internet access.
- Configuring multiple Proxy Servers spread across several different geographic locations.

Now that you have configured the proxy services, it is time to configure the proxy server to provide client access to the Internet. There are many aspects involved in these topics and you can expect plenty of questions on these topics on the Proxy Server exam. You will also need to have a thorough understanding of these issues when the time comes for you to implement Proxy Server in your network.

Critical Information

In the course of reading this book, you have been asked to consider how you will provide Internet access to users in your network. This can be accomplished by using a dial-up connection or by using a dedicated connection. Your internal network can use TCP/IP, or you can configure Proxy Server as an IPX gateway and use IPX/SPX. Single proxy servers can be placed at branch offices, pointing to arrays at central offices.

Configuring Proxy Server to Provide Internet Access through a Dial-Up Connection to an ISP

In order to use the Auto Dial feature of Proxy Server, there are several things that must be done:

- The Remote Access Server (RAS) client must be installed.

WARNING   After installing RAS, IP forwarding is automatically enabled. You should immediately disable it in the TCP/IP properties pages. For more information about RAS, see the *MCSE: NT Server 4 Study Guide*, 2nd ed. (Sybex, 1998).

- Configure RAS for dial out only.

- A phone book entry must be created.

- Remote Access properties must be configured. This consists of starting the Services Control Panel and setting the startup type for Remote Access Auto Dial Manager to disabled, and setting the startup type for Remote Access Connection Manager to automatic.

- The WINS client should be unbound from the Remote Access WAN Wrapper.

- Depending on the ISP, user credentials may need to be reset.

- Dialing services and dialing hours should be set.

- Proxy services should be stopped and restarted.

The Auto Dial function can be configured using Internet Service manager. Do this from the Shared Services section of the Service tab on the properties pages of any of the three proxy services. You can enable Auto Dial for the WinSock and Socks Proxy services, the Web Proxy Primary route, and the Web Proxy Backup route. Allowed dialing hours can be configured here as well. The Auto Dial feature will be automatically engaged in the following situations:

- The Web Proxy service receives a request for an object that is not in cache.

- Active caching begins automatically pre-fetching.

- The WinSock Proxy service receives any request.

- The Socks Proxy service receives any request.

Configuring Proxy Server to Act as an IPX Gateway

Microsoft Proxy Server automatically supports IPX clients after installation. However, the following steps should also be taken in order to allow IPX client access:

- Configure the frame type correctly. If there is an IPX router or NetWare server on the network, IPX will automatically be configured with the correct frame type and network number. If not, these must be manually specified. When you configure a manual frame type, the MSPCLNT.INI file should be configured as follows:

  ```
  [Servers Ipx Addresses]

  Addr1=55555555-000000000001
  ```

- All clients must be either Windows 95 or Windows NT, and must be using 32-bit client software.

- Because of certain problems that can occur with redirection of certain Windows NT services, verify that the following sections of the MSPCLNT.INI file are set as follows:

  ```
  [services]

  Disable=1

  [spoolss]
  ```

```
Disable=1

[rpcss]

Disable=1
```

If IPX/SPX is the only internal protocol, Proxy Server assumes that all TCP/IP requests are destined for the Internet. When a TCP/IP request is received, the WinSock Proxy DLL converts the Windows Socket API parameters to their appropriate IPX/SPX counterparts. The request is then sent to the proxy server. The proxy server then performs the same conversion in reverse and forwards it to the correct destination on the external network. The WinSock Proxy DLL supports virtually all WinSock 1.1 compatible applications. It does not support WinSock 2 applications. The WinSock Proxy DLL combines the following tasks with standard redirection functionality:

Socket() API   When an application uses either UDP or TCP, the WinSock Proxy DLL changes this to the correct IPX/SPX protocol.

Bind() API   When an IP address is given to bind a socket to, the IP address is converted to a local IPX/SPX address. A call to bind to IP_Any is also converted.

Connect() API   When an application connects to an application on the Internet, the address passed to the WinSock Proxy DLL is the IPX address of the internal network adapter on the proxy server.

Sendto() API   The destination address is converted into the IPX address of the internal network adapter on the proxy server.

Recvfrom() API   The source IP address returned is converted from the IPX address of the proxy server to the IP address of the Internet application.

IPX   Is used in place of UDP on the control channel.

Configuring Multiple Microsoft Proxy Servers for Internet Access

There are several considerations when configuring multiple proxy servers to provide Internet access. Multiple proxy servers can work together to provide services to clients using DNS, DHCP, and WINS.

DNS

DNS stands for Domain Naming System and is used to map domain names to IP addresses. Each proxy server must have at least one DNS server IP address configured. A secondary server should be configured for fault tolerance. DNS round robin can be used to provide load balancing. DNS round robin involves assigning multiple IP addresses belonging to each proxy server to one domain name. DNS then cycles through the addresses as requests for resolution of that domain name are received.

DHCP

DHCP stands for Dynamic Host Configuration Protocol. DHCP can be running on a computer running Proxy Server. The internal adapter must have a static IP address assigned, and no default gateway specified. The DHCP server option should be enabled for the internal network adapter only and should be disabled for the external network adapter. There are no special considerations involved in using a proxy server as a DHCP relay.

WINS

A WINS server can be used to configure a multihomed environment. This is similar to DNS round robin. One entry is created containing a list of all of the IP addresses for the proxy servers. The WINS service identifies the source IP address of a client request. It then attempts to locate a proxy server on the same subnet. Failing that, it will attempt to find a proxy server on the same net as the client. If WINS cannot match the client request to a gateway at this point, it picks one at random from the WINS list.

Configuring Multiple Proxy Servers Spread across Several Different Geographic Locations

Configuring proxy servers in a network that spans several geographic locations provides some unique problems. Available bandwidth, connection method, and number of users are all factors that must be considered. Microsoft Proxy Server presents several methods of dealing with these issues.

Arrays

Arrays cause multiple proxy servers to act together as a single logical unit. This increases efficiency in a central location with a large number of users. Arrays can also benefit smaller locations such as branch offices with a smaller number of users and perhaps a slower connection by serving as an upstream proxy server. Figure 2.3 shows a basic array configuration.

FIGURE 2.3: An array of proxy servers

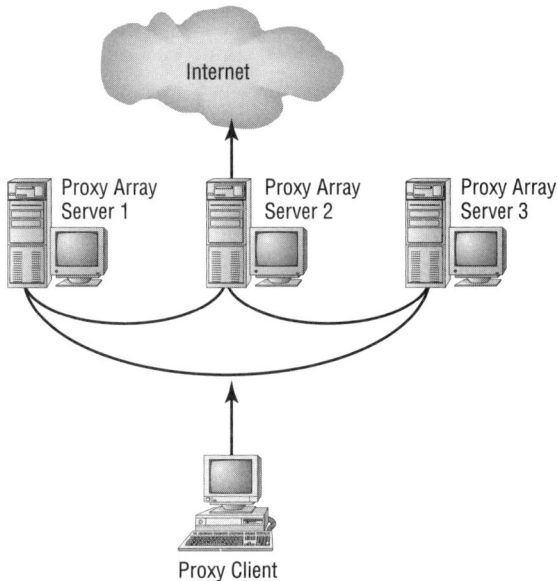

Internet

Proxy Array Server 1

Proxy Array Server 2

Proxy Array Server 3

Proxy Client

Upstream routing

Configuring a single proxy server in a smaller location to point upstream to a proxy array improves caching efficiency and provides load balancing.

Backup Routes

Backup routes can be used in both branch-office situations and central-office situations. At the branch office, a proxy server could be configured to dial a RAS server at the central office for connectivity in the event that the dedicated connection goes down. At the central office, array members could be configured to have a backup route to the external network, which, of course, would increase fault tolerance.

Caching

Arrays should have active caching configured. Branch offices using a single proxy server routing upstream to an array should enable only passive caching. This reduces network congestion over a slow connection while still allowing the branch office to take advantage of the active caching.

Necessary Procedures

Although there are several procedures associated with this objective, many of them are covered by other objectives within this chapter. The necessary procedures unique to this objective are configuring Auto Dial and unbinding the WINS client from the external adapter.

Configuring Auto Dial

1. Start the Internet Service Manager.

2. Select Properties for any of the proxy services. You will see the properties screen with the Services tab selected.

3. From the Shared Services section, click on Auto Dial to see the following Configuration screen:

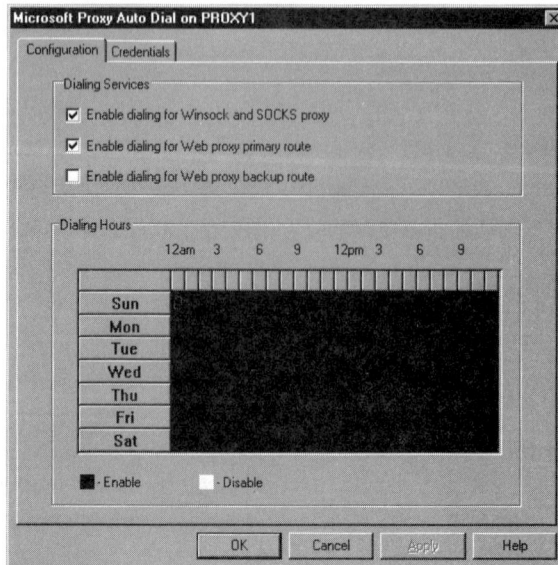

4. From here you can enable Auto Dial for the WinSock and Socks Proxy services, for the Web Proxy primary route, and for the Web Proxy backup route.

5. Configure allowed dialing hours if necessary.

6. Click on the Credentials tab to see the following screen:

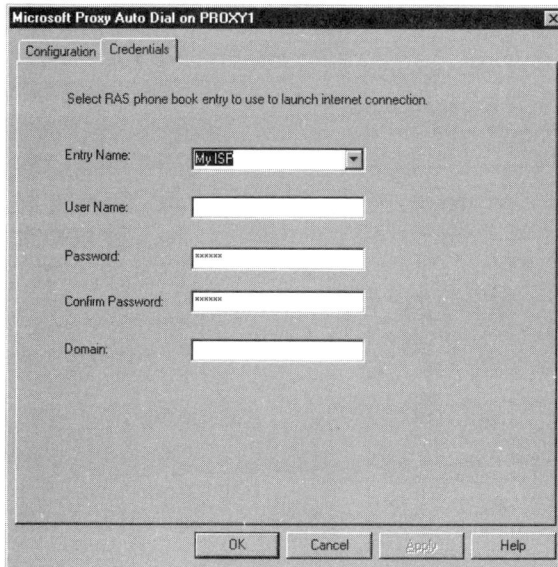

7. Select the phone book entry you have created for this service, and enter the username, password, and domain name if necessary.

8. Click OK, then click OK or Apply.

Unbinding the WINS Client from the External Network Adapter

1. Start Network in Control Panel.

2. Click on the Bindings tab.

3. From the "Show Bindings for" pull-down menu, select Adapters.

4. Click on the plus sign next to the external adapter.

5. Highlight the WINS client and click on Disable.

6. Click OK.

Exam Essentials

Know how to configure Proxy Server to support Auto Dial. RAS must be installed, a phone book entry must be created, Remote Access properties must be configured, and the WINS client should be unbound from the external network adapter.

Know how to configure Auto Dial. Auto Dial is configured using Internet Service Manager. It can be configured for the WinSock and Socks Proxy services, the Web Proxy primary route, and the Web Proxy backup route. Dialing hours can also be configured. Credentials must also be entered.

Know how to configure Proxy Server to support clients using DNS, DHCP, and WINS. Understand how Proxy Server can provide DNS and DHCP services, and how WINS can be used to provide load balancing.

Know how different Proxy Server features can accommodate diverse geographic conditions. Understand how arrays, upstream routing, caching options, and backup routes can be used to provide optimum service in various geographical conditions.

Key Terms and Concepts

Application Programming Interface (API): A set of routines used by an application to have an operating system or another service perform lower level functions.

DHCP: Dynamic Host Configuration Protocol. Provides automatic configuration of TCP/IP settings information to DHCP clients.

DNS: Domain Naming System. DNS is used to map domain names to IP addresses.

DNS round robin: If multiple IP addresses are mapped to the same domain name, DNS servers cycle through the lists of IP addresses each time a request for that domain name is received.

Fault tolerance: The ability to continue services in the event that an individual proxy server or network connection goes down.

MSPCLNT.INI: A global configuration file that is downloaded regularly by proxy server clients.

NetBIOS: Network Basic Input/Output System. NetBIOS is an API used by applications on a local area network.

WINS: Windows Internet Name Service. Provides dynamic and static mapping of NetBIOS names to IP addresses.

Sample Questions

1. When configuring Proxy Server as an IPX gateway, under what circumstances should the frame type in the IPX/SPX properties pages be configured for Auto Detect?

   A. When there is a NetWare server or an IPX router on the network

   B. When there are client computers configured to use IPX/SPX

   C. When there are Unix servers on the network

   D. When Gateway Services for NetWare is installed

   Answer: A. If there is a NetWare server or an IPX router on the network, frame type detection should be set to Auto Detect. Otherwise, the frame type should be specified manually.

2. Which proxy service properties can be used to configure Auto Dial?

   A. Web Proxy service

   B. Socks Proxy service

   C. WinSock Proxy service

   D. WWW service

   Answer: A, B, and C. Auto Dial is configured from the Shared Services section of any of the three Proxy Server services. The WWW service is not a Proxy Server service.

3. Which of the following are settings that should be used when running DHCP on a computer also running Proxy Server?

A. The internal adapter should use a static IP address.

B. The internal adapter should not have a default gateway defined.

C. The external adapter should not have a default gateway defined.

D. The DHCP Server option should be disabled for the external adapter.

Answer: A, B, and D. The internal adapter should use a static IP address and should not have a default gateway defined. The external adapter must have a default gateway defined. And the DHCP Server option should be disabled for the external adapter.

Select and use software configuration management tools (for example, Control Panel, Windows NT Setup, Regedt32).

This objective introduces various tools that can be used to configure and administer Proxy Server. Although Internet Service Manager will be your primary tool for this, there are several other tools that provide valuable assistance. The Proxy Server exam will certainly have questions concerning the use of the alternative tools, and you can expect to encounter real-world situations where they will be helpful.

Critical Information

Configuration management tools that will be discussed under this objective include Regedit and Regedt32, the Services Control Panel, and command line utilities such as Net Start and Net Stop, RemotMSP, and WSPProto. Caution should be used with these utilities, particularly when editing the registry. Of course, Internet Service Manager can be used to accomplish almost everything these tools can accomplish, but there may be situations where you either cannot or do not want to use it.

Regedit and Regedt32

Regedit and Regedt32 are two tools available by default on Windows NT Server. Regedit can be used to import or export registry files, search, edit, add, delete, rename, and create new keys and values.

WARNING Editing the registry directly can be dangerous. If the change can be made through normal configuration tools, such as Internet Service Manager, it should be done there. If you must edit the registry, back it up beforehand and then make one change at a time.

Regedt32 is similar to Regedit with a few important differences. Regedt32 works with individual subtrees in the registry, unlike Regedit, which can span multiple subtrees. Regedt32 can only search for keys—it cannot search for data or values the way Regedit can. And Regedt32 can be used to set permissions, auditing, and ownership for specific keys.

Proxy Server, of course, has its own set of registry settings. Five subkeys are stored within the subkey called:

HKEY_LOCAL_MACHINES\SYSTEM\
CURRENTCONTROLSET\SERVICES.

These are related to Proxy Server functions. Table 2.1 presents a list of subkeys that can be used as a guideline for administration or troubleshooting.

TABLE 2.1: Subkeys

Proxy Service Subkeys	Key Location
Socks Proxy service	\W3PROXY\PARAMETERS\SOCKS
Web Proxy cache	\W3PCACHE\PARAMETERS
Web Proxy service	\W3PROXY\PARAMETERS
Web Proxy publishing	\W3PROXY\PARAMETERS\REVERSEPROXY
WinSock Proxy service	\WSPSRV\PARAMETERS

TABLE 2.1: Subkeys *(continued)*

Proxy Service Subkeys	Key Location
Subkeys Common to All Services:	
Domain filtering keys	\W3PROXY\PARAMETERS\DOFILTER
Packet filtering keys	\MSPADMIN\FILTERS
Proxy Server alerting keys	\MSPADMIN\PARAMETERS\ALERTING
Array membership keys	\W3PROXY\PARAMETERS\MEMBERARRAY\ *ComputerName*
Chained array keys	\W3PROXY\PARAMETERS\CHAINEDARRAY
Backup route array keys	\W3PROXY\PARAMETERS\BACKUPROUTE
Logging values	\MSPADMIN\PARAMETERS

Using RemotMSP from the Command Line

RemotMSP is a command line utility that can be used to perform many simple administration and configuration tasks. Proxy services can be started and stopped, server configurations backed up and restored, access control enabled or disabled, caching enabled or disabled, proxy servers added to or removed from proxy arrays, and more. Entering **remotmsp –h** at the command line gives the following help:

```
C:\msp>remotmsp -h

usage: REMOTMSP <common options> <command> <command
parameters>
Common options:
-C:<remote machine name> -v -h

Commands:
START or STOP or STATUS
SAVE or LOAD
SET
JOIN or REMOVE or SYNC or STATUS
```

Entering the following command would stop the Socks Proxy service on the proxy server named Proxy1:

```
C:\msp>remotmsp -C:proxy1 stop -service:socks
Stopping w3svc service
```

The RemotMSP command is useful in batch scripts, which can be used to manipulate multiple servers. When used from a batch script, RemotMSP returns a result code that can be used to determine the next action in the script.

Using WSPProto from the Command Line

The purpose of WSPProto is fairly straightforward: it is used to add, delete, or edit WinSock Proxy service protocol definitions from the command line. The following is the help message for WSPProto:

```
C:\msp>wspproto
WspProto - WinSock Protocols maintenance Utility
Usage:
WspProto -l
WspProto [-f] <file.wsp>
WspProto [-v] [-f] -a <protocol name> -p:<primary port>
-s:<secondary ports>
e.g. WspProto -a "My Protocol" -p:5555,OUT,TCP -
s:8000,IN,TCP;9000-9010,IN,UDP
WspProto [-v] [-f] -d <protocol name>
WspProto [-v] [-f] -r <old name> <new name>
```

The following would be an example of a bogus protocol added:

```
C:\msp>wspproto -a myprotocol -p:8009,out,tcp -s:8010-
8019,in,tcp
```

This protocol could then be deleted with the following command:

```
C:\msp>wspproto -d myprotocol
```

Net Start Command

The Net Start command can be used to start and stop services. The syntax for this command would be as follows:

```
net start | stop w3svc | wspsrv
```

Starting and stopping the WWW services (w3svc) from the command line will also start and stop the Web Proxy service and the Socks Proxy service. The WinSock Proxy service can be started and stopped using the wspsrv option. This method can be more reliable than using the Services Control Panel to start and stop services.

Services Control Panel

The Services Control Panel can be used to enable or disable a service, and also to control how the service starts. The service can either start automatically when the server boots, or it can be configured to start manually when an administrator starts it from the Services Control Panel. Unused services should be disabled using the Services Control Panel. Starting and stopping services from this Control Panel can be somewhat erratic—using the Net Start command or the RemotMSP command is more reliable.

Necessary Procedures

Procedures for this objective are all alternative methods to accomplish configuration changes, administrative changes, and stopping and starting of services. Tools used to accomplish this include Regedit, Regedt32, the Services Control Panel, RemotMSP, WSPProto, and the Net command.

Using Regedit or Regedt32 to Examine Proxy Server Registry Settings

1. From the Start menu, select Run. Type Regedit or Regedt32 and click OK.

2. Double click on HKEY_LOCAL_MACHINE, or if using Regedt32 select the HKEY_LOCAL_MACHINE window. Double click on SYSTEM.

3. Double click on CurrentControlSet.

4. Double click on Services.

5. Double click on the subkey you wish to view. Be careful not to make any changes.

Using RemotMSP from the Command Line

1. Open a Command Prompt.

2. Change to the C:\MSP directory, or the directory you've installed Proxy Server into.

3. Type **remotmsp –h** and press enter to see the command syntax.

4. Using the help screen for correct syntax, practice stopping and starting services and enabling and disabling access control and caching.

Using WSPProto from the Command Line

1. Open a Command Prompt.

2. Change to the C:\MSP directory, or the directory you've installed Proxy Server into.

3. Type **WspProto** and press enter to see the command syntax.

4. Add a protocol definition using the correct command syntax.

5. Check the WinSock Proxy service properties under the Protocol tab to verify that your protocol has been added.

6. Back at the command prompt, use WSPProto to remove the protocol you just added.

Using the Net Command to Start and Stop Services

1. Start a Command Prompt.

2. Type **net stop** [*service name*], w3svc, or wspsrv.

3. Now type **net start** [*service name*] to start the service again.

Using the Services Control Panel to Enable, Disable, and Modify the Startup Type for a Service

1. Start the Services Control Panel.

2. Select a service, perhaps the FTP Publishing service or the Gopher service.

3. Click Stop to stop the service.

4. Click Start to start the service again.

5. Click Startup. Select Manual or Disabled. Click OK.

Exam Essentials

Know how Regedit and Regedt32 can be used to view and configure Proxy Server services. Proxy Server subkeys are all stored within the subkey called:

HKEY_LOCAL_MACHINES\SYSTEM\
CURRENTCONTROLSET\SERVICES.

Caution should be exercised when changing registry settings.

Know how to disable, enable, stop, start, and configure the startup type for services in the Services Control Panel. The Services Control Panel can be used to configure a service to start automatically or manually, and to enable or disable a service, or to stop or start a service.

Know how to use command line utilities such as RemotMSP, WSP-Proto, and Net to administer, configure, stop, and start Proxy Server services. RemotMSP can be used to stop and start proxy services, and to change many of their configurations as well. WSPProto is used to add, delete, or edit protocols in the WinSock Proxy service. The Net command can be used to start and stop proxy services.

Key Terms and Concepts

Registry: A database used by Windows NT and Windows 95 to store information about configuration.

RemotMSP: A command line tool used to configure Microsoft Proxy Server.

WSPProto: A command line tool used to manipulate protocol definitions for the WinSock Proxy Service.

Sample Questions

1. From the central office of your corporate network, you need to configure a new protocol on multiple proxy servers at several remote branch offices. Which of the following tools would allow you to do this?

   A. Internet Service Manager

   B. RemotMSP

   C. WSPProto

   D. Server Manager

   Answer: A and C. Internet Service Manager and WSPProto can both be used to create a new protocol. Neither RemotMSP nor Server Manager have this functionality.

2. You need to run an automated script to stop and start proxy services on several remote proxy servers. Which utilities could you use to accomplish this?

   A. Internet Service Manager

   B. RemotMSP

   C. WSPProto

   D. The Net command

   Answer: B. Internet Service Manager is not a command line utility and so could not be used in a batch file. WSPProto is used to manipulate protocol definitions. The Net Start and Stop commands only function on the local server. RemotMSP is the correct answer.

3. What are the differences between Regedit and Regedt32? Choose all that apply.

   A. Regedit can set permissions, auditing, and ownership for specific keys. Regedt32 cannot.

   B. Regedit can search for keys, data, or values. Regedt32 can only search for keys.

C. Regedt32 can only work with individual subtrees.

D. Regedit is stored in the WINNT directory. Regedt32 is stored in the WINNT\System32 directory.

Answer: B, C, and D. Answer A is incorrect—it is Regedt32 that can set permissions, auditing, and ownership for specific keys, not Regedit.

Configure auditing.

Auditing is essential to the process of maintaining a secure environment in your proxy server network. Security is an integral part of Proxy Server and of the Proxy Server exam. Auditing can be used to monitor many specific areas of Proxy Server performance. By examining logged information, the network administrator can identify misuses of the internal network, attacks from external sources, and performance problems.

Critical Information

Microsoft Proxy Server has three service logs, one each for Web Proxy service, WinSock Proxy service, and Socks Proxy service. These logs will help you to determine what protocols are being used, to track protocols used by a specific user, to track what time the requests occur, and to determine if the request was successful.

Logging is enabled by default for each service when you install Microsoft Proxy Server. The default location for the log files is C:\WINNT\ SYSTEM32\MSPLOGS. There is also a shared service common to all services that monitors packet filtering. Events logged can be sent to the Windows NT Event log, sent as e-mail to an administrator, or logged to a file. Configuration of proxy service logs was discussed earlier in this chapter. Configuration of packet filter alerting and logging is discussed in detail later in this chapter in the packet filtering objective.

Necessary Procedures

Necessary procedures for this objective include configuring proxy services logging and configuring packet filter alerting and logging.

Configuring Proxy Services Logging

The detailed procedure for configuring proxy services logging can be found under the "Configure the various Proxy Server services" objective earlier in this chapter. Configuring logging is the same for all three proxy services. Logging is enabled by default.

To configure logging, start Internet Service Manager. Select Properties for the service for which you wish to configure logging. Select the Logging tab. Logging should be enabled already.

On the Logging tab, you have the option of setting Regular or Verbose, and setting Log To File to automatically open new log files either daily (the default), weekly, or monthly. You can also limit the number of old log files, you can change the directory the log files are stored in, and you can select Log To SQL/OBDC Database.

Configuring Packet Filter Alerting and Logging

Detailed instructions on configuring packet filter alerting and logging can be found under the "Use packet filtering to prevent unauthorized access" objective later in this chapter. The procedures are very similar to the procedure for configuring logging.

To configure packet filter alerting, start Internet Service Manager. Select Properties for any of the three services. In the Shared Services section, click on Security. Then click on the Alerting tab.

To configure packet filter logging, start Internet Service Manager. Select Properties for any of the three services. In the Shared Services section, click on Security. Then click on the Logging tab.

Exam Essentials

Know how to configure service logging. Review the procedure for configuring logging for all proxy services. These can be configured from the properties pages of each individual service.

Know how to configure packet filter alerting and logging. Both of these are configured by accessing the security options in the Shared Services section for all proxy services. Options include sending events to the Windows NT Event log, sending events in e-mail, and logging events to a file.

Key Terms and Concepts

Packet: A unit of binary information consisting of data plus a header with such information as ID number, source and destination addresses, and error-control data.

Packet filter alerting: A process by which an alert can be sent if the proxy server detects rejected packets, protocol violations, or disk-full events.

Packet filter log: The log where packet filter events are recorded.

Packet filtering: The process of allowing or denying packets based on protocol, local or remote port, direction, and source or destination address.

Windows NT Event log: A Windows NT service that keeps a record of events in the application, security, and system logs. The Event log can be viewed with the Event Viewer.

Sample Questions

1. After installing Proxy Server, what must you do to enable logging for the Web Proxy, WinSock Proxy, and Socks Proxy services?

   A. Install the logging service from the Network Control Panel.

B. Select Enable Logging under the Logging tab of each of the Proxy Server properties pages in Internet Service Manager.

C. Install SQL Server.

D. Nothing

Answer: D. The correct answer is nothing. After installation, logging for all three services is enabled by default. If logging were disabled, you would enable it under the Logging tab of each of the proxy service's properties pages in Internet Service Manager. A database server is only needed if you want to configure the services to log to a database.

Given a scenario, decide which user interface to use to perform administrative tasks.

In previous objectives, many tools that perform administrative tasks have been discussed. Some of them perform some of the same functions. Which tool you decide to use should be based on your knowledge of Proxy Server and the situation at hand. You can expect to see questions concerning this on the Proxy Server exam, and in the real world of Proxy Server administration you need to be familiar with all the tools available to you.

Critical Information

So far you have been introduced to several different administration tools. There are applications such as Internet Service Manager, Regedit, and Regedt32, the Services Control Panel, and command line utilities such as RemotMSP, WSPProto, and Net Start and Net Stop. Let's review the capabilities of each.

Internet Service Manager

The Internet Service Manager can be used to administer all three proxy services: Web Proxy service, WinSock Proxy service, and Socks Proxy service. Let's review the settings that can be configured from the properties pages for each of the three proxy services.

Web Proxy Options

For the Web Proxy service, the following items can be configured:

Permissions: FTP-Read, Gopher, Secure, and WWW protocols can all be assigned permissions.

Caching: Passive and active caching can be enabled and configured, cache size can be set, and cache filters can be defined.

Routing: Primary and backup routes can be defined. Resolving within an array before routing upstream can be enabled.

Publishing: Web publishing, reverse proxying, and reverse hosting can be configured.

Logging: Logging can be configured.

WinSock Proxy Options

For the WinSock Proxy, we have the following items:

Protocols: Protocol definitions can be added, deleted, and edited.

Permissions: Permissions can be applied to defined protocols.

Logging: Logging can be configured.

Socks Proxy Options

For the Socks Proxy, we have the following items:

Permissions: Permissions can be applied based on IP addresses and port numbers.

Logging: Logging can be configured.

Shared Configuration Options

And finally, there are shared configuration items that apply to all proxy services. These can be configured from the Shared Services and

Configuration sections of the Service tab on the properties pages of any of the three proxy services.

Security: Packet filtering, domain filtering, alerting, and logging can all be configured.

Array: Array membership and synchronization can be configured.

Auto Dial: You can enable Auto Dial for specific services and set dialing hours.

Plug-ins: You can connect to a Web page to allow plug-ins to be implemented.

Client Configuration: Configuration settings for clients, browsers, and automatic configuration scripts can be configured.

Local Address Table (LAT): The LAT can be configured.

Server Backup and Server Restore: Backup and restore server configuration can be set.

Regedit and Regedt32

Regedit and Regedt32 can be used to manually change registry settings that apply to Proxy Server. Generally, any change that can be accomplished using normal administration tools should be done in that manner. Editing the registry can be very tricky and a mistake could conceivably force you to reinstall. Registry settings for Proxy Server are stored within the following subkey:

HKEY_LOCAL_MACHINES\SYSTEM\
CURRENTCONTROLSET\SERVICES.

Services Control Panel

The Services Control Panel can be used to start and stop services and to change the startup type of the service to either automatic, manual, or disabled.

RemotMSP

RemotMSP can be used to perform the following tasks:

- Start and stop Proxy services.

- Backup and restore server configurations.

- Enable or disable:

  - Access control

  - Caching

  - Setting for resolving in an array before routing requests upstream

  - Synchronization

  - Internet publishing

- Manipulate arrays, including:

  - Join a server to an array.

  - Remove a server from an array.

  - Synchronize an array.

  - Set a load factor within an array.

TIP Setting the load factor within an array means that you can adjust what percentage of a normal load a particular proxy server will be given. This can only be set from the command line.

RemotMSP can also be used effectively for batch files because it returns result codes to the command line.

WSPProto

WSPProto can be used to add, delete, or edit protocol definitions in the WinSock Proxy service from the command line.

Deciding which of all of these tools you will need to use in a given scenario will depend what your objective is and how that objective must be accomplished. Do you need to perform an automated task at a certain time each day or each week? Then you will need to use command line utilities, which can be run from a batch file. Do you need to create a cache filter? This can only be configured from the Internet Service Manager. Knowing what each utility is capable of will typically answer the question for you.

Necessary Procedures

Procedures for this objective do not involve specific configuration tasks. This objective deals with being familiar with the various tools available to perform configuration tasks.

Exploring Administrative Options

1. Start Internet Service Manager by selecting Start ➤ Programs ➤ Microsoft Proxy Server ➤ Internet Service Manager. Explore the various screens to get a feel for what can be accomplished with this tool.

2. From a Command Prompt, practice using the RemotMSP command. You should know from previous objectives where to access this and how to use Help to display correct syntax. Practice changing various configurations using this tool.

3. From a Command Prompt, practice adding, editing, and deleting WinSock Proxy service protocol definitions with WSPProto.

4. Load Regedit and Regedt32 and become familiar with the differences in the two programs. Examine the registry subkeys pertaining to Proxy Server. Be careful not to make any changes.

Exam Essentials

Know the different administrative tasks that can be performed with applications such as Internet Service Manager, Regedit, Regedt32, and the Services Control Panel.   Internet Service Manager can perform virtually all administrative functions needed. Modifying registry settings with Regedit or Regedt32 will allow you to change some settings that cannot be changed from Internet Service Manager, but caution should be exercised.

Know the different administrative tasks that can be performed with command line utilities such as RemotMSP, WSPProto, and Net Start and Net Stop.   Command line utilities can be called from batch files, and can be used in situations where tools such as Internet Service Manager are not available, e.g., from a workstation.

Key Terms and Concepts

No new terms and concepts were introduced in this objective.

Sample Questions

1. You need to configure dial-in hours for your Auto Dial connection from a branch office to the central office. What will you have to do to configure this?

   A. From a Command Prompt, use RemotMSP.

   B. From a Command Prompt, use WSPProto.

   C. Use Regedit to change the appropriate registry settings.

   D. From the Internet Service Manager, select Properties for any of the three Proxy Server services.

   Answer: D. Auto Dial is a shared configuration setting between the three proxy services. Clicking on this button will allow you to configure dialing hours. Neither RemotMSP nor WSPProto have this capability. Use of Regedit is discouraged when the task can be accomplished with a standard administration tool.

2. You need to permanently disable the Gopher service. Which utility would you use to accomplish this?

   A. RemotMSP

   B. Services Control Panel

   C. Internet Service Manager

   D. WSPProto

   Answer: B. This would be performed using the Services Control Panel. None of the other tools have the capability to permanently disable a service.

3. You need to administer several proxy servers' array memberships across a modem connection. What is the best tool to use?

   A. RemotMSP

B. WSPProto

C. The Services Control Panel

D. Internet Services Manager

Answer: A. Neither WSPProto nor the Services Control Panel have this capability. Internet Services Manager could be used, but because it is interactive, it is inefficient over a slow connection. RemotMSP is the best tool to use in this situation.

Identify the licensing requirements for a given Proxy Server site.

Unlike some other products, licensing for Proxy Server is simple and straightforward. One license is required per Proxy Server installation. No client licenses are required.

Exam Essentials

In a given scenario, know how many Proxy Server licenses are required.   One license is required per Proxy Server. No client licenses are required.

Key Terms and Concepts

No new terms and concepts were introduced in this objective.

Sample Questions

1. You administer a corporate network. You have an array consisting of six proxy servers at the central office. You have four branch offices

each with a single proxy server. You have 2000 client machines total. How many proxy server licenses must you purchase?

A. Ten server licenses, 2000 client licenses

B. Ten server licenses

C. Six server licenses and four client licenses

D. 2000 server licenses

Answer: B. You must have one license per proxy server. No client licenses are required.

Configure Proxy Server arrays.

As your network grows larger, multiple proxy servers will become necessary. In order to provide fault tolerance and load balancing, you need to configure your proxy servers into arrays. Arrays can provide fault tolerance and load balancing.

Critical Information

Configuration of an array can be accomplished with one of two tools: Internet Service Manager and RemotMSP.

Configuring an Array with Internet Service Manager

Configuring an array can be accomplished with the Internet Service Manager by selecting the properties pages for any of the proxy services and clicking on Array. The only option not grayed out at this point is the Join Array button. After clicking this button, type the name of the computer you wish to create an array with. If the computer you type in is not yet part of an array, you will see a message stating this and asking you to type in the name of the array. Once you enter a name, the array is created and you will see a list of array members. Synchronize Configuration Of Array Members is checked by default. This means that you can change array configuration on one proxy server, and that change will be propagated to the rest of the array members. From this screen you can also remove members from the array.

Configuring an Array with RemotMSP

Let's review the syntax for RemotMSP again:

```
C:\msp>remotmsp -h

usage: REMOTMSP <common options> <command> <command
parameters>
Common options:
-c:<remote machine name> -v -h

Commands:
START or STOP or STATUS
SAVE or LOAD
SET
JOIN or REMOVE or SYNC or STATUS
```

The last line gives four actions that can be taken with regard to arrays: Join, Remove, Sync, or Status. Join can be used to create an array. As with the Internet Service Manager, the name of the proxy server you wish to create an array with is used. Here's an example of the correct syntax where proxy2 is the name of the second proxy server:

```
remotmsp join -member:proxy2
```

TIP If you are creating a new array with RemotMSP, the array name will default to "Array name." This can be changed from Internet Service Manager.

The other three commands use the same syntax. Remove will remove a proxy server from the array, Sync will synchronize array configuration, and Status will give you the current status of the array and each member in the array.

Necessary Procedures

Necessary procedures for this objective include configuring an array using Internet Service Manager and using RemotMSP. Expect to encounter several questions regarding arrays on the Proxy Server exam. It is important that you be familiar with the tools available and the process necessary to configure arrays, not just for the exam, but also for when you are asked to do it for real. In order to complete the following exercises, you will need to have at least two computers networked together with Proxy Server installed on both.

Using Internet Service Manager to Configure Arrays

1. Start the Internet Service Manager and select Properties for any of the three proxy services.

2. Click on Array in the Shared Services section. Click on Join Array.

3. You will be asked for the computer name to join an array with. Type in the correct name and click OK.

4. If the other computer is not yet part of an array, you will see a message stating this. Type in a name for the array. Click OK. You will see the screen labeled Array:

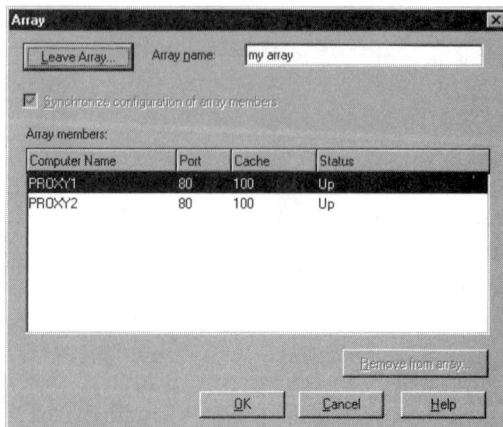

5. You should now see both computers listed in the Array Members list. Click OK, and then click OK or Apply to complete the configuration.

Using RemotMSP to Configure Arrays

1. Start a Command Prompt.

2. Change directories to C:\MSP, or the directory you installed Proxy Server to.

3. Type **RemotMSP join -member:***computername.*

4. Type **RemotMSP status -member:***computername* to see the status of that member in the array.

5. Type **RemotMSP sync -member:***computername* to synchronize the proxy server with the array.

Exam Essentials

Know how to configure an array using Internet Service Manager. Arrays can be configured from the properties pages of any of the proxy services by clicking on the Array button in the Shared Services section.

Know how to configure an array using RemotMSP. RemotMSP can be used from the command line to join an array, remove an array member, see the status of the array, and synchronize the array.

Key Terms and Concepts

Load balancing: The process of dividing client load equally among multiple servers.

Sample Questions

1. You wish to configure an array using Internet Service Manager. To accomplish this, you must configure the properties pages of which proxy service?

   A. WinSock Proxy service

   B. Web Proxy service

C. Socks Proxy service

D. Any of the above

Answer: D. Arrays are configured from the Shared Services section of the properties pages of any of the proxy services.

2. You administer a corporate network that uses a proxy array consisting of 10 member servers. You need to make a configuration change. What must you do to accomplish this?

   A. Administer the configuration changes by physically accessing each proxy server.

   B. Administer the configuration changes by remotely accessing each proxy server.

   C. Make configuration changes to one proxy server—the rest of the servers will receive the changes when the array next synchronizes.

   D. Make configuration changes to each proxy server that has a server downstream from it. The upstream and downstream servers will synchronize the configurations.

   Answer: C. When a configuration change is made to one array member, the change will be propagated to the array members at the next synchronization.

3. Which of the following functions regarding arrays can be accomplished with RemotMSP?

   A. Joining an array

   B. Synchronizing an array

   C. Checking the status of an array

   D. Removing a proxy server from an array

   Answer: A, B, C, D. All of these can be accomplished using RemotMSP.

Configure arrays to provide fault-tolerance for Web Proxy client requests.

Along with load balancing, fault tolerance is one of the principal functions of an array.

Critical Information

An array can provide fault tolerance for Web Proxy clients in two ways: distributed caching using the Cache Array Routing Protocol (CARP) and routing.

Cache Array Routing Protocol (CARP)

As discussed in Chapter 1, Cache Array Routing Protocol (CARP) achieves fault tolerance by using multiple proxy servers arrayed as a single logical cache. The request resolution path is determined by calculations based on the proxy array members' identities and the Uniform Resource Locator (URL). These calculations can take place at the proxy server level or at the browser, if the browser is Internet Explorer. This means that any object requested from cache is at most only two hops away. Figure 2.4 illustrates two paths a request for an object in cache might follow.

The cache object is retrieved either directly by the browser from the proxy server that has the object in cache, or from the correct proxy server by the first array member accessed by the browser. This is called queryless distributed caching. Either the browser or the first proxy server in the array contacted will know the exact location of the object in cache. Because the cache is distributed across multiple proxy servers acting in concert, service is not interrupted if an individual server goes down. Each proxy server in the array maintains a list of which servers are up and which servers are down. Proxy Server will not route requests to servers that are down. If you have created an array and you have caching enabled in the Web Proxy service, CARP will automatically provide this functionality.

FIGURE 2.4: Handling requests from cache

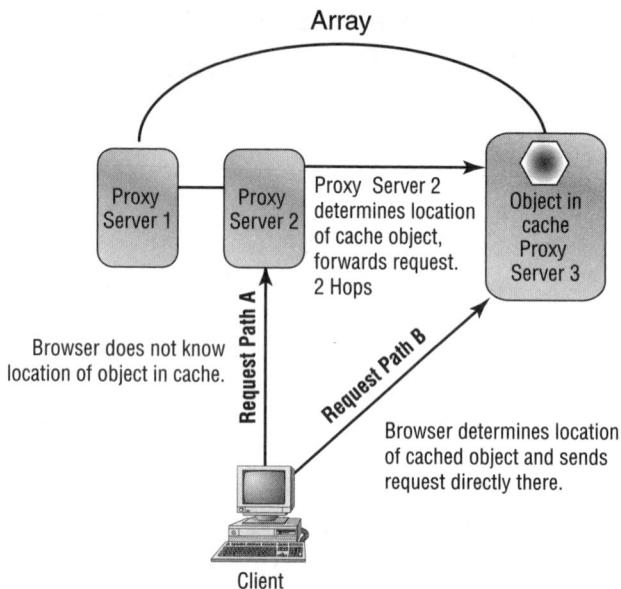

Array

Proxy Server 1

Proxy Server 2

Proxy Server 2 determines location of cache object, forwards request. 2 Hops

Object in cache Proxy Server 3

Browser does not know location of object in cache.

Request Path A

Request Path B

Browser determines location of cached object and sends request directly there.

Client

Routing

By configuring routing in the Web Proxy services properties pages, you can provide fault tolerance in your Web Proxy services. When configuring routing, you can route to an array upstream. This is called upstream routing. Looking back to our network scenarios in Chapter 1, if we have a single proxy server at a branch office, we can configure it to look upstream to an array. This configuration allows the proxy servers at the branch office to take advantage of some of the benefits of the array, such as distributed caching and CARP, without being a member of the array. We can further enhance fault tolerance by configuring each of the proxy servers in the array with a backup route. If each proxy server in the array has a backup route to the external network, then, as long as just one proxy server in the array is still up, clients will be able to access the external network.

Necessary Procedures

Necessary procedures for this objective deal with providing fault tolerance for Web Proxy clients. Web Proxy clients can take advantage of two Proxy Server features that provide fault tolerance: the Cache Array Routing Protocol (CARP) and routing.

Enabling Caching Using Internet Service Manager

1. Start the Internet Service Manager and select Properties for the Web Proxy service.

2. Click on the Caching tab.

3. Put a check in the Enable Caching checkbox.

4. Click OK.

Enabling Caching Using RemotMSP

1. Start a Command Prompt.

2. Change the directory to C:\MSP.

3. Type in the following command to see the syntax shown:

```
C:\msp>remotmsp set -h

Set specific configuration parameter:
Valid SET parameters:
WSPAccessControl={0 | 1}
W3PAccessControl={0 | 1}
EnableDiskCache={0 | 3 | 5 | 7}
ResolveInArray={0 | 1}
EnableSynchronization={0 | 1}
LoadFactor={ 0 < N}
```

4. You have four options for manipulating disk cache settings:

   0—Disable disk caching.

   3—Enable FTP caching only.

   5—Enable HTTP caching only.

   7—Enable HTTP and FTP caching.

5. Type in the command to disable caching if caching is enabled.

6. Type in the command to enable one of the caching options. For example, to enable both HTTP and FTP caching, type the following:

   remotmsp set EnableDiskCache=7

Configuring a Proxy Server to Point to an Upstream Array

1. Start the Internet Service Manager and select Properties for the Web Proxy service.

2. Click on the Routing tab.

3. In the Upstream Routing section, click on Use Web Proxy Or Array.

4. Click on Modify.

5. Type in the name of a proxy server array member.

6. Click OK, then click OK or Apply.

Exam Essentials

Know how arrays can provide fault tolerance in caching. Cache Array Routing Protocol (CARP) achieves fault tolerance by using multiple proxy servers arrayed as a single logical cache. Microsoft emphasizes caching heavily in the Proxy Server exam.

Know how routing can provide tolerance for Web Proxy clients. When configuring routing, you can route to an array upstream. This is called upstream routing. This configuration allows the proxy servers at a branch office to take advantage of some of the benefits of the array, such as distributed caching and CARP, without being a member of the array. This objective is heavily emphasized on the exam.

Key Terms and Concepts

Cache Array Routing Protocol (CARP): A hash-based routing protocol that provides a deterministic request resolution path through an array of proxy servers.

Distributed caching: The process of distributing caching duties across multiple proxy servers acting as a single logical unit.

Queryless distributed caching: Calculations performed either by the browser or by the first proxy server to receive the request are used to determine the exact location of the cached object. Querying proxy servers to discover the location of a cached object is unnecessary.

Request resolution path: The path to a requested object in cache, calculated by the browser or by the first proxy server contacted.

Sample Questions

1. You wish to use RemotMSP to enable only HTTP caching for the Web Proxy service. What command will you type at the Command Prompt?

   A. RemoteMSP set EnableDiskCache=5

   B. RemotMSP set EnableDiskCache=5

   C. RemotMSP set EnableDiskCache=7

   D. WSPProto set EnableDiskCache=7

   Answer: B. Option 5 for the EnableDiskCache parameter enables only HTTP caching. Option 7 enables both HTTP and FTP caching. WSPProto does not provide this function.

2. Which of the following statements describe upstream routing?

   A. It provides load balancing among multiple proxy servers.

   B. It allows a stand-alone proxy server to take advantage of some of the benefits of an array.

   C. It causes multiple proxy servers to act as a single logical unit.

   D. It is a function of the Web Proxy service.

   Answer: B and D. Load balancing can be achieved by configuring an array and using DNS round robin—it is not accomplished through upstream routing. Configuring an array causes multiple proxy servers to act as a single logical unit. Upstream routing allows a single proxy server to take advantage of some of the benefits of an array, and it is a function of the Web Proxy service.

3. Which of the following does an array use to accomplish fault tolerance?

   A. Cache Array Routing Protocol (CARP)

B. Backup route

C. Distributed caching

D. Domain filtering

Answer: A, B, and C. An array can use all of these except domain filtering to accomplish fault tolerance. Domain filtering is used to prevent access to certain external Web sites by internal users.

Use packet filtering to prevent unauthorized access. Tasks include:

- Using packet filtering to enable a specific protocol.
- Configuring packet filter alerting and logging.

Packet filtering is another security function built into Microsoft Proxy Server. Providing filtering security at this level protects against many types of attacks that may be launched by external users or hackers. Packet filtering allows you to configure a list of packet types that are allowed—all others will be denied. Proxy Server will also log packet filter violations so that improper traffic can be monitored. Since one of the principal functions of Proxy Server is security, expect questions concerning this function on the exam.

Critical Information

There are two aspects of packet filtering you can use to secure your network. Packet filtering can be used to filter packets based on the direction of traffic, protocols, local ports, remote ports, and addresses. Packet filter alerting can be used to notify network administrators in the event that certain violation criteria are met.

Using Packet Filtering to Enable a Specific Protocol

A packet is a unit of binary information consisting of data plus a header with such information as ID number, source and destination addresses, and error-control data.

SEE ALSO For more information on IP packets, see the *MCSE: TCP/IP for NT Server 4 Study Guide*, 3rd ed. (Sybex, 1998).

When packet filtering is enabled, Proxy Server examines each packet to determine if it meets the necessary criteria to be considered harmless. If the packet passes inspection, it is allowed to proceed. In order to enable packet filtering, you must have an external adapter configured. If you are using a modem or an ISDN adapter for external access, Auto Dial must be configured before packet filtering can be enabled. Also, packet filtering only applies to the external interface.

There are two different procedures for adding new packet filter definitions: predefined filters and custom filters. Predefined filters include the following:

- DNS Lookup
- ICMP All Outbound
- ICMP Ping Response
- ICMP Ping Query
- ICMP SRC Quench
- ICMP Timeout
- ICMP Unreachable
- PPTP Call
- PPTP Receive
- SMTP
- POP3
- Identd
- HTTP Server (port 80)
- HTTPS Server (port 443)
- NetBIOS (WINS client only)
- NetBIOS (All)

The predefined packet filter can be defined to allow local IP addresses by the default external adapter IP address, a specific proxy IP address, or an internal client IP address. The remote host can be limited to a specific host IP address, or any IP address.

You may need to define a packet filter not included above. In this case you can define a custom filter. When defining a custom packet filter, you can specify the protocol ID from the following choices: Any, ICMP, TCP, and UDP. The filter can be defined for outgoing packets, incoming packets, or both. The local port allowed can also be specified as any port, a specified port, or a dynamic port that can range from 1025 to 5000. The remote port can be specified also as any port or as a specified port. The remote port cannot be dynamic. As with the predefined filters, you can define allowed local IP addresses by the default external adapter IP address, a specific proxy IP address, or an internal client IP address. The remote host can be limited to a specific host IP address or to any IP address.

Once you have finished defining packet filters, any packet received by Proxy Server that does not meet the criteria established will not be allowed into the internal network. Keep in mind that improper packet filter definitions can create security holes. If you need to return to a clean slate, simply click on the Reset Defaults button. This returns the definitions to those installed by default and removes any you have added.

Another option that can be enabled is filtering of IP fragments. Enabling this option increases security by preventing address spoofing and FRAG attacks.

Dynamic filtering means that ports are opened and closed as needed for transmission. Ports are closed immediately after transmit or receive operations. If this is enabled, it is not necessary to unbind services from the external adapters, as the packet filtering process will block improper packets. Dynamic filtering greatly reduces the amount of necessary administration. However, if applications accessing the Internet are being run from the same server running Proxy Server, static filtering definitions are necessary.

Configuring Packet Filter Alerting and Logging

Packet filter alerting and logging allow you to be notified of instances of packet violations such as packets sent to unused ports or dropped packets. These alerts can be sent to an e-mail address, to the Windows NT system Event log, to a log file, or to any combination.

Packet filtering can be configured from the Shared Services section of the properties pages of any proxy service. Clicking the Security button and then the Alerting tab will bring you to the configuration screen. There are three types of events that you can configure to generate an alert:

Rejected packets   This monitors dropped IP packets or frame anomalies on the external network adapter.

Protocol violations   This monitors illegal IP packets on the external network adapter.

Disk full   This monitors failures caused by a full disk, and is triggered when any of the volumes containing the service logs or packet log become full.

An alert can be generated if one of these events occurs more than x number of times per second. The default is one event per second, except for the rejected packets event, which has a default of 20 per second. When this condition is met, an alert can either be sent to an e-mail address, reported to the Windows NT Event log, or both. Clicking the Configure Mail button allows you to configure mail server and account information. Microsoft recommends sending e-mail alerts to an internal mail server to avoid problems.

Logging can be configured by clicking on the Logging tab and is configured in the same fashion as proxy service logging. Security logging can be configured to log in regular format or in verbose format. It can be configured to log to a text file or to a SQL/OBDC database. If logging to a text file is selected, it can be configured to create a new log file daily, weekly, or monthly. The number of old log files can be limited, and all services can be stopped if the disk becomes full. By default the log files are stored in *drive*:\root\SYSTEM32\MSPLOGS, although this location can be changed. Security log files are named in the following format: PF*yymmdd*.LOG. If you choose to log to a

SQL/OBDC database, you must provide the following information: the OBDC Data Source Name (DSN), the table name, and the user-name and password for the database.

Necessary Procedures

Increased security for all services is the goal of this objective. Packet filtering is used to apply secure parameters at the packet level, and is applied to the external network adapter. Using packet filter alerting and logging can help you monitor violations of security parameters. Expect to encounter questions regarding these topics on the Proxy Server exam, and being able to configure them in real world situations is vital to the security of your network. Necessary procedures for this objective include using predefined filters, using custom filters, and configuring packet filter alerting.

Using Predefined Packet Filters

1. Start the Internet Service Manager and select Properties for any of the three proxy services.

2. In the Shared Services section, click on Security. You will see the following screen:

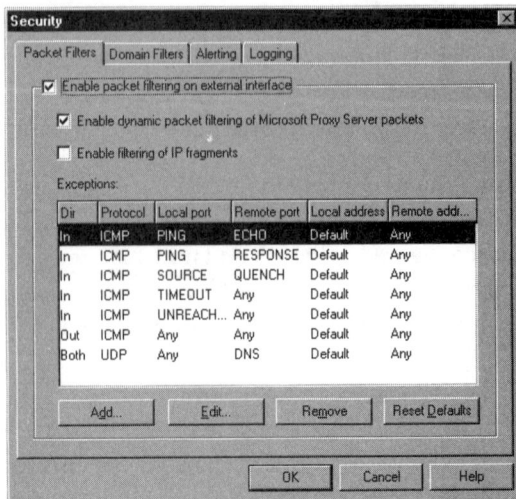

3. Ensure that "Enable Packet Filtering On External Interface" is checked.

4. Click Add.

5. Select Predefined filter.

6. From the pull-down menu, choose the protocol you wish to add to the packet-filtering list. Some of the filters are already in place by default. Choose one that is not, such as Identd.

7. Select a local and remote port option.

8. Click OK.

Defining Custom Packet Filters

1. Start the Internet Service Manager and select Properties for any of the three proxy services.

2. In the Shared Services section, click on Security. Ensure that "Enable Packet Filtering On External Interface" is checked.

3. Click Add. You will see the following screen:

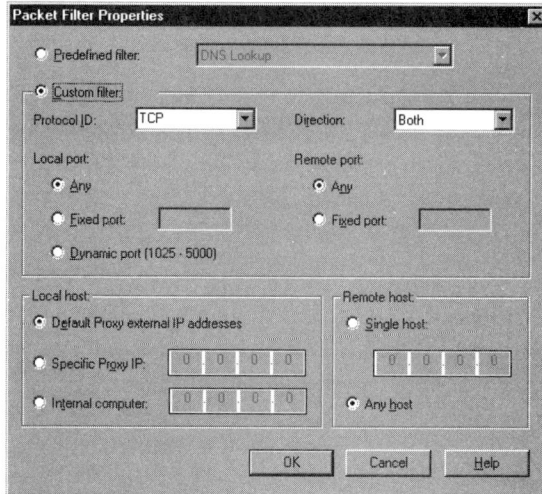

4. Select Custom Filter. Then select a protocol from the Protocol ID pull-down menu.

5. Define the direction to which you wish to apply the filter from the Direction pull-down menu: Both, In, or Out.

6. Define the local port: Any, Fixed, or Dynamic.

7. Define the remote port: Any or Fixed.

8. Define the local host: the default external adapter, a specific proxy server IP address, or an internal computer.

9. Define the remote host: a Single Host or Any Host.

10. Click OK twice.

Configuring Packet Filter Alerting

1. Start the Internet Service Manager and select Properties for any of the three proxy services.

2. In the Shared Services section, click on Security.

3. Click on the Alerting tab to see the following screen:

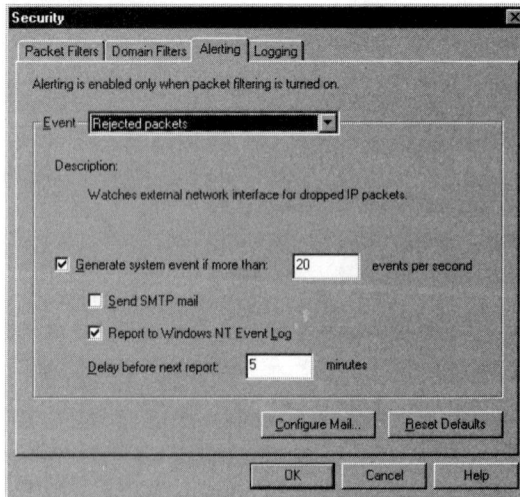

4. Choose the event for which you wish to configure alerting from the Event pull-down menu.

5. Make sure there is a check in the Generate System Event checkbox. Enter the number of events per second that will trigger this alert.

6. Put a check in the Send SMTP Mail checkbox.

7. Click on Configure Mail and configure the mail server account information. Click OK.

8. Make sure there is a check in the Report To Windows NT Event Log checkbox.

9. Adjust the delay between reports if necessary.

10. Click OK.

Configuring Packet Filter Logging

Logging is enabled by default.

1. To configure logging, start Internet Service Manager by selecting Start ➤ Programs ➤ Microsoft Proxy Server ➤ Internet Service Manager.

2. Select Properties for any proxy service. Under the Shared Services section, click on Security. Click on the Logging tab. You will see the following screen:

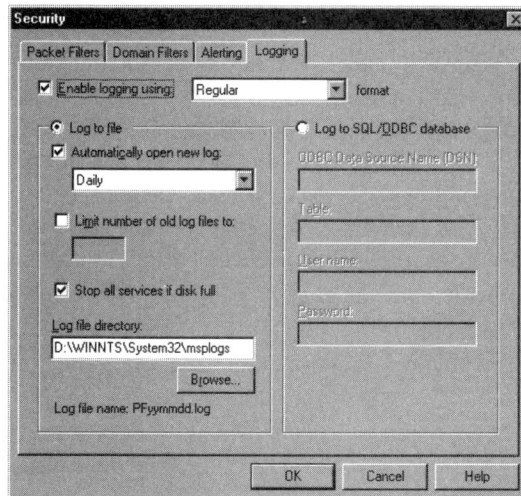

3. Logging should be enabled already. Select Regular or Verbose from the pull-down menu.

4. By default, Log To File will be selected. If you leave this enabled, you have the option to automatically open new log files daily (the default), weekly, or monthly.

5. You can limit the number of old log files by putting a check in the next box, and entering a number.

6. "Stop All Services If Disk Full" is checked by default—uncheck it if you wish.

7. You can also change the directory the log files are stored in by clicking Browse.

8. You can also select Log To SQL/OBDC Database. If you select this, Log To File is automatically deselected.

9. Once Log To SQL/OBDC Database is selected, you enter an OBDC Data Source Name (DSN), a Table, a Username, and a Password.

10. Click OK and you are done.

Exam Essentials

Know how to create packet filtering definitions using both pre-defined and custom filters. Predefined filters include basic filters you may need in order for your network to function. Custom filters can be used to create packet filters needed but not included in the predefined filters. Internet Service Manager is used to define packet filters.

Know how to configure packet filtering alerting and logging. Packet filtering alerting can be used to generate alerts when specific events occur. These alerts in turn can either generate an e-mail message notifying a network administrator, or they can be sent to the Windows NT Event log, or be logged to a text file, or any combination of the three.

Key Terms and Concepts

Dynamic packet filtering: When this is enabled, the proxy server opens and closes TCP/IP ports as needed for transmission.

Internet Control Message Protocol (ICMP): Part of the TCP/IP protocol suite that handles control and error messages.

IP address spoofing: The process of sending a packet with a fake source address in an attempt to gain access to an internal network.

Static packet filtering: TCP/IP ports are manually enabled or disabled by the administrator.

Sample Questions

1. You administer a corporate network that accesses the Internet through a proxy server. You have configured packet filtering to block a specific protocol from a specific remote host. You wish to receive an e-mail alert when packets using that protocol are received from that remote host. For which event should you configure alerts?

   A. Protocol violations

   B. Disk full

   C. Rejected packets

   D. TCP

   Answer: C. Protocol violations occur when the packet does not follow standard protocol structure. Disk full events occur when the volume containing the packet logs or the service logs becomes full. TCP is a protocol, not a packet-filtering event. Rejected packets is correct because, when an incoming packet meets the criteria of a defined filter, the packet is rejected or dropped.

2. What is the effect of using dynamic packet filtering on services bound to the external network adapter?

   A. IP forwarding is disabled.

   B. Unbinding specific services from the external network is unnecessary.

   C. There is no effect on services bound to the external network adapter.

   D. Protocol violations on the external network adapter will be reported to the Windows NT Event log.

Answer: B. When dynamic filtering is enabled, unbinding specific services from the external network adapter is not necessary. IP forwarding is enabled or disabled from the TCP/IP properties pages. Protocol violations can be reported to the Windows NT Event log, but this is a separate configuration issue.

3. Which of the following protocols can be used to define a custom packet filter?

   A. SPX

   B. ICMP

   C. TCP

   D. UDP

   Answer: B, C, and D. SPX is not part of the TCP/IP protocol suite. ICMP, TCP, and UDP are valid options.

Configure hierarchical caching.

Hierarchical caching is achieved by linking multiple proxy servers together. Benefits of hierarchical caching include improved cache performance and load balancing. Caching is heavily emphasized in the Proxy Server exam. Familiarity with all aspects of caching is a must. Knowing how to configure caching in your network will also allow you to maximize the benefits of using Proxy Server.

Critical Information

Routing is used to configure a proxy server to look upstream to either an array or another proxy server. When a request is received, if the downstream proxy server does not contain the object in cache, the request is forwarded to the upstream proxy. The upstream proxy either services the request from its own cache, routes the request to another member of the array that contains the object in cache, or forwards the request either to its upstream proxy or array, or directly to the Internet, depending on the configuration. Since each proxy server is linked to its upstream partner in a hierarchical fashion, this is called hierarchical caching. It is also sometimes referred to as chaining or cascaded proxying. Figure 2.5 illustrates a simple example of hierarchical caching.

FIGURE 2.5: Hierarchical caching

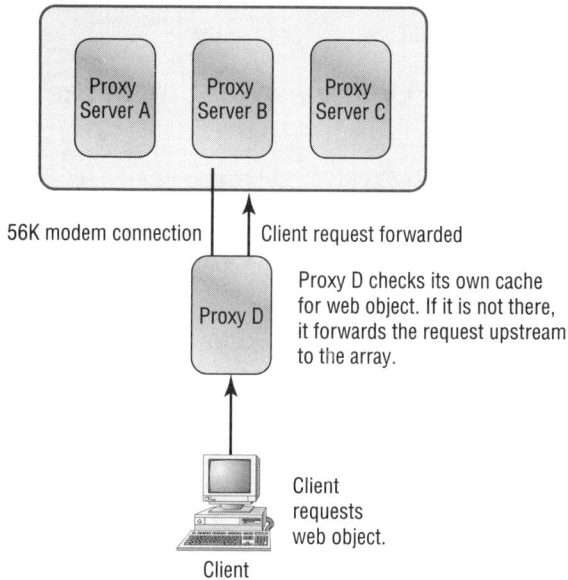

When Proxy Server D receives a request for an object that it does not have in cache, it forwards the request upstream to the array. The first proxy server in the array to receive the request checks to see if it has the object in its cache or if any of the other member servers in the array has the object in its cache. At most, the request will take one hop through the array, either to the correct array member to service the request or on to its next upstream path if the object is not in the array cache. This process is transparent to the user. Better cache performance is achieved because the caching duties are divided between the stand-alone proxy server and the upstream array.

Necessary Procedures

Configuring hierarchical caching is really the same procedure as configuring routing. The proxy server is configured to route requests to an upstream partner. Therefore the necessary procedure associated with this objective is to configure upstream routing in the Web Proxy service.

Configuring Upstream Routing in the Web Proxy Service

1. Start the Internet Service Manager and select Properties for the Web Proxy service.

2. Click on the Routing tab to see the following screen:

```
Web Proxy Service Properties For proxy1                            [X]

  Service | Permissions | Caching | Routing | Publishing | Logging |

  ┌─ Use this Http Via header alias for the local server ─────────────┐
  │ PROXY1                                                            │
  └──────────────────────────────────────────────────────────────────┘

  ┌─ Upstream Routing ───────────────────────────────────────────────┐
  │   ○ Use direct connection                                        │
  │   ● Use Web Proxy or array:    Proxy2          [ Modify... ]      │
  │   ┌─ ☑ Enable backup route ──────────────────────────────────┐   │
  │   │   ● Use direct connection                                │   │
  │   │   ○ Use Web Proxy or array:              [ Modify... ]    │   │
  │   └──────────────────────────────────────────────────────────┘   │
  └──────────────────────────────────────────────────────────────────┘

  ┌─ Routing within array ───────────────────────────────────────────┐
  │   ☐ Resolve Web Proxy requests within array before              │
  │      routing upstream                        [ Advanced... ]      │
  └──────────────────────────────────────────────────────────────────┘

              [   OK   ]   [ Cancel ]   [ Apply ]   [ Help ]
```

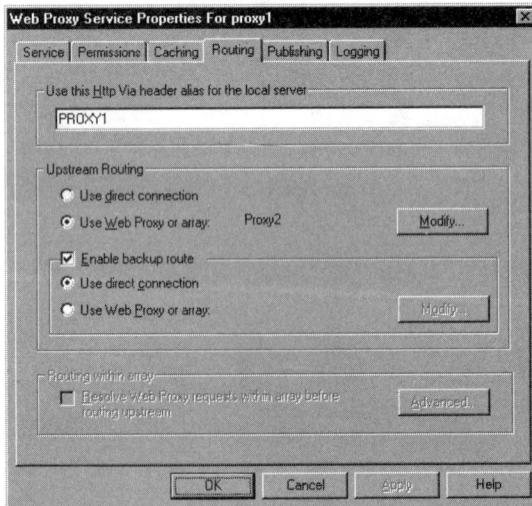

3. In the Upstream Routing section, select Use Web Proxy Or Array.

4. Click on Modify and you will see the screen labeled Advanced Routing Options.

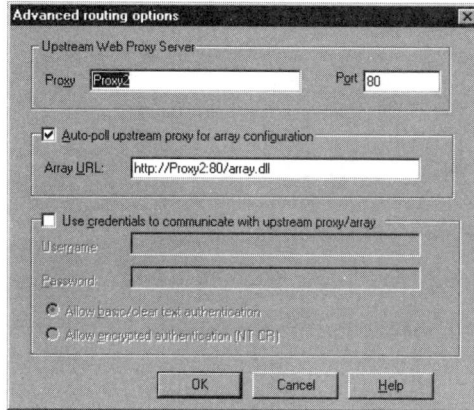

5. Type the name and port number of the upstream Web proxy server.

6. Click OK, and then click OK or Apply.

Exam Essentials

Know how to configure hierarchical caching. Hierarchical caching is configured using the routing configuration screen of the Web Proxy service and specifying an upstream Web Proxy or an array.

Know the benefits of hierarchical caching. The benefits of hierarchical caching are improved cache performance and load balancing.

Know how client requests are handled when hierarchical caching is configured. Requests for objects not contained in cache are sent upstream either to a proxy server or to an array. The upstream proxy server either services the request, forwards the request to another member in the array if that member has the object in cache, or forwards the request to its upstream path, either another proxy server or directly to the Internet.

Key Terms and Concepts

Hierarchical caching: The forwarding of a client request to an upstream proxy server or an array. Also known as chaining or cascaded proxying

Sample Questions

1. Hierarchical caching can also be called which of the following?

   A. Cascaded proxying

   B. Distributed caching

   C. Active caching

   D. Chaining

   Answer: A and D. Distributed caching takes place within an array. Active caching is the process of pre-downloading frequently requested sites. Chaining and cascaded proxying are both alternate names for hierarchical caching.

2. Choose two benefits of hierarchical caching:

   A. Increased security

   B. Load balancing

   C. Improved caching performance

   D. Fault tolerance

   Answer: B and C. Security is not a function of hierarchical caching. Hierarchical caching does not by itself provide fault tolerance. Load balancing and improved caching performance are benefits of hierarchical caching.

CHAPTER

3

Setting Up and Managing
Resource Access

Microsoft Exam Objectives Covered in This Chapter:

- Grant or restrict access to the Internet for selected outbound users and groups who use the various Proxy Server services to access the Internet. *(pages 145 – 150)*

- Grant or restrict access to specific Internet sites for outbound users. *(pages 151 – 157)*

- Choose the location, size, and type of caching for the Web Proxy service. *(pages 157 – 161)*

- Configure active caching and passive caching. *(pages 161 – 165)*

- Implement Web publishing to enable reverse proxying. *(pages 165 – 168)*

- Back up and restore Proxy Server configurations. *(pages 169 – 173)*

- Implement reverse hosting. *(pages 174 – 178)*

This chapter focuses on some of the methods you can use to control access to resources on your internal network by external users, and to control access to external resources by internal users. There are internal security issues, such as restricted access to the Internet using domain filtering and access control permissions. In many corporate situations, there may be particular sites to which management wishes to deny access. Management may also wish to limit various groups of users to certain protocols. There are inbound security issues that can be addressed by implementing reverse proxying and reverse hosting. It's a fact of life that there are hackers out there on the Internet who will try to cause whatever trouble they can. Running a public Web site is an open invitation to many of these people to get past whatever security measures you have. Proxy Server efficiency can be enhanced by choosing and implementing correct caching options. When implementing Proxy Server, network usability should be enhanced, not degraded. And finally, being able to back up and restore Proxy Server configurations will provide a measure of stability to your Proxy Server network.

Grant or restrict access to the Internet for selected outbound users and groups who use the various Proxy Server services to access the Internet.

In the planning stages of your Proxy Server implementation, you should have made, or been given, some policy decisions regarding the amount and type of access that internal users in your network are allowed. Proxy Server provides several methods that you can use to implement these policies.

Critical Information

Each proxy service provides a mechanism for enforcing outbound access policies. Being familiar with options offered by each is essential for you to be able to implement the security policies of your corporation.

Web Proxy Service

The Web Proxy service allows four protocol options on which to assign permissions:

- FTP Read
- Gopher
- Secure
- WWW

In order to access these options, access control must be enabled. You can then select one of the options listed above and assign to a user or group either Read access for FTP Read or Gopher, or Full access for Secure or WWW.

TIP For administration purposes, you should create groups and assign various permissions to them and then add or remove users to and from the groups as needed.

WinSock Proxy Service

The WinSock Proxy service presents numerous protocol options for which permissions can be assigned. In addition, unlike the Web Proxy service, new protocols can be defined as needed. In order to assign protocol permissions for the HTTP protocol, go to the Permissions tab of the WinSock Proxy service properties pages. Again, access control must be enabled. Select HTTP from the pop-up Protocol menu, and click on Edit. You can then choose a group or user to give access to this protocol. Any user not given access or not belonging to a group given access will be denied use of the HTTP protocol. Permissions for other WinSock Proxy protocols are configured in the same manner.

Socks Proxy Service

The Socks Proxy service is somewhat different in its application of permissions. By default, all Socks requests are denied. You can permit or deny requests to or from a Domain/Zone, an IP subnet, or All. You select a port number or a range of port numbers to apply this permission to. When you select the port number, you need to define the permission as applying to a number Equal To the port number listed (EQ), Not Equal To (NEQ), Greater Than (GT), Less Than (LT), Greater Than Or Equal To (GE), or Less Than Or Equal To (LE). Although not as advanced as the WinSock Proxy service, the Socks Proxy service has the advantage of wide support on both Windows and non-Windows platforms.

Necessary Procedures

Procedures involved in this objective include configuring protocol permissions in the Web Proxy service, the WinSock Proxy service, and the Socks Proxy service.

Setting Protocol Permissions for the Web Proxy Service

1. Start Internet Service Manager by selecting Start ➤ Programs ➤ Microsoft Proxy Server ➤ Internet Service Manager and select Web Proxy service Properties.

2. Click on the Permissions tab.

3. Enable Access Control if it is not enabled.

4. From the Protocol pull-down menu, select the protocol for which you will assign permissions.

5. Click Edit.

6. Click Add. Select the correct user or group.

7. Click OK twice.

8. Click OK or Apply.

Setting Protocol Permissions for the WinSock Proxy Service

1. Start Internet Service Manager by selecting Start ➤ Programs ➤ Microsoft Proxy Server ➤ Internet Service Manager, and select the WinSock Proxy service Properties.

2. Click on the Permissions tab.

3. Select the protocol you need to assign permissions to and click Edit.

4. Assign access to the appropriate groups or users. Click OK twice to return to the Internet Service Manager.

Setting Protocol Permissions for the Socks Proxy Service

1. Start Internet Service Manager by selecting Start ➤ Programs ➤ Microsoft Proxy Server ➤ Internet Service Manager and select the Socks Proxy service Properties.

2. Click on the Permissions tab.

3. Click Add. You will see the screen labeled Socks Permission.

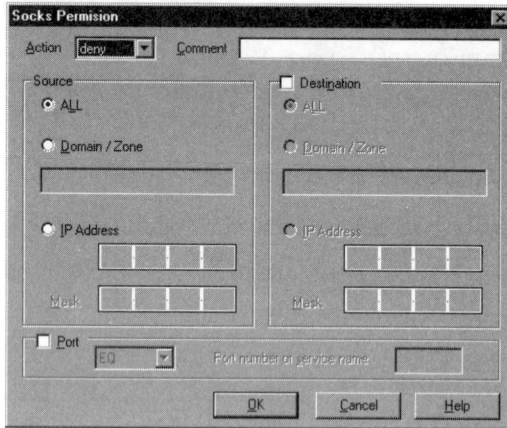

4. Select Action: Deny or Permit. Select Source or Destination.

5. Enter a short comment in the Comment field for easy recognition later.

6. Select All, Domain/Zone, or IP Address depending on your needs.

    A. If you select Domain/Zone, type in the name of the domain.

    B. If you select IP Address, enter the IP address and the subnet mask to create a range.

7. Click on the Port checkbox to activate it.

8. Type in the port number or service name.

9. Select the qualifier, i.e., EQ (equal), GT (greater than), etc.

10. Click OK.

Exam Essentials

Know where to modify protocol permissions and the differences in the permissions between Web Proxy, WinSock Proxy, and Socks Proxy services. Web Proxy service can only apply permissions to FTP, Gopher, Secure, and WWW. WinSock Proxy service can apply permissions to a wide range of protocols, and more can be added. The Socks Proxy service applies permit or deny permissions to TCP/IP port numbers.

Know how to apply protocol permissions to a specific user or group. Permissions can be applied to a specific user or group with either the Web Proxy service or the WinSock Proxy service. The Socks Proxy service permissions are applied globally.

Key Terms and Concepts

Socks Proxy service: This service provides transparent redirection of client requests for a wide variety of platforms. Microsoft Proxy Server 2 supports Socks version 4.3a.

Web Proxy service: This service supports CERN-compliant Web browsers running on any platform.

WinSock Proxy service: This service provides transparent support through the use of APIs for redirection of Windows-based client requests.

Sample Questions

1. You need to assign permissions for non-secure World Wide Web access in the Web Proxy service. Which protocol would you assign permissions to?

   A. HTTP

   B. HTTPS

   C. WWW

   D. Secure

   Answer: C. The protocols available to assign permissions in the Web Proxy service include FTP Read, Gopher, Secure, and WWW. Secure is used for HTTPS, or secure Web pages. The correct answer is WWW.

2. You need to allow permissions to use RealAudio to a group of managers in your corporation. What is the best way to accomplish this?

   A. From the WinSock Proxy service properties pages, add a protocol definition defining the correct port numbers and protocols for RealAudio. Assign permissions for the managers group to this protocol.

   B. From the WinSock Proxy service properties pages, assign permissions to the HTTPS protocol for the managers group.

   C. From the Web Proxy service, assign permissions for the managers group to the predefined RealAudio protocols.

   D. From the WinSock Proxy service properties pages, assign permissions for the managers group to the predefined RealAudio protocols.

   Answer: D. Adding a protocol definition for RealAudio is not necessary as there is already a predefined protocol in the WinSock Proxy service. HTTPS is not used by RealAudio. The Web Proxy service cannot be used by RealAudio and this proxy service does not have a predefined protocol for it.

3. You need to allow access from a specific external IP address on a particular port into your internal network. Which proxy service would you configure to accomplish this?

   A. Socks Proxy service

   B. Web Proxy service

   C. Secure Proxy service

   D. WinSock Proxy service

   Answer: A. The Socks Proxy service is the only service that has this functionality. Neither the Web Proxy service nor the WinSock Proxy service can apply permissions based on source address. There is no Secure Proxy service.

Grant or restrict access to specific Internet sites for outbound users.

In the previous section blocking or permitting access by protocol was discussed. Another way to implement restrictions on outbound Internet access is not to limit the entire protocol, but merely to deny access to individual Web sites that may be objectionable for one reason or another. This is called domain filtering.

Critical Information

Two strategies can be used when implementing domain filtering. By default, access to all sites can be either granted or denied. A list of exceptions to this can then be configured. Domain filters are configured from the Shared Services section of any of the three proxy services. Clicking on the Security button and then on the Domain Filters tab will present you with the configuration screen. If access to all Internet sites is granted by default, then any sites listed in the filter will be denied, but all others will be allowed. If access to all Internet sites is denied by default, then any sites listed in the filter will be allowed, and all others will be denied.

When configuring the filter list, a single IP address or DNS name can be entered, a group of IP addresses can be entered using an IP address and a subnet mask, or a domain can be specified. If a domain such as sybex.com is entered, then all sites within that domain would be either allowed or denied, depending on the configuration. These filters are applied globally and cannot be assigned to a specific user or group.

TIP The use of asterisks or wildcards in domain filtering is not necessary or permitted.

Once domain filtering is enabled it is applied to all HTTP, FTP, and Gopher requests. When a request is received that contains a domain name, the filtering list is examined for that domain name and for the IP address to which the domain name resolves. If the request received contains an IP address, the filtering list is searched for that address. However, if the filtering list contains at least one domain name, then reverse resolution is used to find the domain name for the address. The list is then searched for that domain name. If access to a site is restricted by IP address, all IP addresses mapped to the same domain name will also be restricted. This prevents users from bypassing filtering restrictions by using the IP address instead of the domain name.

When using domain filtering with the WinSock Proxy service, filters should be created for both the IP address and the domain name. A WinSock application converts a domain address to an IP address and then attempts to access the site. If the default filtering mode is set to denied, both an IP address filter and a domain name filter must be in effect for the request to succeed.

For the Socks Proxy service, domain filtering should be configured from the Permissions tab of the Socks Proxy service properties pages. Sites can be denied by IP address only, by IP address and subnet mask, or by domain name.

Necessary Procedures

The only procedure associated with this objective is implementing domain filtering. For the Web Proxy and WinSock Proxy services, this is configured from the Shared Services section of the properties pages of any of the proxy services. For the Socks Proxy service, this is configured from the Permissions tab of the Socks Proxy service properties pages.

Configuring Domain Filtering for the Web Proxy and WinSock Proxy Services

1. Start Internet Service Manager by selecting Start ➤ Programs ➤ Microsoft Proxy Server ➤ Internet Service Manager, and then select Properties for any of the three services.

2. In the Shared Services section, click on Security.

3. Click on the Domain Filters tab.

4. Click on Enable Filtering. You will see the following screen:

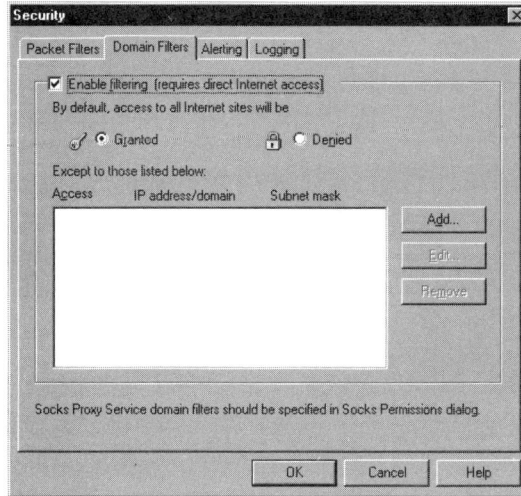

5. Select either Granted or Denied to grant or deny access to all sites by default.

6. Click Add. You will see the screen labeled "Deny Access to."

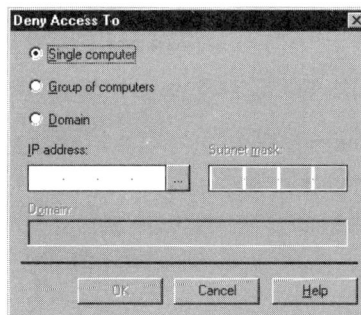

7. Enter either an IP address for a single computer, an IP address and a subnet mask for a group of computers, or a domain name.

8. Click OK.

Configuring Domain Filtering for the Socks Proxy Service

1. Start Internet Service Manager by selecting Start ➤ Programs ➤ Microsoft Proxy Server ➤ Internet Service Manager. Select the Socks Proxy service properties.

2. Click on the Permissions tab.

3. Click Add. You will see the Socks Permission screen:

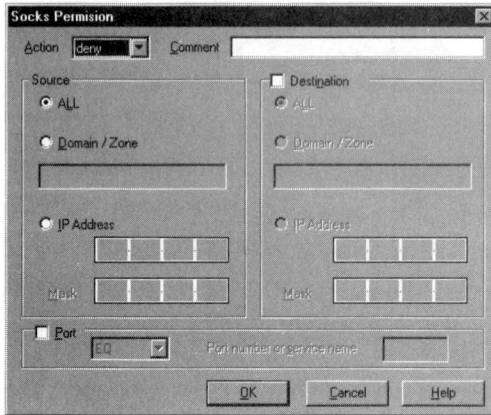

4. Select Action: Deny or Permit. Select Destination.

5. Enter a short comment in the Comment field for easy recognition later.

6. Select either Domain/Zone or IP Address, depending on your needs.

   A. If you select Domain/Zone, type in the name of the domain.

   B. If you select IP Address, enter the IP address and the subnet mask to create a range.

7. Click OK, then click OK or Apply.

Exam Essentials

Know how to configure domain filtering for the Web Proxy and WinSock Proxy services. Domain filtering for the Web Proxy and WinSock Proxy services are configured from the Shared Services section of any of the proxy service properties pages. All sites can be either granted or denied access by default, and a list of exceptions can be implemented.

Know how to configure domain filtering for the Socks Proxy service. Domain filtering for the Socks Proxy service is configured from the Permissions dialog box of the Socks Proxy service properties pages. Access to sites can be filtered on the basis of IP address only, a range of IP addresses, or a domain name.

Key Terms and Concepts

Domain filtering: The process of denying or allowing access to a specific site by IP address or domain name.

Reverse resolution: The process of resolving a domain name from an IP address.

Sample Questions

1. You are implementing domain filtering and need to allow access only to the mydomain.com domain. How do you accomplish this?

   A. Select Deny Access To All Sites By Default and create a domain filter for the mydomain.com domain name.

   B. Select Grant Access To All Sites By Default and create a domain filter for the mydomain.com domain name.

   C. Select Deny Access To All Sites By Default and create a domain filter for *.mydomain.com.

   D. Select Deny Access To All Sites By Default and create a separate filter for each site in the mydomain.com domain.

   Answer: A. In order to allow access to only this domain, you must select the Deny Access To All Sites By Default option. The use of wildcards is not necessary or permitted. Creating a separate filter for each site in the domain is not necessary, since when you enter only the domain, Proxy Server will automatically do this.

2. You administer a corporate network, and have implemented domain filtering. You have filtered some sites by domain name. You wish to deny access to the site www.mydomain.com. whether it is requested by IP address or by domain name. Which of the following would accomplish this?

   A. Configure a domain filter denying access to the domain name, and configure another allowing access to the IP address.

   B. Configure a domain filter for its IP address only.

   C. Configure a domain filter for .mydomain.com.

   D. Configure a domain filter for its domain name only.

   Answer: B and D. Allowing an IP address while filtering a domain name would not accomplish the objective. A filter for .mydomain.com would filter all sites in that domain, which is not what was specified. When a request is received using a domain name, Proxy Server will resolve the domain for an IP address and then check the filtering list for that address. If a request is received using an IP address and there is at least one domain name in the filtering list, Proxy Server will use reverse resolution to get the domain name and then check for that name in the filtering list.

3. You need to deny access by several Unix workstations to a site with the IP address 172.16.29.190. Where would you go to configure this?

   A. The Shared Services section of any of the three proxy services' properties pages

   B. The Permissions dialog box of the Socks Proxy service properties pages

   C. The Permissions dialog box of the WinSock Proxy service properties pages

   D. The Shared Services section of the Socks Proxy service properties pages

   Answer: B. Socks Proxy service domain filters should be configured from the Permissions dialog box of the Socks Proxy service properties pages. Unix workstations can only use the Socks Proxy service. The Shared Services section of the three proxy services can only configure domain filters for the Web Proxy and WinSock Proxy services.

Choose the location, size, and type of caching for the Web Proxy service.

In order for Proxy Server to provide efficient service to users, it is essential that caching be configured correctly. The size and location of the cache can have a dramatic effect on the level of service provided to the end user. Configuring the type of caching, passive or active, also greatly impacts the amount of latency encountered by users.

Critical Information

The size and location of the cache is first configured during installation. Cache can only be configured on an NTFS partition of 5MB or larger. This is a change from Microsoft Proxy Server 1, which allowed caching on a FAT partition. Higher cache performance will be accomplished by placing the cache on a separate physical disk from the disk containing the main proxy installation and the disk containing the operating system. The recommended minimum size for cache is calculated by starting with 100MB and adding an additional 0.5MB for each client workstation. The size of the cache can be fine-tuned after experimenting with typical proxy server usage. It should be large enough that, under normal load, caching does not run out of space. Once Proxy Server is installed, the Setup program should not be used to adjust the size or location of cache. Instead, these changes should be made using the Web Proxy service properties pages in Internet Service Manager. If you use Internet Service Manager to decrease cache size, some cache objects may be deleted. If you set the cache size to zero, all cached objects are deleted. Increasing the cache size has no effect on the data stored in cache.

TIP Each time the Web Proxy service is started, it verifies the integrity of cache. If you attempt to change the cache configuration before it is finished, you will receive an error message. You must wait until verification is complete to make configuration changes.

Once the size and location of the cache is configured correctly, there are two types of caching that can be utilized: passive caching and active caching.

Passive caching: When passive caching is used, all objects stored in cache have a Time-to-Live, or a TTL. The TTL determines how long an object will be stored in cache before it is updated from the originating site. With passive caching all objects requested are stored in cache, with a TTL defined either by the source HTML or by the TTL settings configured in the cache properties of Proxy Server.

Active caching: Active caching will automatically update an object when the object's TTL is close to expiration. The algorithm used by active caching to determine when an object will be updated includes the popularity of the object, the TTL of the object, and server load. When server load is high, objects will only be updated if the TTL will expire in less than a minute. When server load is low, objects will be updated if they are at least 50% expired. This causes the bulk of active caching to take place during times of low network usage, such as during the night. However, active caching may update cached objects even during periods of high utilization.

TIP When using Auto Dial, active caching will be disabled during times when Proxy Server is not allowed to dial out.

Necessary Procedures

Procedures defined in this objective include configuring the location and size of caching, and configuring the two types of caching. Configuring active and passive caching are discussed in detail in the next objective. So, in this objective only the first procedure will be discussed.

Configuring the Location and the Size of Caching

1. Start Internet Service Manager by selecting Start ≻ Programs ≻ Microsoft Proxy Server ≻ Internet Service Manager, and then select Web Proxy service Properties.

2. Click on the Caching tab.

3. Click on Cache Size. You will see the screen labeled Microsoft Proxy Server Cache Drives.

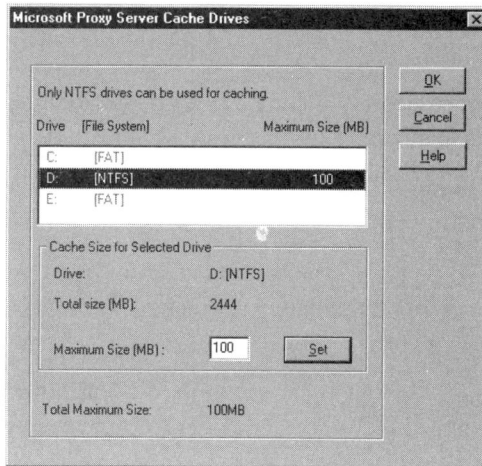

4. Highlight the drive on which you will configure caching. Note that if there are FAT partitions, you will be unable to select them.

5. Type in the maximum cache size in megabytes, and click Set. Click OK.

6. Click OK or Apply.

Exam Essentials

Know how to choose the size and location of caching. Caching must take place on an NTFS partition of 5MB or larger. Caching will be more efficient if placed on a different physical disk than the Proxy Server partition and the partition containing the operating system.

Know how to choose the type of caching. There are two types of caching: passive caching and active caching. Passive caching caches all objects requested. If the Time-to-Live (TTL) of a cache object is expired and that object is requested again, the object is updated from the originating site. Active caching uses a combination of a cached object's popularity, its TTL, and the server load to automatically refresh cached objects before their TTL expires.

Key Terms and Concepts

Active Caching: The process of downloading frequently requested sites in advance during periods of low network utilization.

Caching: The process of storing requested objects on disk in a local server.

FAT: A file system, supported by all Windows operating systems, which uses a table to keep track of segments of disk space used for file storage.

NTFS: A file system supported by Windows NT that offers enhanced security, file system recovery, object-oriented applications, and support for very large storage media.

Passive Caching: The process of storing requested sites in cache so that subsequent requests for those sites can be served locally.

Time-to-Live: The amount of time an object will be stored in cache before it must be updated from the origin site.

Sample Questions

1. Which file system must be used on the partition you will use for caching?

   A. FAT

   B. HPFS

   C. FAT32

   D. NTFS

Answer: D. Only NTFS can be used with Proxy Server 2 for caching.

2. What criteria does the active caching process use to determine when an object will be updated?

   A. Time-to-Live

   B. Cache size

   C. Popularity of object

   D. Current proxy server load

   Answer: A, C, and D. The three criteria used by active caching are the TTL, the popularity of the object, and the current proxy server load. The cache size is not taken into account in these calculations.

3. You administer a corporate network with 1,500 client workstations. What is the minimum recommended cache size?

   A. 1.5GB

   B. 850MB

   C. 750MB

   D. 100MB

   Answer: B. The formula used to calculate the minimum recommended cache size is 100MB + 0.5MB for each client workstation. In this case, that is equal to 850MB.

Configure active caching and passive caching.

Efficient Internet access is one of the biggest advantages of using Microsoft Proxy Server. Active and passive caching play a large part in providing that efficiency. The default cache settings are likely to suit your needs. However, if you need more precise control over the cache, it is available in the Advanced Cache Settings section. As mentioned previously, caching is emphasized in the Proxy Server exam.

Critical Information

Configuration settings for caching can be accessed from the Caching tab of the Web Proxy service properties pages. For passive caching there are three different settings available:

Updates are more important (more update checks): When this option is selected, the Time-to-Live (TTL) for all objects will be set to 0, unless the object has its own TTL specified. This is useful for sites with highly volatile information such as stock quotes, search pages, etc.

Equal importance: When this option is selected, the TTL for all objects without a TTL specified will be set to 20% of the object's age, assuming the object provides Proxy Server with a Time Last Modified. It also specifies a minimum TTL of 15 minutes and a maximum of 1,440 minutes.

Fewer network accesses are more important (more cache hits): When this option is selected, the TTL is set to 40% of the object's age, again assuming that the object is without its own TTL and the object provides Proxy Server with a Time Last Modified. It specifies a minimum TTL of 30 minutes and a maximum of 2,880 minutes.

For all of these options, if FTP Caching is enabled, the default TTL is 1,440 minutes. By clicking on the Advanced button, you can specify all of these settings yourself. You can also specify a limit to the size of an object in cache. By default, no limit is set. In the Advanced Cache Policy screen you can also determine how long Proxy Server will serve an object from cache if the object cannot be updated from the source Web site. The default is 50% of the TTL. From this screen, you can also create cache filters. You can create a filter specifying that all or part of a particular site should be either always cached or never cached.

Active caching also has three settings:

- Faster user response is more important (more pre-fetching)

- Equal importance

- Fewer network accesses are more important (less pre-fetching)

Necessary Procedures

Procedures necessary for this objective include configuring both passive and active caching. Both of these are properties of the Web Proxy service.

Configuring Passive Caching and Active Caching

1. Start Internet Service Manager by selecting Start ➤ Programs ➤ Microsoft Proxy Server ➤ Internet Service Manager.

2. Select Properties for the Web Proxy service.

3. Click on the Caching tab. You will see the following screen:

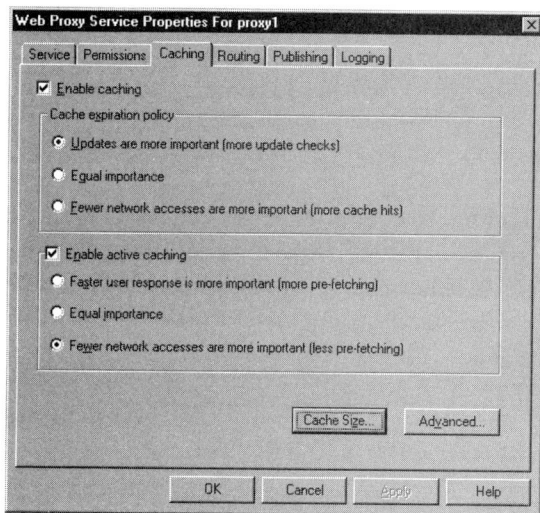

4. To enable passive caching, check the Enable Caching box.

5. Under Cache expiration policy, select one of the three options:

   A. Updates Are More Important (More Update Checks)

   B. Equal Importance

   C. Fewer Network Accesses Are More Important (More Cache Hits)

6. If you wish to change the default settings for caching, click on the Advanced button.

7. To configure active caching, make sure the Enable Active Caching box is checked. Then select one of the three options:

   A. Faster User Response Is More Important (More Pre-Fetching)

   B. Equal Importance

   C. Fewer Network Accesses Are More Important (Less Pre-Fetching)

Exam Essentials

Know how to configure passive caching. Passive caching is configured from the Web Proxy service properties pages. Three options are available: more update checks, equal importance, and fewer network accesses. Advanced configuration settings can also be used to control the Time-to-Live (TTL) of objects, the size of cache objects, and cache filters.

Know how to configure active caching. Active caching is also configured from the Web Proxy service properties pages. Active caching offers three options: faster response, equal importance, and fewer network accesses.

Key Terms and Concepts

Cache filtering: Specifying sites either to always be cached or to never be cached.

FTP caching: The caching of FTP objects.

Pre-fetching: The process of downloading Web objects in advance.

Sample Questions

1. Which of the following is a valid definition of active caching?

   A. The process of storing frequently requested objects in disk space on a local server

B. The process of caching objects as they are requested

C. The process of downloading frequently requested sites in advance during periods of low network utilization

D. The amount of time an object will be stored in cache before it must be updated from the original site

Answer: C. Active caching is the process of downloading frequently requested sites in advance during periods of low network utilization.

2. Which proxy services allow clients to take advantage of active caching?

A. WinSock Proxy service

B. Web Proxy service

C. Socks Proxy service

D. WWW Proxy service

Answer: B. Only the Web Proxy service uses caching. There is no WWW Proxy service.

Implement Web publishing to enable reverse proxying.

Reverse proxying enables Proxy Server to intercept incoming requests to an internal Web server and to respond for that server. This provides a measure of security for an internal Web server that might be considered an insecure server. Because the proxy server handles requests, the external user never sees the internal server. Often, Web sites that are made available to the general public are an invitation to hackers to see what kind of trouble they can cause. Placing the Web server behind the protection of the proxy server provides an important layer of security against hackers.

Critical Information

When Web publishing is enabled, there are three ways you can configure Proxy Server to deal with incoming Web requests:

Discarded: All Web requests will be discarded by default.

Sent to the local Web server: All Web requests will be sent to the local Web server by default.

Sent to another Web server: All Web requests will be sent to another Web server on the internal network by default.

This means that the external user will not actually see the Web server they are accessing. If the content they are accessing is not stored on the remote server, they will be unable to access the local server for this content. All they can access is the remote server. Figure 3.1 shows an example of reverse proxying.

FIGURE 3.1: An example of reverse proxying

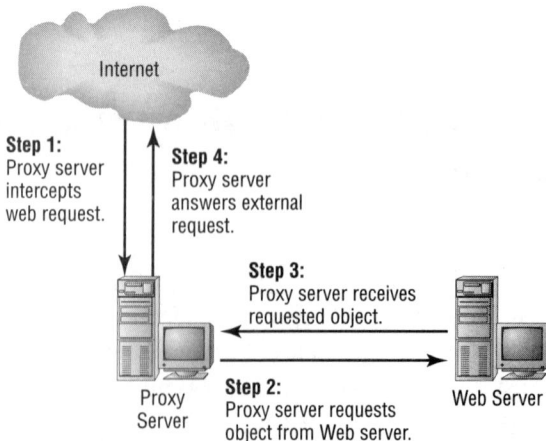

Necessary Procedures

There is only one procedure associated with this objective. Configuring reverse proxying with Web publishing provides valuable added security to your network.

Configuring Reverse Proxying with Web Publishing

1. Start Internet Service Manager by selecting Start ➤ Programs ➤ Microsoft Proxy Server ➤ Internet Service Manager.

2. Select Properties for the Web Proxy service.

3. Click on the Publishing tab.

4. Put a check in the Enable Web Publishing box. You will see the following screen:

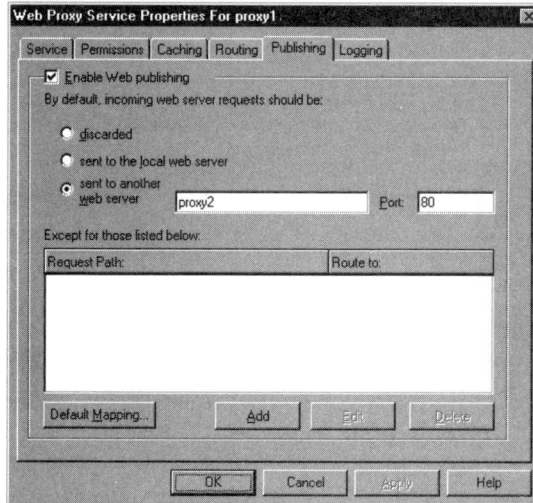

5. Choose either "Sent to The Local Web Server" or "Sent to Another Web Server."

6. Click OK or Apply.

Exam Essentials

Know how to configure reverse proxying with Web publishing.
Reverse proxying is configured from the Web Proxy service properties pages on the Publishing tab. Reverse proxying can be configured to listen for all incoming Web requests and respond on behalf of the internal Web server.

Key Terms and Concepts

Publishing: The process of a Web server sitting behind a proxy server and publishing content on the Internet.

Reverse Proxying: The process of a proxy server listening for and responding to incoming Web requests on behalf of an internal Web server.

Sample Questions

1. You administer a proxy server network with a Web server running on a separate computer. You wish to configure reverse proxying for an internal Web server. What else must you do to have the proxy server route all Web requests to that server?

   A. Select "Sent to Local Web Server" in the Publishing dialog box.

   B. Select "Sent to Another Web Server" and type in the URL of the server and the port number the server is using for Web services.

   C. Select Discarded in the Publishing dialog box.

   D. Nothing

   Answer: B. Selecting "Sent to Local Web Server" will route requests to the Web server running on the proxy server computer. Selecting Discard will result in all Web requests being discarded, as will doing nothing, since this is the default setting when Web publishing is enabled.

2. Which proxy service must be configured to allow reverse proxying?

   A. Web Proxy service

   B. WinSock Proxy service

   C. Socks Proxy service

   D. WWW service

   Answer: A. Reverse proxying is configured from the Web Proxy service properties pages.

Back up and restore Proxy Server configurations.

Proxy Server configurations can be backed up to a file and also restored from that file. This can be a valuable tool to provide continued proxy services in the event that a Proxy Server installation has become damaged. Microsoft has made this process very easy with Proxy Server.

Critical Information

Server backup and server restore can be performed from the Configuration section of any of the three proxy services. The default location for proxy server configuration files is C:\MSP\CONFIG. They are named in the following format: MSP*yyyymmdd*.MPC. Proxy Server can be saved to any directory, although for maximum security the use of NTFS partitions is recommended. Configuration files can also be named anything if RemotMSP is used to perform the backup.

When restoring configuration files, there are two options: full restore and partial restore. A full restore will restore all Proxy Server configuration parameters. A partial restore will only restore non-computer-specific configuration parameters. The following is a list of configuration parameters that will not be restored when performing a partial restore:

- Location and size of cache

- Location of service logs and packet filtering logs

- Packet filtering configuration information

- Configuration information for Auto Dial

- Server alias used for routing in the "HTTP Via" header

- Server intra-array IP address

- Any registry keys that cannot be configured using Internet Service Manager

Partial restores can be used between proxy servers when permissions are identical. Full restores are typically used when rebuilding a server or when restoring a previous configuration.

RemotMSP can also be used both to back up and to restore proxy server configurations. The correct syntax to back up a proxy server configuration is as follows: `RemotMSP SAVE -File:<local file name>`. The correct syntax for restoring proxy server configuration using RemotMSP is seen by typing the Help command at a Command Prompt:

```
C:\msp>remotmsp load -h

Load configuration from a backup file.
usage: REMOTMSP LOAD -File:<local file name> -
LEVEL:<level>
<level> is FULL or PARTIAL
```

Necessary Procedures

Procedures for this objective consist of backing up server configurations, and restoring server configurations. Both procedures provide a much-needed solution to enhance Proxy Server 2 stability compared to earlier versions.

Backing up a Proxy Server Configuration Using Internet Service Manager

1. Start Internet Service Manager by selecting Start ➤ Programs ➤ Microsoft Proxy Server ➤ Internet Service Manager.

2. Select Properties for any of the three proxy services. You will see the Services tab selected.

3. In the Configuration section, click on Server Backup to see the following screen:

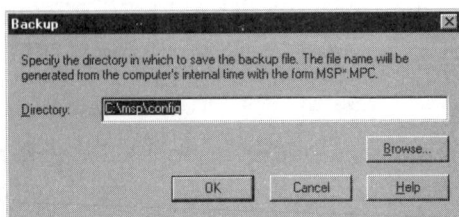

4. You can accept the default directory, or click Browse to choose another directory.

5. Click OK.

Backing up a Proxy Server Configuration Using RemotMSP

1. Start a Command Prompt.

2. Type in the Help command to see the correct syntax:

```
RemotMSP save -h
```

3. Type in the correct command to perform the backup:

```
RemotMSP save file:<local file name>
```

Restoring a Proxy Server Configuration Using Internet Service Manager

1. Start Internet Service Manager by selecting Start ➢ Programs ➢ Microsoft Proxy Server ➢ Internet Service Manager.

2. Select Properties for any of the three proxy services. You will see the Services tab selected.

3. In the Configuration section, click on Server Restore to see the following screen:

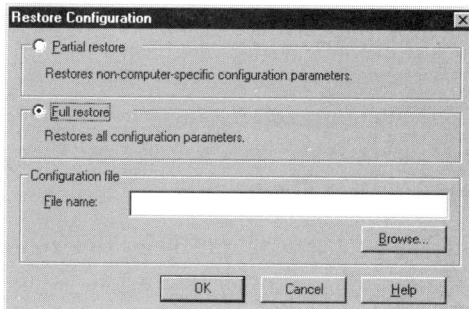

4. Select either Partial Restore or Full Restore.

5. Either type in the path and the name of the configuration file to restore or click Browse to locate it.

6. Click OK.

Restoring a Proxy Server Configuration Using RemotMSP

1. Start a Command Prompt.

2. Type in the Help command to see the correct syntax:

   ```
   RemotMSP load -h
   ```

3. Type in the correct command to perform either a full or partial restore:

   ```
   RemotMSP load file:<local file name> -level:<level>
   ```

Exam Essentials

Know how to back up proxy server configurations. Either Internet Service Manager or RemotMSP can be used to back up proxy server configurations. The default location for these files is C:\MSP\CONFIG. When using RemotMSP, the files can be named anything. When using Internet Service Manager, the files are named in the following format: MSP*yyyymmdd*.MPC.

Know how to restore proxy server configurations. Either Internet Service Manager or RemotMSP can be used to restore proxy server configurations. Either a partial or a full restoration can be performed. A partial restore only restores non–computer-specific settings. A full restore will restore all configurations settings.

Key Terms and Concepts

Auto Dial: A service available with Proxy Server that uses a dial-up connection to provide Internet access to clients.

RemotMSP: A command line utility that can be used to administer proxy servers.

Sample Questions

1. Which of the following is a proxy configuration backup file?

A. WSPCFG.INI

B. MSPCLNT.INI

C. W3981023.LOG

D. MSP19980727.MPC

Answer: D. Proxy configuration files by default are named in the format MSP*yyyymmdd*.MPC. The other files named are specific proxy server files used for different purposes.

2. You administer a corporate network. You need to restore a proxy server configuration. Specifically, you need to restore packet filtering configuration information that has been corrupted. Which of the following would accomplish this?

A. Use Internet Service Manager to restore a proxy server configuration, specifying a partial restore.

B. Use RemotMSP to restore a proxy server configuration, specifying a partial restore.

C. Use Internet Service Manager to restore a proxy server configuration, specifying a full restore.

D. Use RemotMSP to restore a proxy server configuration, specifying a full restore.

Answer: C and D. Either Internet Service Manager or RemotMSP can be used to restore proxy server configurations. However, a partial restore will not restore packet filtering configuration. Only a full restore will accomplish this.

Implement reverse hosting.

Reverse hosting is similar to reverse proxying but extends to the next logical step by maintaining a list of servers that are permitted to publish to the Internet. Proxy Server then listens for requests and responds on behalf of multiple servers sitting behind it. This is an extremely valuable feature, as it allows you to hide all of your servers behind the proxy server, thereby protecting them from hackers.

Critical Information

As with reverse proxying, reverse hosting is configured from the properties pages of the Web Proxy service under the Publishing tab. However, to configure reverse hosting, all incoming Web requests should be discarded by default. Mappings are then added to provide paths to various Web servers sitting downstream from the proxy server. These mappings connect virtual paths belonging to the proxy server to the actual path of a Web server. For instance, your proxy server might have a domain name http://www.mydomain.com. You might have a mapping defined for http://www.mydomain.com/guests/. Requests to this URL would be routed to an entirely different server in the internal network. You could also have an entirely different domain name still mapped to the proxy server IP address, such as http://www.myotherdomain.com . This could also be routed to an entirely separate internal server. Some legacy Web browsers do not provide the full publishing server name in their request. For these browsers you should configure a default mapping to which all of their requests will go.

Tighter security can be provided by putting the Web servers publishing to the Internet in a separate domain from the proxy server, and configuring a one-way trust. This is illustrated in Figure 3.2. Then, if a hacker were able to get past the proxy server, chances are damages would be limited to the proxy server domain, leaving the Web servers untouched.

FIGURE 3.2: Using separate domains and one-way trust

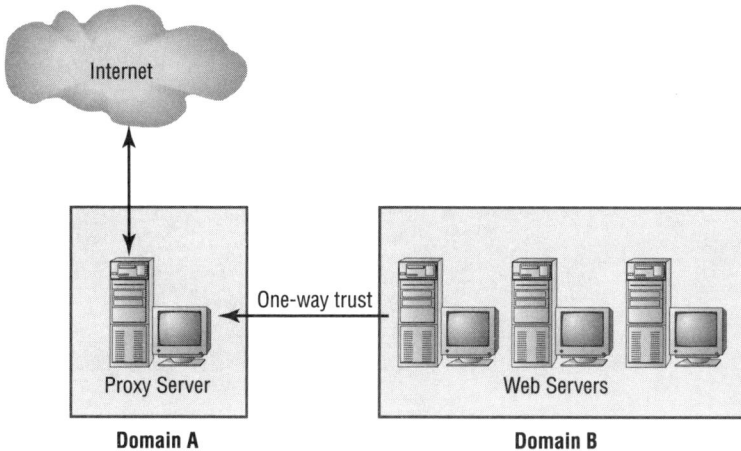

SEE ALSO For a detailed discussion of trust relationships, see the *MCSE: NT Server 4 in the Enterprise Study Guide*, 2nd ed. (Sybex 1998).

Necessary Procedures

The only procedure associated with this chapter is implementing reverse hosting. Although this is configured using the same tools as implementing reverse proxying, there are significant differences.

1. Start Internet Service Manager by selecting Start ➢ Programs ➢ Microsoft Proxy Server ➢ Internet Service Manager.

2. Select Properties for the Web Proxy service.

3. Click on the Publishing tab to see the following screen:

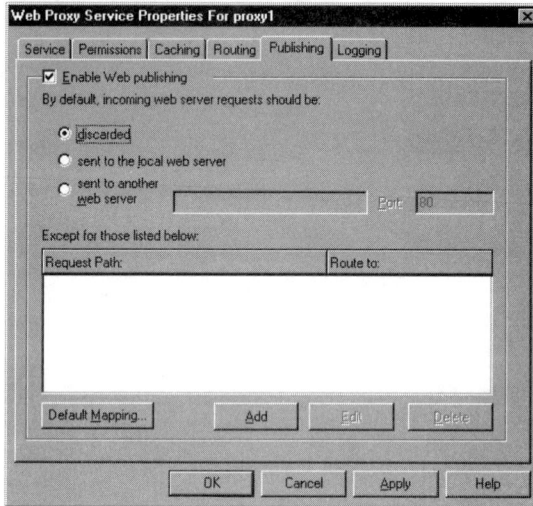

4. Under "By Default, Incoming Web Server Request Should Be," select Discarded.

5. Click Add to see the screen labeled Mapping.

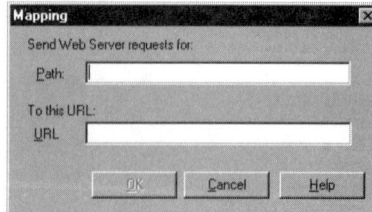

6. Type in the URL that the proxy server should listen for and the URL that those requests should be sent to.

7. Click OK.

8. At this point, you may be asked to enter a default mapping. Enter a URL if you wish.

9. Click OK. Click OK or Apply.

Exam Essentials

Know how to configure reverse hosting. Reverse hosting is configured from the Publishing tab of the Web Proxy service properties pages. Mappings can be configured to route incoming requests to internal servers without identifying those servers to the external user.

Key Terms and Concepts

One-way trust: A trust relationship configured so that one domain will have access to the resources in a second domain, but the second domain will not have access to the resources in the first domain.

Reverse hosting: The process of a proxy server listening for and responding to incoming Web requests on behalf of multiple servers sitting behind the proxy server.

Sample Questions

1. You have configured reverse hosting on your network, and have several Web servers that publish content to the Internet. You receive complaints from some users that they cannot access your Web sites. After investigation, you discover that they are using very old Web browsers. What should you do to solve this problem?

A. Configure reverse proxying instead of reverse hosting.

B. Configure Web publishing to send all Web requests to the local server.

C. Create a default mapping for incoming Web requests.

D. Disable packet filtering.

Answer: C. Reverse proxying will not work in this situation because there are multiple Web servers publishing content to the Internet. Sending all Web requests to the local server will not work for the same reason. Packet filtering would have no effect on this problem.

Because the users having the problem are all using old Web browsers, we can assume that the problem is caused by them. Creating a default mapping for incoming Web requests should solve their problem.

2. Which proxy service is used to configure reverse hosting?

   A. Web Proxy service

   B. WinSock Proxy service

   C. Socks Proxy service

   D. WWW service

   Answer: A. The properties pages for the Web Proxy service are used to configure reverse hosting.

CHAPTER

4

Integration and Interoperability

Microsoft Exam Objectives Covered in This Chapter:

▶ **Use the Proxy Server client Setup program to configure client computers.** *(pages 180 – 190)*

▶ **Configure Proxy Server and Proxy Server client computers to use the Proxy Server services. Configurations include:** *(pages 190 – 203)*
- Microsoft Internet Explorer client computers
- Netscape Navigator client computers
- Macintosh client computers
- UNIX client computers
- Client computers on an IPX-only network

▶ **Configure a RAS server to route Internet requests.** *(pages 203 – 212)*

▶ **Write JavaScript to configure a Web browser.** *(pages 212 – 215)*

▶ **Change settings in Mspclnt.ini.** *(pages 216 – 221)*

Now that you have installed and configured Proxy Server, it's time to let everyone use it. Depending on your network, you may have many different client configurations. There may be clients using IPX or TCP/IP, Netscape or Internet Explorer, Windows or Macintosh or Unix, etc. All of these clients will need to be able to use the proxy server.

▶ Use the Proxy Server client Setup program to configure client computers.

For Windows-based computers, the client Setup program can be used to automate much of the client configuration. Much of the configuration is provided automatically, but to be able to tailor the configuration to fit your needs, you must be familiar with every aspect of it.

Critical Information

When Microsoft Proxy Server is installed, a share is created called MSPCLNT. The default directory this share is created from is C:\MSP\ CLIENTS. This directory contains a Setup program that can be used to configure both WinSock Proxy and Web Proxy clients. This Setup program can also be run from the command line or can be accessed using a Web browser to connect to the URL http://*servername*/ msproxy/. The Setup program uses information stored in the file named MSPCLNT.INI. Internet Service Manager can be used to configure the information in this file.

Client configuration can be configured using Internet Service Manager. From the properties pages of any of the proxy services, click on the Client Configuration button. In the Client Installation/Configuration screen, there are three sections. The first deals with the setup for WinSock Proxy clients. The second deals with Web browsers, which use the Web Proxy service. The third section is used to configure the auto-configuration script that can be used by Web browsers.

Using Setup to Configure WinSock Proxy Clients

WinSock clients can connect to the proxy server using the computer name, the DNS name, the IP address, a manually entered array name, or a group of IP addresses for an array.

NOTE   Manual configuration requires that you edit the MSPCLNT.INI file. This is discussed later in this chapter.

The Setup program will make the following changes to the client computer:

- The Proxy Server client application is installed.

- The WINSOCK.DLL file is replaced by a proxy server version of WINSOCK.DLL.

- The Local Address Table (LAT) contained in the file MSPLAT.TXT and the file MSPCLNT.INI are copied to the C:\MSPCLNT directory on the client computer.

- A new control panel icon, WSP Client, is added. From this icon, the client can point to a new proxy server, the WinSock Proxy client can be enabled and disabled, and the use of IPX/SPX can be forced.

- A program group is added with options to run the Setup program again or to uninstall the proxy client.

Using Setup to Configure Client Web Browsers

Client configuration can be used to automatically configure Web browsers. When this option is enabled, the computer name, DNS name, or IP address of the proxy server is specified, as well as the port number. There is also an option to configure Web browsers to use automatic configuration. When this is enabled, the configuration will automatically use the default address for the configuration URL:

```
http://servername:80/Array.DLL?Get.Routing.Script
```

This URL can be changed to a custom location.

Using Setup to Configure Automatic Configuration Scripts

The automatic configuration script can be configured as follows:

To use the proxy server for local servers   All internal traffic to local servers will be forced to go through the proxy server.

To bypass the proxy server for specific ranges of IP addresses
Requests for those IP addresses will not go through the proxy server.

To bypass the proxy server for specific domains   Requests for those domains will not go through the proxy server.

To configure a back-up route   In the event that the proxy server goes down, the client computer can be configured either to access the Internet directly or to route traffic to a second proxy server.

Using the Command Line to Run Setup

The Setup program can be launched from the command line with the following options:

Setup /g *filename*   Generates a log of installation activity.

Setup /q   Displays progress bars and the completion dialog box, but does not prompt the user for settings.

Setup /q1   Displays progress bars, but does not display the completion dialog box and does not prompt the user for settings.

Setup /qt   Does not display progress bars or the completion dialog box, does not prompt the user for settings, and automatically restarts the computer upon completion if necessary. This option is not available to 16-bit clients.

Setup /r   Reinstalls the proxy server client.

Setup /u   Uninstalls the client application but leaves shared components. This option can be used together with the /q1 and /qt switches, e.g., `Setup /q1 /u`.

Setup /y   Installs the client without copying files.

Necessary Procedures

Necessary procedures for this objective all deal with client configuration, including configuration of WinSock Proxy clients, Web Proxy clients, and automatic configuration scripts.

Configuring Proxy Server to Configure WinSock Proxy Clients

1. Start Internet Service Manager by selecting Start ➤ Programs ➤ Microsoft Proxy Server ➤ Internet Service Manager.

2. Select the Service tab of the properties pages for any of the three proxy services.

3. Click on Client Configuration to see the screen labeled Client Installation/Configuration.

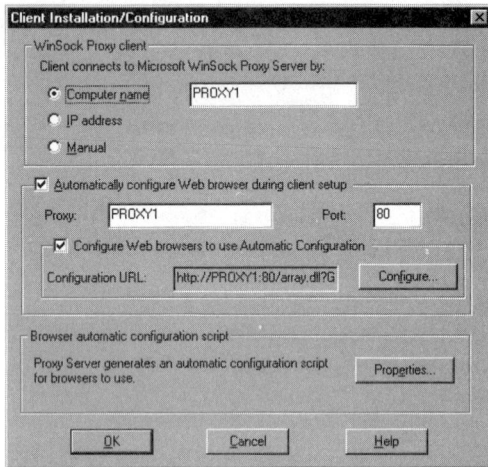

4. In the WinSock Proxy Client section, select either Computer Name or IP Address. (The Manual setting is discussed later in this chapter.) Type in either a computer name, a DNS name, or an IP address.

5. Click OK, then click OK or Apply.

Configuring Proxy Server to Set Up Client Web Browsers

1. Start Internet Service Manager by selecting Start ➤ Programs ➤ Microsoft Proxy Server ➤ Internet Service Manager.

2. Select the Service tab of the properties pages for any of the three proxy services.

3. Click on Client Configuration to see the screen labeled Client Installation/Configuration.

4. Make sure the checkbox labeled "Automatically Configure Web Browser During Client Setup" is checked.

5. The name of the proxy server and the port number should already be set. Verify that they are correct.

6. Make sure that there is a check in the checkbox labeled "Configure Web Browsers to Use Automatic Configuration."

7. To change from the default URL to a custom URL, click on Configure. You will see the screen labeled Configuration URL For Clients.

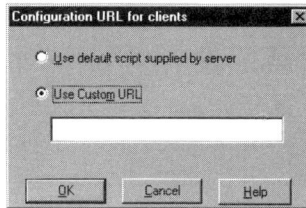

8. From here you can either select to use the default script, or you can specify a custom URL.

9. Click OK twice, then click OK or Apply.

Using Setup to Configure the Automatic Configuration Script

1. Start Internet Service Manager by selecting Start ➤ Programs ➤ Microsoft Proxy Server ➤ Internet Service Manager.

2. Select the Service tab of the properties pages for any of the three proxy services.

3. Click on Client Configuration to see the screen labeled Client Installation/Configuration.

4. In the Browser Automatic Configuration Script section, click on Properties to see the screen labeled Advanced Client Configuration.

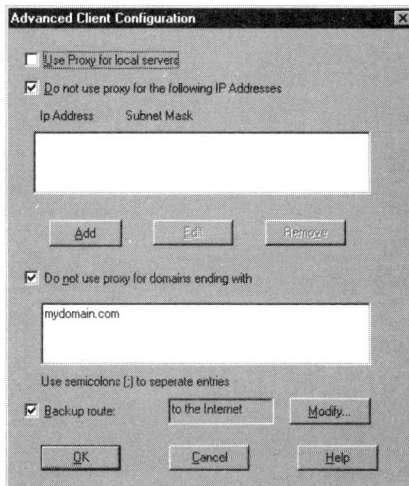

5. If you want to use the proxy server for local servers, put a check in the first checkbox.

6. To configure IP addresses for which the client should bypass the proxy server, click on Add. Type in an IP address and a subnet mask.

7. To configure domains for which the client should bypass the proxy server, put a check in the checkbox labeled "Do Not Use Proxy for Domains Ending with."

8. Type in the domains. Use semicolons to separate multiple entries.

9. If you wish to configure a backup route, put a check in the Backup Route checkbox.

10. Click on Modify to see the screen labeled Configure Backup Route.

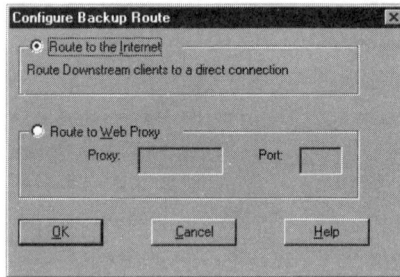

11. Select either "Route to the Internet" or "Route to Web Proxy." For routing to a Web proxy, enter the server name of the proxy and the port number.

12. Click OK three times and then click OK or Apply.

Running the Client Setup Program

1. The Setup program can be accessed either through the MSPCLNT share on the proxy server or by using a Web browser to go to http://*servername*/Msproxy.

2. Once started, the Setup program will check for a previous installation.

3. If a previous installation is found, the screen labeled Microsoft Proxy Client 2.0 Setup will appear.

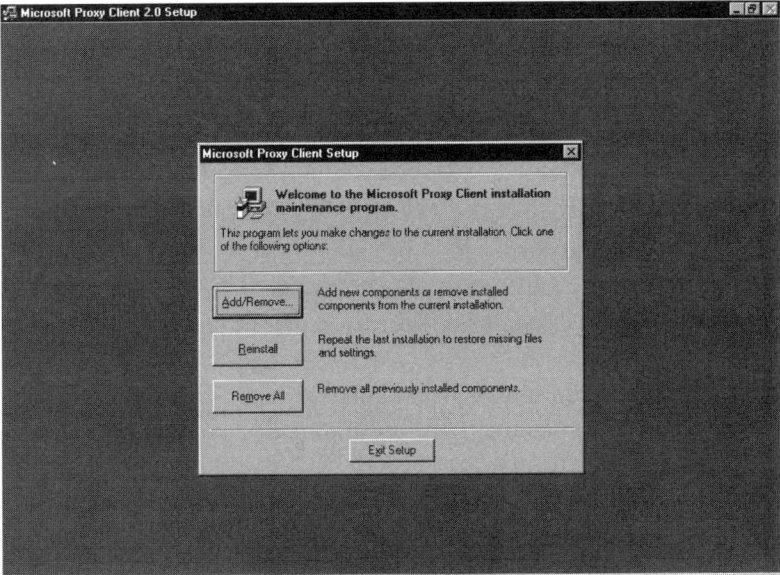

4. From here, you have the option to add or remove components (Add/Remove), to repeat the last installation (Reinstall), or to uninstall the client (Remove All).

5. If a previous installation is not found, you are asked to select an installation folder. The default is C:\MSPCLNT.

6. You will know that the installation was successful when you see the following dialog box:

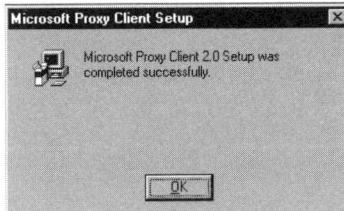

Exam Essentials

Know how to configure Microsoft Proxy Server to set up WinSock Proxy clients. Configuration for WinSock Proxy clients is accessed from the properties pages of any of the three proxy services by clicking on the Client Configuration button. WinSock Proxy clients can be configured to access the proxy server by server name, by DNS name, by IP address, or using a manual configuration.

Know how to configure Microsoft Proxy Server to set up client Web browsers. The settings for automatic configuration of client Web browsers are accessed from the properties pages of any of the three proxy services by clicking on the Client Configuration button. Client browsers can be configured with the proxy name and port number and can be configured to use automatic configuration. A custom URL can be configured if the default URL for automatic configuration is not being used.

Know how to configure the automatic configuration script. Configuration for the automatic configuration script is accessed from the properties pages of any of the proxy services by clicking on the Client Configuration button and then clicking on the Properties button. Browsers can be configured to use the proxy server for local servers or not to use the proxy server for specific IP addresses or domains. They can also be configured with a backup route.

Know how to access and run the Proxy Server client Setup program. The Proxy Server client Setup program can be accessed either from the MSPCLNT share on the proxy server or by using a Web browser to open the URL http://*servername*/Msproxy. The Setup program can be used to add or remove components, to reinstall using the previous settings, or to uninstall the Proxy client.

Key Terms and Concepts

Domain Naming System (DNS): This is a naming system that is used to map domain names to IP addresses.

Uniform Resource Locator (URL): This is a naming convention that is used to specify the protocol used, the location of the computer, and the directory or file name on the Internet.

Web Proxy service: This service supports CERN-compliant Web browsers running on any platform.

WinSock Proxy service: This service provides transparent support through the use of APIs for redirection of Windows-based client requests.

Sample Questions

1. What is the default directory for the Proxy Server client Setup program?

   A. C:\MSPCLNT

   B. C:\CLIENTS

   C. C:\MSP\MSPCLNT

   D. C:\MSP\CLIENTS

   Answer: D. C:\MSPCLNT is the default directory for installation on the client computer. MSPCLNT is the share name containing the client Setup application. C:\CLIENTS is not a directory associated with the proxy server. C:\MSP\CLIENTS is the correct answer.

2. You administer a corporate network that uses Microsoft Proxy Server to connect to the Internet. You wish to configure client Setup to automatically configure Internet Explorer Web browsers to take advantage of caching. How is this accomplished?

   A. Configure the properties of each Web browser to access the Internet through the proxy server.

   B. Use Internet Service Manager to configure the WinSock Proxy client configuration section in the Client Configuration screen.

   C. Use Internet Service Manager to configure the proxy client Setup program to automatically configure client browsers to access the Internet through a proxy server.

   D. Use Internet Service Manager to set the correct configuration, then push the changes out to each client computer.

Answer: C. Configuring the properties of each Web browser to access the Internet through the proxy server would work, but it is not automatic. The WinSock Proxy client configuration has no effect on caching. Internet Service Manager is not capable of pushing these changes out to client computers. The correct solution is to use Internet Service Manager to configure the proxy client Setup program to automatically configure client Web browsers.

3. You administer a network using Microsoft Proxy Server. You wish to automatically configure client Web browsers so that they will bypass the server when accessing the site www.domain.com. How can this be accomplished?

   A. Using Internet Service Manager, configure the client Setup so that automatic configuration of Web browsers is used. Configure the automatic configuration script properties so that the proxy will not be used when the domain www.domain.com is requested.

   B. Use the Web browser settings to make an exception for www.domain.com, so that requests for it will bypass the proxy server.

   C. Configure a static filter for www.domain.com.

   D. Configure Web Publishing to allow access to www.domain.com.

   Answer: A. Using the Web browser settings to accomplish this means repeating the procedure for each client computer. Neither static filtering nor Web Publishing accomplishes the objective.

Configure Proxy Server and Proxy Server client computers to use the Proxy Server services. Configurations include:

- Microsoft Internet Explorer client computers
- Netscape Navigator client computers
- Macintosh client computers
- UNIX client computers
- Client computers on an IPX-only network

So far, the configuration methods discussed have dealt with Windows-based computers on a network using TCP/IP. Most networks are not this one-dimensional. Typically, a variety of operating systems and Web browser software must be supported. Additionally, you may use IPX/SPX instead of TCP/IP on your internal network. All of these factors require special consideration when configuring client computers.

Critical Information

There are generally only two Web browsers you need to worry about when configuring your network: Internet Explorer and Netscape Navigator. Operating systems you will need to take into account include Windows, Macintosh, and Unix. In addition, if you are using IPX/SPX on your network, there are special considerations for Windows 95 and Windows NT clients.

Web Proxy Client Considerations

When configuring client computers to use the Web Proxy service, keep the following information in mind:

- Do not configure Web browser helper applications (RealAudio, for example) to be Web Proxy clients.

- IPX clients should be configured to point to the proxy server using an IP address, not a computer name or a DNS name.

- With 16-bit applications, you may need to enter additional information during a client logon procedure.

WinSock Proxy Client Considerations

When configuring client computers to use the WinSock Proxy service, the following points are important:

- Do not configure WinSock applications to use the proxy server, even if the application supports this functionality.

- When using a Web browser, clients should be configured to point to the proxy server using an IP address, not a computer name or a DNS name. This also applies to any Windows sockets application.

- With 16-bit applications, you may need to enter additional information during a client logon procedure.

- Client computers running Windows for Workgroups should have a domain name set for client logon. If this is not done, the first time the WinSock Proxy client application redirects an application, a user-credentials dialog box will appear.

- Windows NT clients whose operating systems have been upgraded should have the WinSock Proxy client software reinstalled.

- The WinSock Proxy client software should be disabled if you are running a Socks client application through the Socks Proxy service.

For some applications, such as Exchange, there are specific steps that must be taken in order to work with Proxy Server. This is accomplished either by creating application-specific settings in the MSPCLNT.INI or by creating a file called WSPCFG.INI and placing it in the folder that contains the executable file in question. The WinSock Proxy client will first check the Disable entry in the [Common Configuration] section of the MSPCLNT.INI. If the value is one, the WinSock Proxy service is disabled. If the value is zero, the client looks for a WSPCFG.INI file in the application directory. If it finds that, it looks for a [*WSP Client*] section, where *WSP Client* is the name of the application. If this section does not exist, it looks for the [Common Configuration] section. If this section also does not exist, it looks for the same sections in the MSP-CLNT.INI file. Only the first section found in this process is used. The following parameters can be configured in the WSPCFG.INI file:

Disable   When this is set to one, the WinSock Proxy service is disabled.

NameResolution   By default all dot-convention names are redirected. You can force local name resolution by setting this value to L or force redirection by setting the value to R.

LocalBindTcpPorts   This defines a TCP port, list, or range that is bound locally.

LocalBindUdpPorts   This defines a UDP port, list, or range that is bound locally.

RemoteBindTcpPorts   This defines a TCP port, list, or range that is bound remotely.

RemoteBindUdpPorts   This defines a UDP port, list, or range that is bound remotely.

ServerBindTcpPorts   This defines a TCP port, list, or range used by a server application.

ProxyBindIp   This specifies an IP address or list that is used when binding with a corresponding port. This is used when multiple servers that use the same port need to bind to different ports on the proxy server.

KillOldSession   When enabled, this means that, if the proxy server holds a session from a previous instance of an application, that session will be terminated before a new session is generated.

Persistent   When enabled, this means that, if the proxy server is stopped and restarted, the client computer will send keep-alive messages to the server. The client will then try to restore the session when the server restarts.

ForceProxy   This is used to force a specific WinSock application to use a specific proxy server. The syntax for this setting is Force-Proxy=[*tag*]:[*entry*], where *tag* equals I for IP address, X for IPX address, or N for a name. If N is used, the WinSock Proxy service will only work over IP.

ForceCredentials   When enabled, this setting forces the use of alternate user credentials stored locally using the CREDTOOL.EXE application provided with Proxy Server. The user credentials must refer to an account that can be authenticated by the proxy server.

NameResolutionForLocalHost   This option specifies how the LocalHost computer name is resolved. Setting this value to L returns the IP address of the local computer. Setting the value to P returns the IP addresses of the proxy server computer. Setting the value to E returns only the external IP addresses of the proxy server computer.

Configuring Microsoft Internet Explorer Clients

If proxy server client setup is configured to automatically configure Web browsers, the browsers will be configured as clients when the client Setup program is executed. Internet Explorer can also be configured manually as a Web Proxy client. The configuration is accessed by clicking on the View menu option in Internet Explorer and then selecting Internet Options. From there, click on the Connection tab. From this screen you can configure the browser to access a specific proxy server by entering the name of the server and port number, and you can configure the browser not to use the proxy server for local servers. By clicking on the Advanced button, you can configure the browser to point to different proxy servers for each of the following protocols:

- HTTP
- Secure
- FTP
- Gopher
- Socks

By default the same proxy server will be used for all protocols. You can also configure the browser to bypass the proxy server for specific sites.

Internet Explorer can also be configured to use the automatic configuration script stored on the proxy server. This script is configured from the Client Installation/Configuration screen in Internet Service Manager. The default URL for this script is `http://servername:80/array.dll?Get.Routing.Script`.

Configuring Netscape Navigator Clients

If Netscape Navigator is configured to be the default Web browser on the client computer, the Proxy Server client Setup program will configure it as a Web Proxy client application. This configuration can also be done manually. There are some minor differences in the configuration method between different versions of Netscape Navigator.

Configuring Netscape Navigator 2.*x* and 3.*x*

The proxy configuration for Netscape Navigator 2.*x* and 3.*x* is accessed by clicking on the Options menu, selecting Network Preferences, and clicking on the Proxies tab. You have three options:

- No Proxies

- Manual Proxy Configuration. Much like Internet Explorer, you can configure a different proxy for each protocol. You can also configure a list of domains for which the proxy server will be bypassed.

- Automatic Proxy Configuration. The URL for the automatic configuration script is entered here. Again, the default URL is `http://servername:80/array.dll?Get.Routing.Script`.

Configuring Netscape Navigator 4.0*x*

As this book goes to press, the most current version is Navigator 4.06. The proxy configuration for Netscape Navigator 4.0x is accessed by clicking on the Edit menu, selecting Preferences, clicking on the plus sign next to Advanced, and then clicking on Proxies. Once the configuration is accessed, the options are exactly the same as previous versions of Netscape.

Configuring Macintosh Clients

To configure a Macintosh client to be a Web Proxy client, the browser used must be configured with the name of the proxy server and the port number. Configurations for Internet Explorer and Netscape Navigator on Macintosh have some minor differences from the Windows versions, but the concepts are the same. Macintosh clients can also use the Socks Proxy service. Proxy Server supports version 4.3a of Socks.

Configuring Unix Clients

As with Macintosh clients, when configuring a Unix client to be a Web Proxy client, the Unix Web browser must be configured with the name of the proxy server and the port number. Configuration procedures for Internet Explorer and Netscape Navigator on Unix are identical to the

Windows versions. Unix clients can also use the Socks Proxy service. Proxy Server supports version 4.3a of Socks.

Configuring Clients on an IPX-Only Network

Note that Proxy Server does not support the use of IPX with Windows 3.1 or Windows for Workgroups 3.11 clients. Proxy Server does support the Novell Client32 or Client for IntranetWare (32-bit) IPX stack on Windows 95 clients. For Windows NT clients, the following settings should be verified in the MSPCLNT.INI file to prevent refreshing or redirection of some Windows NT services:

```
[Services]
Disable=1
[Spoolss]
Disable=1
[Rpcss]
Disable=1
```

If your network has NetWare servers or IPX routers, the [Servers Ipx Addresses] section of the MSPCLNT.INI should already be configured correctly. If it does not, you will need to add the following:

```
[Servers Ipx Addresses]
Addr1=55555555-000000000001
```

Also, if your network has NetWare servers or IPX routers, the frame type detection can be set to Auto. Otherwise, manual frame type detection should be used.

Necessary Procedures

Procedures associated with this objective involve client configuration of the two most popular Web browsers in use at this time: Internet Explorer and Netscape Navigator.

Configuring Internet Explorer As a Web Proxy Client

1. Start Internet Explorer. Click on the View menu and select Internet Options.

2. Click on the Connection tab to see the following screen:

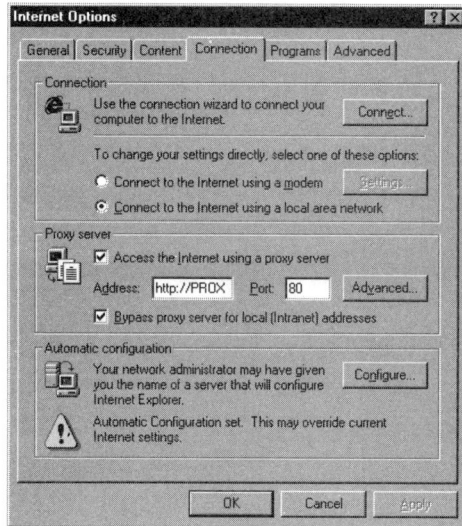

3. Make sure there is a check in the checkbox labeled "Access the Internet Using a Proxy Server."

4. Type the name of the proxy server in the Address box and the port number in the Port box.

5. Click on Advanced.

6. If needed, change proxy servers used for individual protocols by removing the check from the checkbox labeled "Use the Same Proxy Server for All Protocols," and then type in the proxy server name and port number for each protocol.

7. In the Exceptions section, type in domain names for which the proxy server should not be used. Separate multiple entries with semicolons.

8. Click OK.

9. To enable automatic configuration, click on the Configure button in the Automatic Configuration section.

10. Type in the URL for the automatic configuration script.

11. Click Refresh to update the settings immediately.

12. Click OK, then click OK or Apply.

Configuring Netscape Navigator 2.*x* and 3.*x* As a Web Proxy Client

1. Start Netscape Navigator.

2. Click on the Options menu and select Network Preferences.

3. Click on the Proxies tab of the Preferences screen to see the screen shown here. From this screen, you can choose between manual and automatic proxy configuration.

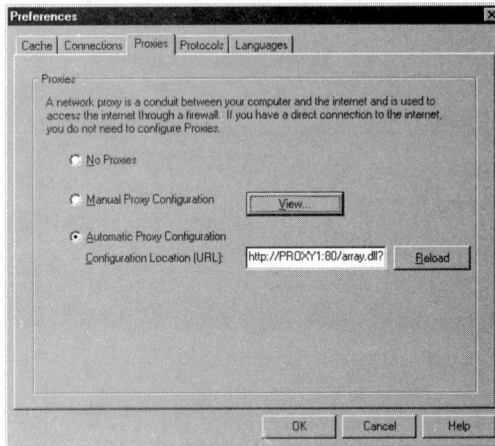

4. For manual configuration, select Manual Proxy Configuration.

    A. Click on View to see the screen labeled Manual Proxy Configuration.

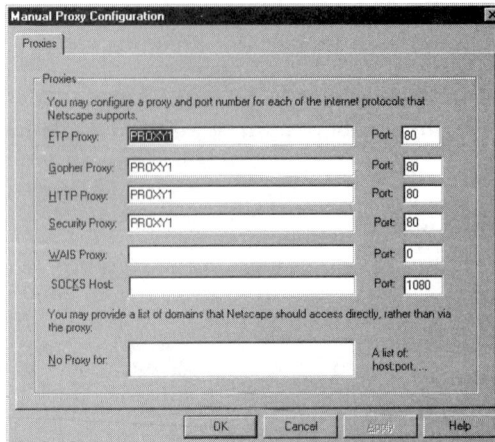

B. Type in the correct proxy server name and port number for each protocol.

C. Next to "No Proxy for," type in any domain names that should bypass the proxy server.

D. Click OK.

5. For automatic configuration, in the Proxies tab of the Preferences screen, select Automatic Proxy Configuration.

    A. Type in the correct URL.

    B. Click Reload to update the settings immediately.

    C. Click OK.

Configuring Netscape Navigator 4.0*x* As a Web Proxy Client

1. Start Netscape Navigator.

2. Click on the Edit menu and select Preferences.

3. Click on the plus sign next to Advanced.

4. Click on Proxies to see the screen labeled Preferences, shown here. From this screen, you can choose between manual and automatic proxy configuration.

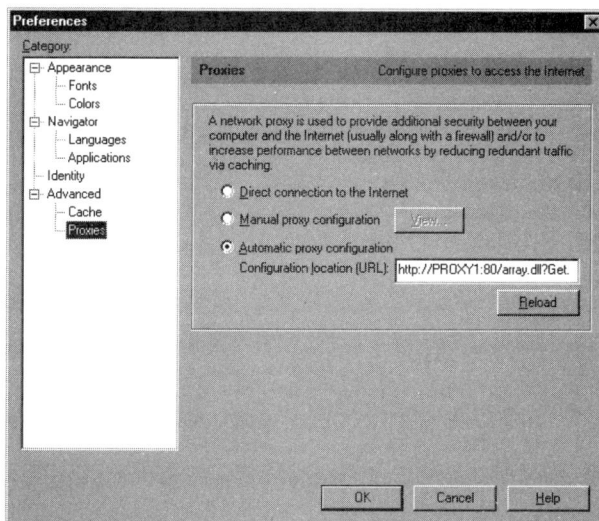

5. For manual configuration, select Manual Proxy Configuration.

    A. Click on View to see the screen labeled Manual Proxy Configuration.

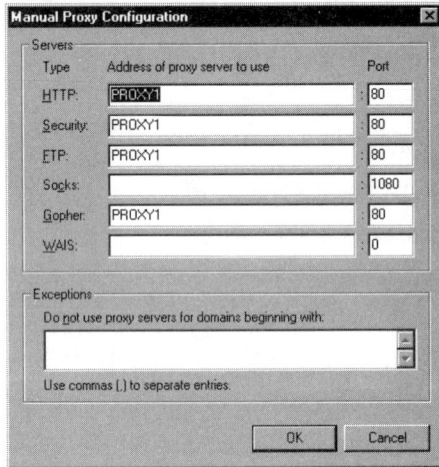

    B. Type in the correct proxy server name and port number for each protocol.

    C. In the Exceptions section, type any domains for which requests should bypass the proxy server.

    D. Click OK.

6. For automatic configuration, in the Proxies tab of the Preferences screen, select Automatic Proxy Configuration.

    A. Type in the correct URL.

    B. Click Reload to update the settings immediately.

    C. Click OK.

Exam Essentials

Know how to configure Internet Explorer to be a Web Proxy client. Internet Explorer can use manual or automatic proxy configuration. With manual configuration, each protocol can use a different proxy server. Requests for specific sites can be configured so that they bypass the proxy server.

Know how to configure Netscape Navigator to be a Web Proxy client. As with Internet Explorer, Netscape Navigator can use manual or automatic proxy configuration. With manual configuration, each protocol can use a different proxy server. Requests for specific sites can be configured to bypass the proxy server.

Know how to configure Macintosh and Unix clients. Macintosh and Unix clients must be configured with the name and port number of the proxy server. Configuration of Internet Explorer and Netscape Navigator is similar to the Windows versions.

Know how to configure IPX client computers. Proxy Server does not support Windows 3.1 and Windows for Workgroups 3.11 using IPX. Windows 95 (IPX-based) computers using a 32-bit client are supported. If there are NetWare servers or IPX routers on the network, auto frame type detection should be used. If not, manual frame type detection should be configured.

Key Terms and Concepts

File Transfer Protocol (FTP): This is an Internet standard protocol that is used to transfer files between computers.

Helper applications: These are applications that are used to help Web browsers deal with different file types, such as GIF, JPEG, Quicktime, RealAudio.

Hypertext Transfer Protocol (HTTP): This is an Internet standard protocol that is used on the World Wide Web.

IPX/SPX: This abbreviation is short for Internetwork Packet Exchange/Sequenced Package Exchange, a routable network protocol that is used primarily in NetWare-based networks.

Secure Sockets Layer (SSL): This is a protocol that uses data encryption and decryption to provide secure communication.

Socks Proxy service: This service provides transparent redirection of client requests for a wide variety of platforms. Microsoft Proxy Server 2 supports Socks version 4.3a.

Sample Questions

1. You are configuring Netscape Navigator on a Unix computer to take advantage of caching on a proxy server. What must be done to accomplish this?

   A. Install a Socks client on the Unix computer and configure it to use the Socks Proxy service.

   B. Install a Socks client on the Unix computer and configure it to use the Web Proxy service by specifying the DNS name or IP address.

   C. Configure Netscape Navigator to point to the DNS name or IP address and the port number of the proxy server in its proxy configuration.

   D. Install the proxy server client application on the Unix computer.

   Answer: C. The Socks Proxy service does not support caching and a Socks client cannot be configured to use the Web Proxy service. The proxy server client application cannot be installed on a Unix computer.

2. Which proxy services can a Macintosh client use?

   A. Web Proxy service

   B. WinSock Proxy service

   C. WWW service

   D. Socks Proxy service

   Answer: A and D. Macintosh clients cannot use the WinSock Proxy service. The WWW service is not a proxy service.

3. You administer a network consisting of client computers using Windows for Workgroups 3.11, Windows 95, and Windows NT. You

use only IPX on your internal network. How can you configure all client computers to use the proxy server?

A. Install 32-bit NetWare clients on Windows for Workgroups 3.11 and Windows 95. Install the proxy server client application.

B. Install 32-bit NetWare clients on the Windows 95 computers. Configure the Windows 95 and Windows NT computers to use the WinSock Proxy service. Configure the Windows for Workgroups 3.11 computers to use the Web Proxy service.

C. Configure the Windows for Workgroups 3.11 computers to use the Socks Proxy service. Install the proxy server client application on the Windows 95 and Windows NT computers.

D. This cannot be done.

Answer: D. Proxy Server 2 does not support Windows 3.1 or Windows for Workgroups 3.11 using the IPX protocol. In order for these computers to use the Web Proxy service or the Socks Proxy service, they must be using TCP/IP.

Configure a RAS server to route Internet requests.

Routing and Remote Access Service (RRAS) is an add-on product that, combined with Proxy Server 2, can greatly enhance functionality and security.

Critical Information

RRAS provides routing between dial-up networks. Typically RRAS is used to create Virtual Private Networks (VPN), which use the Point-to-Point Tunneling protocol.

SEE ALSO For more information on Virtual Private Networks (VPN) and the Point-to-Point Tunneling protocol, see *MCSE: Proxy Server 2 Study Guide* (Sybex, 1998)

Before installing RRAS, you should make the following preparations:

- Remove previous versions of the Remote Access Service and Multi-Protocol Routing version 1.

WARNING When you remove the services, you also erase the previous configurations for these services.

- Pause the SNMP service.

- Install all necessary hardware for the server to function as a router.

During setup, you can choose any combination of three different RRAS installation options:

Remote Access Service   Provides support for client dial-up networking.

LAN routing   Provides support for LAN-to-LAN routing.

Demand dial routing   Provides support for routing over WANs and dial-up media, such as ISDN and PPTP.

When RRAS is used with Proxy Server 2, the following considerations apply:

- If packet filtering is enabled, the predefined filters PPTP Receive and PPTP Call must be enabled.

- The RRAS hot fix must be applied.

- If the proxy server is a departmental server, packet filtering should be disabled.

- An edge server connecting to the Internet should have packet filtering enabled with the predefined packet filters. No custom filters should be configured.

- An edge server with an extranet or a LAN barrier segment will have a third network adapter installed. An extranet in this context is a secure zone between the internal network and the Internet. Usually routing is enabled between the Internet and the extranet LAN. The computers on the extranet LAN communicate directly with the Internet. All communication between the extranet LAN and the internal network should pass through the proxy server. All computers on the extranet should use legal, non-private IP addresses. These addresses should not be included in the Local Address Table (LAT) of the proxy server. Figure 4.1 illustrates a possible extranet configuration.

F I G U R E 4.1: An extranet configuration

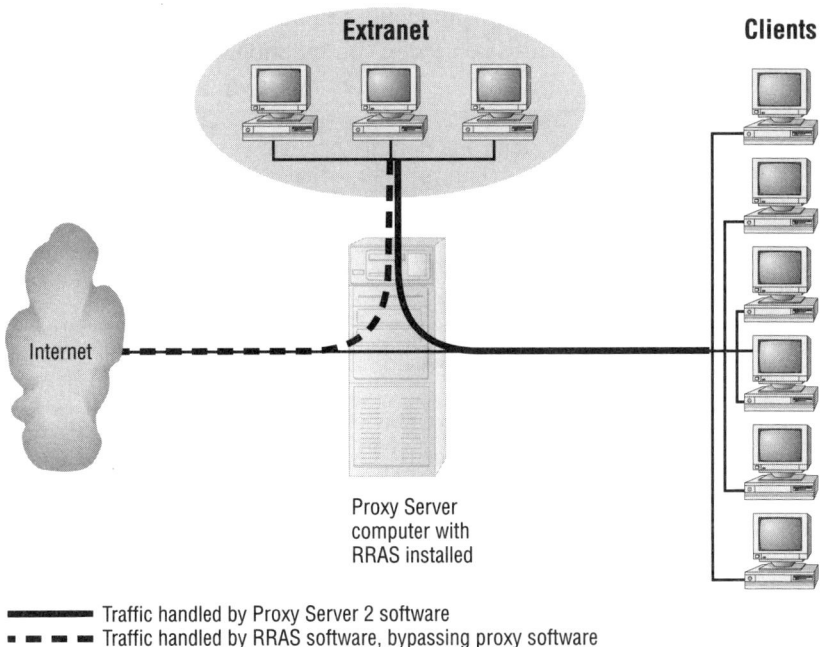

━━━━ Traffic handled by Proxy Server 2 software
■ ■ ■ ■ Traffic handled by RRAS software, bypassing proxy software

TIP Instead of using a proxy server to control traffic between the extranet and the internal network, you could use RRAS to perform this function if IP forwarding is enabled. However, this configuration is not recommended.

Once RRAS is installed, it can be administered from the Routing and RAS Admin tool found in the Administrative Tools (Common) section of the Start menu. RRAS supports two routing protocols:

Open Shortest Path First (OSPF)   A routing protocol that routes packets according to the least expensive path. RRAS supports Bay Networks, implementation of OSPF.

Routing Information Protocol (RIP)   A distance-vector–based interior gateway protocol. RRAS supports RIP version 2 for Internet Protocol.

Both OSPF and RIP are used to provide dynamic administration of network routes. However, there may be situations where you do not want to use either of these protocols. RRAS also supports the use of static routes. Static routes are manually administered by the network administrator and can also be used in combination with OSPF and RIP.

SEE ALSO   Routing and Remote Access Service is a very powerful and complicated tool. For more information on RRAS, see *MCSE: Proxy Server 2 Study Guide* (Sybex, 1998).

Necessary Procedures

Procedures associated with this objective include installing Routing and Remote Access Service (RRAS) and administering the methods RRAS uses to route Internet traffic.

Installing Routing and Remote Access Service (RRAS)

1. Obtain the RRAS Setup file and the RRAS hot fix from Microsoft's Web site.

2. Execute the RRAS Setup file. After the Setup program finishes extracting files, you will be asked to choose an installation folder. The default location is C:\PROGRAMFILES\ROUTING. You can accept this, type in a different location, or browse to a different location. Then click OK.

3. A dialog box will appear, asking if you want to continue installation. Click Yes. Next you will see the screen labeled Routing And Remote Access Setup.

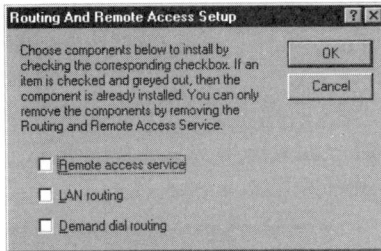

4. Here you have three options: Remote Access Service, LAN Routing, and Demand Dial Routing. Select the services you require and click OK.

5. If you selected the option to install the Remote Access Service or Demand Dial Routing, you will now go through the RAS setup process. After you select a modem, you will see the screen labeled Remote Access Setup.

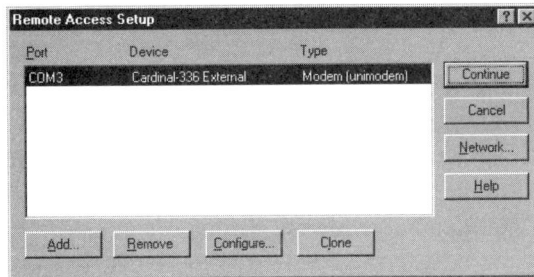

6. Click on Configure to see the screen labeled Configure Port Usage.

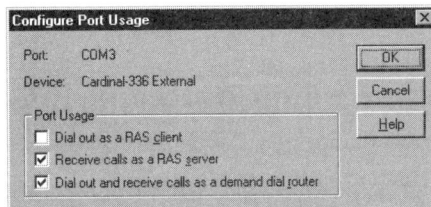

7. You have three options:

   A. Dial out As a RAS Client.

   B. Receive Calls As a RAS Server.

   C. Dial out and Receive Calls As a Demand Dial Router.

8. Choose the options you need. Click on Continue.

9. If you selected Receive Calls As a RAS Server, you will see the screen labeled RAS Server TCP/IP Configuration.

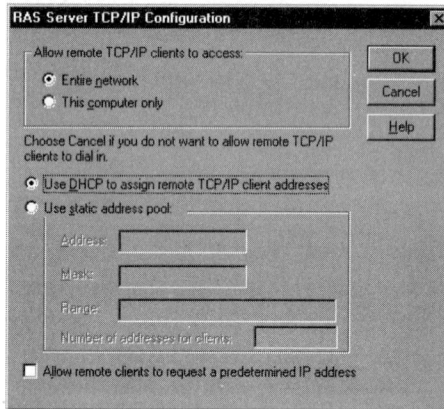

10. From this screen you can allow RAS clients to see only the server or the entire network and to use DHCP or a static address pool for IP address assignment. You can also allow clients to request a pre-determined IP address.

11. Click OK.

12. Click Close and restart the server when prompted.

13. Apply the RRAS hot fix by executing the hot fix file. Restart the server when prompted.

Adding a Routing Protocol to RRAS

1. Start the Routing and RAS Admin tool by clicking on Start ➤ Programs ➤ Administrative Tools (Common) ➤ Routing and

RAS Admin. You will see the screen labeled Routing and RAS Admin.

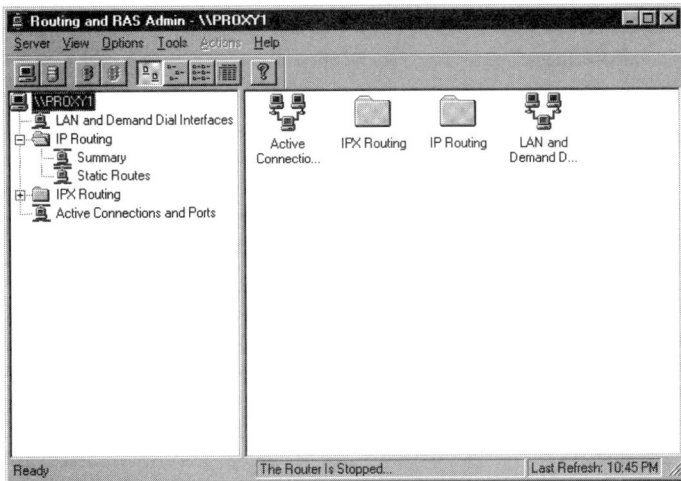

2. Click on the plus sign next to IP Routing.

3. In the IP Routing section, right click on Summary and select Add Routing Protocol to see the screen labeled Select Routing Protocol.

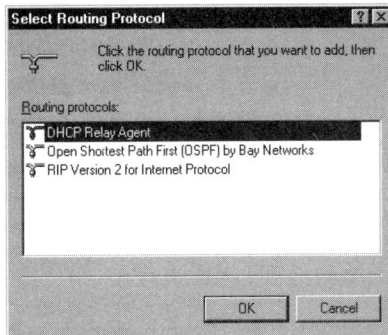

4. Select the routing protocol you require and click OK.

Adding a Static Route

1. Start the Routing and RAS Admin tool by clicking on Start ➣ Programs ➣ Administrative Tools (Common) ➣ Routing and RAS Admin. You will see the screen labeled Routing and RAS Admin.

2. Right click on Static Routes. Select Add Static Route to see the following screen:

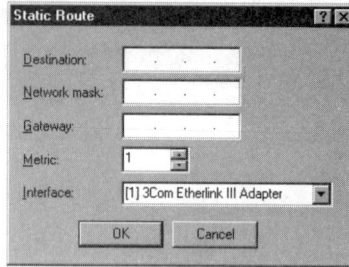

3. Type in the destination IP, the subnet mask, and the gateway address to that network. Click OK.

Exam Essentials

Know how to install Routing and Remote Access Service. The Routing and Remote Access Service installation file and the RRAS hot fix can be obtained from Microsoft's Web site. If the Remote Access Service is installed, it must be uninstalled before installing RRAS. The RRAS hot fix must be installed after the RRAS installation or Proxy Server 2 will not function properly.

Know how to use RRAS to route Internet requests. Review the procedures used to add routing protocols and static routes to RRAS.

Key Terms and Concepts

Extranet: This is a secure zone between the intranet and the Internet.

Open Shortest Path First (OSPF):   This is a routing protocol that routes packets according to the least expensive path. RRAS supports Bay Networks implementation of OSPF.

Point-to-Point Tunneling Protocol (PPTP):   This is a networking protocol that allows users to access corporate networks securely across the Internet.

Routing Information Protocol (RIP): This is a distance-vector–based interior gateway protocol. RRAS supports RIP version 2 for Internet protocol.

Simple Network Management Protocol (SNMP): This is a standard protocol that is used to monitor networks.

Static route: This is a manually defined path to a remote network.

Virtual Private Networks (VPN): This is a logical network spanning diverse locations that is made secure by the use of PPTP.

Sample Questions

1. Which of the following are routing protocols supported by RRAS?

   A. Routing Information Protocol (RIP)

   B. Internet Gateway Routing Protocol (IGRP)

   C. Border Gateway Protocol (BGP)

   D. Open Shortest Path First (OSPF)

   Answer: A and D. IGRP is a Cisco proprietary interior gateway protocol. BGP is an exterior gateway protocol used within autonomous systems. Neither is supported by RRAS.

2. After installing RRAS, what should you do to make it work with Proxy Server 2?

   A. Edit the registry so that it refers to Proxy Server 1 instead of Proxy Server 2.

   B. Reapply Service Pack 3.

   C. Apply the Proxy Server 2 hot fix.

   D. Apply the RRAS hot fix.

   Answer: D. Neither editing the registry nor reapplying Service Pack 3 will help. There is not currently a Proxy Server 2 hot fix. Only applying the RRAS hot fix will cause Proxy Server 2 to function properly with RRAS.

3. Which of the following information must you provide when configuring an IP static route?

A. Network mask

B. Gateway

C. Routing protocol

D. Destination

Answer: A, B, and D. When configuring a static route, the destination, network mask, gateway, and metric must be defined. A routing protocol cannot be specified.

Write JavaScript to configure a Web browser.

Using the client configuration setup to configure automatic configuration scripts was discussed previously in this chapter. These configuration scripts are written in JavaScript. JavaScript is a programming language used with client Internet applications.

WARNING Microsoft has developed its own implementation of Sun Microsystem's JavaScript language called JScript. JScript is an object-oriented language that must be run with an interpreter either on a Web server or a Web browser. However, this objective requires a knowledge of the older JavaScript, not of Microsoft's JScript.

Critical Information

When a client Web browser requests the configuration script from the proxy server, it is delivered in JavaScript. Understanding how this configuration works and being able to manipulate it is essential for you to be able to configure Web browsers on your network properly.

Mostly this configuration can be done from within the Internet Service Manager.

The default script provided automatically by Proxy Server is very complicated and lengthy. Those who are familiar with JavaScript may prefer to write their own scripts, which have the potential to be much simpler. For example:

```
function FindProxyForURL(url, host)
{
if (dnsDomainIs(host, ".mydomain.com") ||
dnsDomainIs(host, ".myotherdomain.com") ||
isInNet(host, "172.16.41.91", "255.255.255.255"))
return "DIRECT";
else
return "PROXY 172.16.24.10:80;
}
```

This script causes the Web browser to bypass the proxy server for domains ending in mydomain.com or myotherdomain.com and for the IP address 172.16.41.91. The proxy server address and port number is also assigned.

NOTE   For the exam, Microsoft does not expect you to know how to write an automatic configuration script. Even though this objective is not emphasized on the exam, a knowledge of automatic configuration scripts is important on the job.

Necessary Procedures

Although a knowledge of the configuration options available when configuring automatic configuration scripts is important, a detailed knowledge of JavaScript is not necessary when taking the Proxy Server exam. However, a basic knowledge of custom automatic configuration scripts is helpful.

Implementing a Custom Automatic Configuration Script

1. Start any text editor, such as Notepad. Using the following outline, create a script appropriate for your network, replacing the italicized words with the correct information:

```
function FindProxyForURL(url, host)
{
if (dnsDomainIs(host, "domain") ||
dnsDomainIs(host, "domain") ||
isInNet(host, "IP address", "255.255.255.255"))
return "DIRECT";
else
return "PROXY proxy server address:port number;
}
```

2. Make the script available on your Web server.

3. Start the Internet Service Manager, select Properties for any of the proxy services, and click on Client Configuration.

4. In the Configuration URL section, click on Configure to see the screen labeled Configuration URL For Clients.

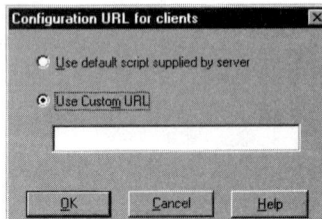

5. Select Use Custom URL and type in the correct URL.

6. Click OK twice.

7. Click OK or Apply.

Exam Essentials

Know how to create and use a custom automatic configuration script. Understand how a simple automatic configuration script works and know how to configure Proxy Server so that client Web browsers will automatically use this script.

Key Terms and Concepts

JavaScript: This is a programming language that is used with client Internet programs and was developed by Sun Microsystems.

JScript: This is Microsoft's implementation of JavaScript.

Sample Questions

1. What programming language is used in automatic configuration scripts?

   A. Perl

   B. JavaScript

   C. CGI

   D. C++

   Answer: B

2. What software tool is required to create a custom automatic configuration script?

   A. A compiler

   B. Any text editor

   C. Internet Service Manager

   D. Java Virtual Machine

   Answer: B. Any text editor can be used to create a custom automatic configuration file.

Change settings in Mspclnt.ini.

When you installed Proxy Server, a file was created named MSPCLNT.INI and placed in the default directory C:\MSP\CLIENTS. Client computers download this file each time they restart and every six hours thereafter. There are certain situations that may require that this file be edited.

Critical Information

There are two ways to edit the MSPCLNT.INI file:

- Use a text editor to modify the file.
- Reinstall Proxy Server, specifying the new configuration information in the Client Installation/Configuration dialog box.

After the MSPCLNT.INI file has been modified, each client will download it. If necessary, the configuration can be manually updated by the client from the WSP Client icon in Control Panel.

The following is an example of an MSPCLNT.INI file:

```
[Internal]
scp=9,10
Build=2.0.372.2
[wspsrv]
Disable=1
[inetinfo]
Disable=1
[services]
Disable=1
[spoolss]
Disable=1
[rpcss]
Disable=1
```

```
[kernel32]
Disable=1
[mapisp32]
Disable=0
[exchng32]
Disable=0
[outlook]
Disable=0
[raplayer]
RemoteBindUdpPorts=6970-7170
LocalBindTcpPorts=7070
[rvplayer]
RemoteBindUdpPorts=6970-7170
LocalBindTcpPorts=7070
[net2fone]
ServerBindTcpPorts=0
[icq]
RemoteBindUdpPorts=0
ServerBindTcpPorts=0,1025-5000
NameResolutionForLocalHost=P
[Common]
WWW-Proxy=PROXY1
Set Browsers to use Proxy=1
Set Browsers to use Auto Config=1
WebProxyPort=80
Configuration Url=http://PROXY1:80/
array.dll?Get.Routing.Script
Port=1745
Configuration Refresh Time (Hours)=6
Re-check Inaccessible Server Time (Minutes)=10
Refresh Give Up Time (Minutes)=15
Inaccessible Servers Give Up Time (Minutes)=2
Setup=Setup.exe
[Servers Ip Addresses]
Name=PROXY1
[Servers Ipx Addresses]
[Master Config]
Path1=\\PROXY1\mspclnt\
```

Tables 4.1 and 4.2 define some of the key entries in the MSPCLNT.INI.

TABLE 4.1: Key Entries in the MSPCLNT.INI Common Section

Entry	Description
WWW-Proxy	Client Web browsers will be configured to use the proxy server named here.
WebProxyPort	Client Web browsers will use the port number specified to communicate with the proxy server.
Configuration URL	Gives the URL that the browser will use to obtain the automatic configuration script.
Set Browsers to Use Proxy	Setting this value to one will cause client Web browsers to use the proxy server defined in the WWW-Proxy entry.
Inaccessible Servers Give Up Time (Minutes)	If all proxy servers are marked as inaccessible, this interval determines how long the client will wait before trying again. The default is two minutes.
Refresh Give Up Time (Minutes)	The amount of time a client will wait to attempt to update its configuration if a previous attempt failed. The default is 15 minutes.
Re-check Inaccessible Server Time (Minutes)	The amount of time a client will wait before redirecting a request to a specific inaccessible server. The default is 10 minutes.
Configuration Refresh Time (Hours)	The interval in hours between each client request for an updated copy of the Local Address Table (LAT).
Port	The port the proxy server uses for the control channel. It will rarely need to be changed.

T A B L E 4.2: Key Entries in Other Sections of MSPCLNT.INI

Section	Entry	Description
[Servers Ipx Addresses]	Addr1	The IPX address of the server, or of multiple servers if an array is being used.
[Servers Ip Addresses]	Addr1	The computer or DNS name of the proxy server.
[Master Config]	Path1	A UNC path to the shared directory containing the client configuration files; if an array is being used, it will contain paths to the shared directories of all array members.

If you are using an array and either you do not have a DNS server or you have IPX clients on your network, you will need to make a special configuration change to the MSPCLNT.INI file. In the C:\MSP\CLIENTS directory of each proxy server, there is a file called LOCAL_ADDR .DUMP. This file contains all of the IP and IPX addresses for each server. You should collect the addresses for all of the servers and merge them into the [Servers Ip Addresses] and [Servers Ipx Addresses] sections. You will have to manually copy this information to each server in the array.

Necessary Procedures

Necessary procedures relating to this objective involve making changes to the MSPCLNT.INI file and updating those changes to client computers.

Editing the MSPCLNT.INI File

1. Using a text editor, load the MSPCLNT.INI. The default location is C:\MSP\CLIENTS.

2. Practice changing the various entries listed previously for this objective.

Forcing a Client Configuration Update

1. Start the WSP Client in Control Panel. You will see the screen labeled Microsoft WinSock Proxy Client.

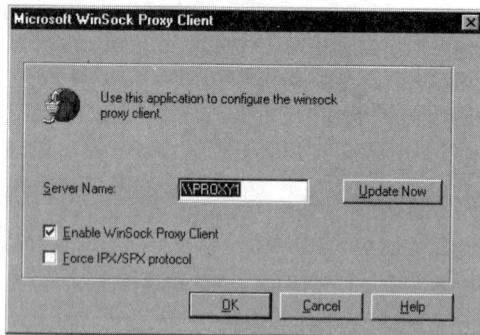

2. Click on Update Now.

3. You will see a dialog box telling you that the operation was completed successfully. Click OK. Click OK again.

4. Click Restart Windows Now.

Exam Essentials

Know how to change settings in the MSPCLNT.INI file.   Review Tables 4.1 and 4.2 and be sure you understand what the different entries mean and how they affect client performance.

Know how to force a client configuration update.   Client configuration can be updated from the WSP Client icon in Control Panel.

Key Terms and Concepts

There are no new terms or concepts for this objective.

Sample Questions

1. What file contains the information needed to configure the MSPCLNT.INI file so that IPX clients can take advantage of an array?

   A. MSPCLNT.INI

   B. WSPCFG.INI

   C. LOCAL_ADDR.DUMP

   D. PROXY.INI

   Answer: C. The LOCAL_ADDR.DUMP file contains the IP and IPX addresses for each server. These addresses should be merged into the [Servers Ip Addresses] and [Servers Ipx Addresses] sections of the MSPCLNT.INI.

2. What administration tool can be used to force a client computer to update its configuration?

   A. Internet Service Manager

   B. WSP Client icon in Control Panel

   C. RemotMSP

   D. Any text editor

   Answer: B

CHAPTER

5

Monitoring and Optimization

Microsoft Exam Objectives Covered in This Chapter:

▶ **Configure Proxy Server to log errors when they occur.**
(pages 225 – 241)

▶ **Monitor performance of various functions by using Microsoft Windows NT Performance Monitor. Functions include HTTP and FTP sessions.** *(pages 242 – 248)*

▶ **Analyze performance issues. Performance issues include:**
(pages 249 – 257)

- Identifying bottlenecks
- Identifying network-related performance issues
- Identifying disk-related performance issues
- Identifying CPU-related performance issues
- Identifying memory-related performance issues

▶ **Optimize performance for various purposes. Purposes include:**
(pages 257 – 261)

- Increasing throughput
- Optimizing routing

▶ **Use Performance Monitor logs to identify the appropriate configuration.** *(pages 261 – 266)*

▶ **Perform Internet traffic analysis by using Windows NT Server tools.** *(pages 266 – 270)*

▶ **Monitor current sessions.** *(pages 270 – 272)*

Y ou've finished installing and configuring Proxy Server and installing and configuring Proxy Server clients. However, the job is not finished yet. Most network administrators are very familiar with the often-heard complaint, "The network is slow!" It is natural for users to blame any network-related problem on the proxy server. It is essential that you be able to identify and resolve Proxy Server performance problems. Being able to identify bottlenecks related to the network, disk usage, memory usage, and CPU usage will assist you in this task. Motivated network administrators attempt to identify potential problems in advance so that users are never inconvenienced by them.

Configure Proxy Server to log errors when they occur.

One of the first things to check when trying to determine if the proxy server is experiencing performance problems is whether or not it is logging any errors. Dealing with known problems may eliminate many problems of which you are not yet aware.

Critical Information

Microsoft Proxy Server has three service logs, one each for Web Proxy service, WinSock Proxy service, and Socks Proxy service. These logs help you to determine what protocols are being used, to track protocols used by a specific user, to track what time the requests occur, and to determine if the request was successful.

Logging for proxy services and for packet filtering can be configured to use regular format or verbose format. It can be configured to log to a text file or to a SQL/OBDC database. If logging to a text file is selected, a new log file will be created daily, weekly, or monthly. The number of old log files can be limited and the services can be stopped if the disk becomes full. By default the log files are stored in $drive$:\$root$\SYSTEM32\ MSPLOGS, although this location can be changed. The default names for log files are as follows:

- W3*filename*.LOG for the Web Proxy service
- WS*filename*.LOG for the WinSock Proxy service
- SP*filename*.LOG for the Socks Proxy service
- PF*filename*.LOG for packet filter events

How frequently the log files are created will determine the specific name of the file. For example, for the WinSock Proxy service, files would be named as follows:

- SP*yymmdd*.LOG for daily logs

- SPW*yymmw*.LOG for weekly logs

- SPM*yymm*.LOG for monthly logs

In this format, *yy* is a number between 0 and 99 indicating the year, *mm* is a number between 01 and 12 indicating the month, *dd* is a number between 01 and 31 indicating the day of the month, and *w* is a number from one to five indicating the week of the month. Text log files are created as comma delimited files. This means that a comma separates each field of information from the next field. This is so that you can easily export the information contained in the log files into another format, such as an Excel spreadsheet.

If you choose to log to a SQL/OBDC database, you must provide the following information: the OBDC Data Source Name (DSN), the table, the username, and the password for the database.

Logging in Regular Format

When configured to log in regular format, the Web Proxy, WinSock Proxy, and Socks Proxy logs will contain the information shown in Table 5.1.

TABLE 5.1: Proxy Service Log Information

Field Name	Information Field Type	Description
Client Computer Name (ClientIP)	Client	This is the name of the computer making the request. If active caching is enabled, this will be the same as the "Proxy Name" field.

T A B L E 5.1:   Proxy Service Log Information *(continued)*

Field Name	Information Field Type	Description
Client User Name (Client-UserName)	Client	This is the Windows NT username for the current user on the computer making the request.
Destination Name (DestHost)	Connection	This is the domain name for the computer responding to the request. If the request is serviced from the Web Proxy cache, this value may be a hyphen.
Destination Port (DestHostPort)	Connection	This is the port number reserved on the remote computer servicing the connection.
Log Date (Take over Time)	Server	This is the date the event was logged.
Log Time (LogTime)	Server	The time the event was logged.
Object Name (URL)	Object	For the Web Proxy service, this contains the contents of the URL request. Neither the WinSock Proxy service nor the Socks Proxy service uses this field.
Object Source (ObjectSource)	Object	Neither the WinSock Proxy nor the Socks Proxy services use this field. For the Web's Proxy service, this is the source used to serve the request. See Table 5.2 for possible values.
Protocol Name (Protocol)	Connection	For the Web Proxy service, this field indicates the protocol used for transfer, such as HTTP, FTP, and so on. For the WinSock Proxy service, this indicates the destination port for the socketed application.

TABLE 5.1: Proxy Service Log Information *(continued)*

Field Name	Information Field Type	Description
Result Code (ResultCode)	Object	For the Web Proxy service, this field indicates either a Windows error code for values less than 100, an HTTP status code for values between 100 and 1000, or a Windows Sockets error code for values between 10,000 and 11,004. For the WinSock Proxy service, this field will indicate either a Windows error for values less than 100, or a Windows Sockets error code for values between 10,000 and 11,004. Typically there will be two log entries; one for connection establishment, and one for connection termination. Some of the supported values are shown in Tables 5.3 and 5.4.
Service Name (Service)	Server	The value indicates the name of the active service being logged. CERN-Proxy refers to Web Proxy service logging, WSProxy indicates WinSock Proxy service logging, and SOCKS indicates Socks Proxy service logging.

ObjectSource Values

Neither the WinSock Proxy nor the Socks Proxy services uses this field. For the Web Proxy service, this is the source used to service the request. Possible values are given in Table 5.2.

TABLE 5.2: ObjectSource Values for the Web Proxy Service

Value	Description
0	No source information available, cache.
Inet	Internet.

T A B L E 5.2: ObjectSource Values for the Web Proxy Service *(continued)*

Value	Description
Member	Another member of an array.
NotModified	A refresh has been requested and the object has not been modified.
NVCache	The object was obtained from cache but the object could not be verified to source.
Upstream	The object was returned from an upstream proxy cache.
Vcache	The object was obtained from cache and verified to the source.
VFInet	The source was the Internet. The object has been verified to the source and has been modified.

ResultCode Values

For the Web Proxy service, the ResultCode field indicates either a Windows error code for values less than 100, an HTTP status code for values between 100 and 1000, or a Windows Sockets error code when the value is between 10,000 and 11,004. Some of the supported values are shown in Table 5.3.

T A B L E 5.3: ResultCode Values for the Web Proxy Service

ResultCode Value	Description
200	OK, successful connection
201	Created
202	Accepted
204	No content
301	Moved permanently
302	Moved temporarily

T A B L E 5.3: ResultCode Values for the Web Proxy Service *(continued)*

ResultCode Value	Description
304	Not modified
400	Bad request
401	Unauthorized
403	Forbidden
404	Not found
500	Internal server error
501	Not implemented
502	Bad gateway
503	Service unavailable
10060	Connection timed out
10061	Connection refused by destination
10065	Host unreachable
11001	Host not found

For the WinSock Proxy service, the ResultCode field will indicate either a Windows error, for values less than 100, or a Windows Sockets error code for values between 10,000 and 11,004. In addition, the error codes shown in Table 5.4 may be used.

T A B L E 5.4: ResultCode Values for the WinSock Proxy Service

ResultCode Value	Description
0	Successful connection.
13301	The connection was rejected by the proxy server because of filtering or protocol permissions.

T A B L E 5.4: ResultCode Values for the WinSock Proxy Service *(continued)*

ResultCode Value	Description
20000	Normal connection termination.
20001	Abortive connection termination.

Logging in Verbose Format

Verbose logging includes all of the information listed in regular format logging, as well as the fields listed in Table 5.5.

T A B L E 5.5: Verbose Format Log Information

Field Name	Information Field Type	Description
Authentication Status (Client-Authenticate)	Client	This field indicates if the service request is using an authenticated client connection.
Bytes Received (BytesRecvd)	Connection	For the Web Proxy service, the number of bytes received from the remote computer. A value of a hyphen, a zero, or a negative number indicates either that this information was not provided by the remote computer or that no bytes were received from the remote computer.
Bytes Sent (BytesSent)	Connection	For the Web Proxy service, the number of bytes sent to the remote computer. A hyphen, a zero, or a negative number indicates either that the information was not provided by the remote computer or that no bytes were sent to the remote computer.

TABLE 5.5: Verbose Format Log Information *(continued)*

Field Name	Information Field Type	Description
Client Agent (ClientAgent)	Client	For the Web Proxy service, this value contains specialized header information from the client browser to be used when processing the proxy request. For the WinSock Proxy service this value contains the name of the client application generating the request.
Client Platform (ClientPlatform)	Client	The Web Proxy service does not use this field. For the WinSock Proxy service, the value indicates the operating system of the client computer. Possible values are shown in Table 5.6.
Destination Address (DestHostIP)	Connection	The IP address of the remote computer servicing the connection. A hyphen may indicate that the object was served from cache.
Object MIME (MimeType)	Object	For the Web Proxy service, this is the current object's Multipurpose Internet Mail Extensions (MIME) type.
Operation (Operation)	Connection	For the Web Proxy service, this value specifies the current operation, such as GET, PUT, POST, and HEAD. For the WinSock Proxy service, this value specifies the current socket API call, such as Connect( ), Accept( ), SendTo( ), RecvFrom( ), GetHostByName( ), and Listen( ).
Processing Time (ProcessingTime)	Connection	This is the processing time in milliseconds needed by the proxy server to process the current request.
Proxy Name (ServerName)	Server	This is the name of the proxy server computer.

TABLE 5.5: Verbose Format Log Information *(continued)*

Field Name	Information Field Type	Description
Referring Server Name (Referred-Server)	Server	The name of the downstream proxy server that routed the request to the upstream proxy server.
Transport (Transport)	Connection	For the Web Proxy service, this is always TCP/IP. For the WinSock Proxy service, this can be TCP/IP, UDP, or IPX/SPX.

ClientPlatform Values

The Web Proxy service does not use the ClientPlatform field. For the WinSock Proxy service, the value indicates the operating system of the client computer. Possible values include those given in Table 5.6.

TABLE 5.6: ClientPlatform Values

ClientPlatform Values	Operating System of the Client Computer
0:3.1	Windows 3.1
0:3.11	Windows for Workgroups
0:3.95	Windows 95 (16-bit)
1:3.11	Win32
2:4.0	Windows 95 (32-bit)
3:3.1	Windows NT 3.1
3:3.5	Windows NT 3.5
3:3.51	Windows NT 3.51
3:4.0	Windows NT 4.0

Packet Filter Logging

Packet filter logging can be configured with regular or verbose logging formats. Table 5.7 lists the information recorded with regular logging.

T A B L E 5.7: Packet Filter Information Recorded with Regular Logging

Field Name	Information Field Type	Description
Destination-Address	Local	This is the IP address of the destination (local) computer, usually the proxy server.
DestinationPort	Local	This is the service port number used by the destination (local) computer to maintain the connection with the source computer. This is only valid if the protocol used is TCP, UDP, or ICMP.
FilterRule	Filter	Possible values are either zero for dropped packets or one for accepted packets. Only dropped packets are logged by default.
Interface	Filter	This is the interface the packet was received on. This field is reserved for future use.
PFlogTime	General	This is the date and time the packet was received.
Protocol	Remote	This is the transport protocol used during the connection, such as TCP, UDP, or ICMP.
SourceAddress	Remote	This is the IP address of the source, or remote, computer.
SourcePort	Remote	The port number that the source, or remote, computer is using to maintain the connection. This field is only valid if the protocol is TCP, UDP, or ICMP.

Verbose packet filter logging includes all of the information logged with the regular format, as well as the fields listed in Table 5.8.

T A B L E 5.8: Verbose Packet Filter Logging

Field Name	Information Field Type	Description
IPHeader	Packet	This value contains the entire IP header of the packet that generated the alert event.
Payload	Packet	This value consists of a partial listing of the data packet, after the IP header, that generated the alert event.
TcpFlags	Packet	This value indicates the TCP flag value in the IP header of a TCP data packet. Possible values are ACK, FIN, PSH, RST, SYN, and URG.

Windows NT System Event Log

Proxy Server also uses the Windows NT System Event log to record events associated with proxy services. These event logs contain the name of the service that logged the event. The following is a list of event source names that appear in the system event log:

MSProxyAdmin: Proxy Server administrative events

PacketFilterLog: Packet filter alert events (filtered frames)

NOTE When a packet event occurs in a proxy service, it is logged by that service. PacketFilterLog entries only refer to packet filter alert events.

SocksProxy: Socks Proxy service events

SocksProxyLog: Socks Proxy logging events

WebProxyCache: Web Proxy caching events

WebProxyLog: Web Proxy logging events

WebProxyServer: Web Proxy service events

WinSockProxy: WinSock Proxy service events

WinSockProxyLog: WinSock Proxy logging events

NOTE When Web publishing is configured, related events are logged in the WWW service log.

Necessary Procedures

Procedures necessary to this objective include configuring logging for the three proxy services and configuring packet filter logging.

Configuring Proxy Service Logging

Configuring logging is the same for all three proxy services. Logging is enabled by default.

1. To configure logging, start Internet Service Manager by selecting Start ➤ Programs ➤ Microsoft Proxy Server ➤ Internet Service Manager.

2. Select Properties for the service for which you wish to configure logging.

3. Select the Logging tab. You will see a screen similar to the following, depending upon which service you selected:

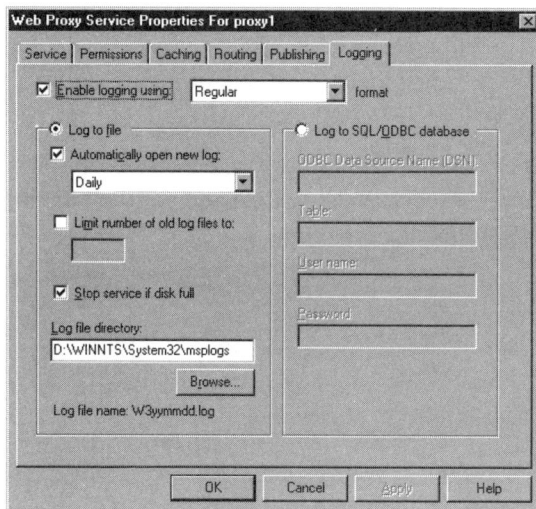

4. Logging should be enabled already. Select Regular or Verbose from the pull-down menu.

5. By default, Log To File will be selected. If you leave this enabled, you have the option to automatically open new log files either daily (the default), weekly, or monthly.

6. You can limit the number of old log files by putting a check in this box and entering a number.

7. "Stop Disk Service If Full" is checked by default. Uncheck it if you wish.

8. You can also change the directory the log files are stored in by clicking Browse.

9. You can also select Log To SQL/OBDC Database. If you select this, Log To File is automatically deselected. Once Log To SQL/OBDC Database is selected, you must enter an OBDC Data Source Name (DSN), a table, a username, and a password.

10. Click OK and you are done.

Configuring Packet Filter Logging

Logging is enabled by default.

1. To configure logging, start Internet Service Manager by selecting Start ➤ Programs ➤ Microsoft Proxy Server ➤ Internet Service Manager.

2. Select Properties for any proxy service. Under the Shared Services section, click on Security. Click on the Logging tab. You will see the following screen:

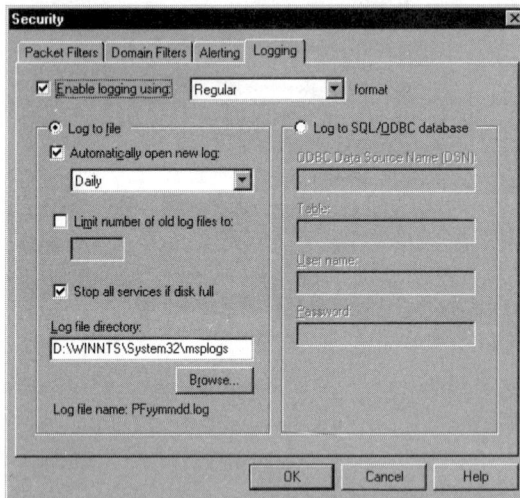

3. Logging should be enabled already. Select Regular or Verbose from the pull-down menu.

4. By default, Log To File will be selected. If you leave this enabled, you have the option to automatically open new log files daily (the default), weekly, or monthly.

5. You can limit the number of old log files by putting a check in this box and entering a number.

6. "Stop All Services If Disk Full" is checked by default. Uncheck it if you wish.

7. You can change the directory the log files are stored in by clicking Browse.

8. You can select Log To SQL/OBDC Database. If you select this, Log To File is automatically deselected.

9. Once Log To SQL/OBDC Database is selected, you must enter an OBDC Data Source Name (DSN), a Table, a Username, and a Password.

10. Click OK and you are done.

Exam Essentials

Know how to configure logging for proxy services.   Review the procedures for configuring logging for all proxy services. These can be configured from the properties pages of each individual service.

Know how to configure packet filter logging.   Packet filtering can be used to generate an alert when a specific event occurs. These alerts in turn can generate an e-mail message notifying a network administrator, be sent to the Windows NT Event log, be logged to a text file, or any combination of the three.

Know the differences between regular and verbose logging. Review the types of information logged in regular and verbose logging formats.

Key Terms and Concepts

Application Programming Interface (API):   This is a set of routines used by an application to have an operating system or another service perform lower level functions.

Internet Control Message Protocol: This is part of the TCP/IP protocol suite that handles control and error messages.

Packet filtering: This is the process of allowing or denying packets based on protocol, local or remote port, direction, and source or destination address.

Socks Proxy service: This service provides transparent redirection of client requests for a wide variety of platforms. Microsoft Proxy Server 2 supports Socks version 4.3a.

Transmission Control Protocol (TCP): Part of the TCP/IP protocol suite, TCP provides reliable, full duplex, connection oriented transport.

User Datagram Protocol (UDP): Part of the TCP/IP protocol suite, UDP provides connectionless-oriented transport.

Web Proxy service: This service supports CERN-compliant Web browsers running on any platform.

WinSock Proxy service: This service provides transparent support through the use of APIs for redirection of Windows-based client requests.

Sample Questions

1. You administer a corporate network using Microsoft Proxy Server and consisting entirely of Windows 95 computers. You wish to find out which employees are using RealAudio. What is the best way to find this out?

   A. Examine the packet filter logs.

   B. Examine the WinSock Proxy service logs.

   C. Examine the Web Proxy service logs.

   D. Use Performance Monitor to log activity for the RealAudio protocol.

   Answer: B. Neither the packet filter logs nor the Web Proxy logs contains the information you need. Performance Monitor also does not provide this information. RealAudio uses the WinSock Proxy service, therefore the needed information is contained in those log files.

2. You administer a corporate network using Microsoft Proxy Server. Your internal network uses TCP/IP only. You have noticed that Don,

an employee, is using his computer after hours to surf the Internet. Don uses Netscape Navigator, which is configured to access the Internet through the proxy server. What should you do to find out if the sites he is visiting are appropriate or not?

A. Enable packet filter logging and examine the log files.

B. Enable WinSock Proxy service logging and examine the log files.

C. Enable Web Proxy service logging and examine the log files.

D. Enable Socks Proxy service logging and examine the log files.

Answer: C. Since Don is using a CERN-compliant Web browser configured to access the Internet through a proxy server, he must be using the Web Proxy service. Therefore the information needed is contained in the Web Proxy service logs.

3. You need to know the destination IP addresses for each request processed by the Web Proxy service. How must you configure logging to accomplish this?

A. Configure Web Proxy service logging to log to a SQL/OBDC database.

B. Configure Web Proxy service logging to log events to the Windows NT System Event log.

C. Enable Web Proxy service logging.

D. Configure Web Proxy service logging to log in verbose format.

Answer: D. Configuring the Web Proxy service to log to a SQL/OBDC database or just enabling Web Proxy service logging does not cause Proxy Server to log the destination address for each request. The Web Proxy service cannot be configured to log events to the Windows NT System Event log. The destination address for each request processed is only logged if logging is enabled in the verbose format.

Monitor performance of various functions by using Microsoft Windows NT Performance Monitor. Functions include HTTP and FTP sessions.

Windows NT Performance Monitor is a powerful tool provided with Windows NT that can be used to monitor many different aspects of server performance. Proxy Server also takes advantage of this tool by installing several new counters that can be used to monitor aspects associated with its various functions. Using this information enables you to analyze the performance of your proxy server and take steps to optimize that performance.

Critical Information

WARNING   Enabling disk performance counters can have a slight adverse effect on disk performance.

When Proxy Server is installed, the following counter objects are installed into Performance Monitor:

> **Web Proxy Server Service Counters:**   Relate to the Web Proxy service and the Socks Proxy service.

NOTE   Although the Socks Proxy service is separate from the Web Proxy service and could logically have its own counter object, these counters are instead integrated into the Web Proxy Server Service counter object.

> **Web Proxy Server Cache Counters:**   Relate to caching performed by the Web Proxy service.

WinSock Proxy Server Service Counters: Relate to the WinSock Proxy Server.

Packet Filtering Counters: Relate to packet filtering.

Pre-Selected Performance Monitor Counters

A shortcut is placed into the Start Menu under Microsoft Proxy Server that loads Performance Monitor with several of the most important counter objects pre-selected.

% Processor Time-Process (INETINFO instance):   The amount of processor time used by a particular instance or individual process. In this counter the INETINFO instance is measured. This is the Internet Information Services (IIS) process. This counter will give you a good idea of how much a particular process is occupying the CPU's time.

% Processor Time-Process (WSPSrv instance):   The same counter, this time measuring the WSPSrv instance. This is the WinSock Proxy service process.

Active Sessions: This measures the number of active sessions for the WinSock Proxy service.

Cache Hit Ratio (%):   The percentage of requests served from cache compared to the number of total requests. This counter helps you in determining if the cache size needs to be adjusted or if the use of cache filters is appropriate.

Request/Sec: The rate of requests made to the Web Proxy Server

Current Average Milliseconds/Request: The mean time, in milliseconds, used to service a request. This counter, in combination with the Request/Sec counter, can be monitored to see if increased server load is causing a corresponding increase in latency.

Other Important Performance Monitor Counters

In addition to these counters, there are several others you should be familiar with:

Active Refresh Bytes Rate: This is the number of bytes of data per second downloaded from the Internet to refresh popular cached

URLs in advance. This counter can be used to determine if adjustments in the active caching configuration are needed.

FTP Requests: This is the number of FTP requests that the Web Proxy service has received.

HTTP Requests: This is the number of HTTP requests that the Web Proxy service has received.

Total Actively Refreshed URLs: This is the total number of popular URLs in the cache that active caching has caused to be refreshed from the Internet. This counter also assists in determining if the active caching configuration is optimized.

DNS Cache Entries: This is the number of DNS domain name entries currently cached by the Web Proxy service. If requests fail for machines whose IP address has recently changed, it is most likely because the DNS cache has not been cleared.

Maximum Users: This is the maximum number of users that have been connected to the Web Proxy service at one time. This counter helps determine server usage.

Total Failed Socks Sessions: This is the total number of client requests that were not serviced by the Socks Proxy service because the client did not have access rights or because of an initial protocol error. This will give you a general indication that there is a problem with Socks clients.

Total Socks Sessions: This is the number of Socks Proxy client sessions.

Frames Dropped Due to Protocol Violations: This is the number of frames dropped due to protocol anomalies. This counter can alert you to possible attempted security violations.

Performance Monitor can also be configured to generate alerts when a particular monitored item passes a threshold limit. The Performance Monitor alert system uses the Windows NT messenger service.

Packet Filter Counters

There are several performance counters associated with packet filtering that you should be aware of. These counters can give you a good indication of the state of security on your network.

NOTE Packet filtering must be enabled for these counters to be activated.

Packet filter counters measure the effectiveness of the packet filtering service capabilities of Proxy Server. The following counters are specific to the packet filtering functions:

Frames Dropped Due to Filter Denial: This is the number of frames dropped due to data rejection by dynamic packet filters.

Frames Dropped Due to Protocol Violations: This is the number of frames dropped due to protocol anomalies.

Total Dropped Frames: This is the number of dropped or filtered frames.

Total Incoming Connections: This is the number of inbound connections created through filtered interfaces.

Total Lost Logging Frames This is the number of dropped frames that could not be logged.

SEE ALSO There are many other counters available in the counter objects associated with Proxy Server. For a more complete listing see *MCSE: Proxy Server 2 Study Guide* (Sybex, 1998).

Necessary Procedures

Using Performance Monitor to monitor proxy server functions is the only procedure necessary to this objective.

Monitoring Proxy Server Performance with Performance Monitor

1. Select Start ➤ Programs ➤ Microsoft Proxy Server ➤ Monitor Microsoft Proxy Server Performance, to load Performance Monitor with the default Proxy Server counters added. Alternatively, select Programs ➤ Administrative Tools (Common) ➤ Performance Monitor to load it without the default Proxy Server counters. You will see the screen labeled Performance Monitor.

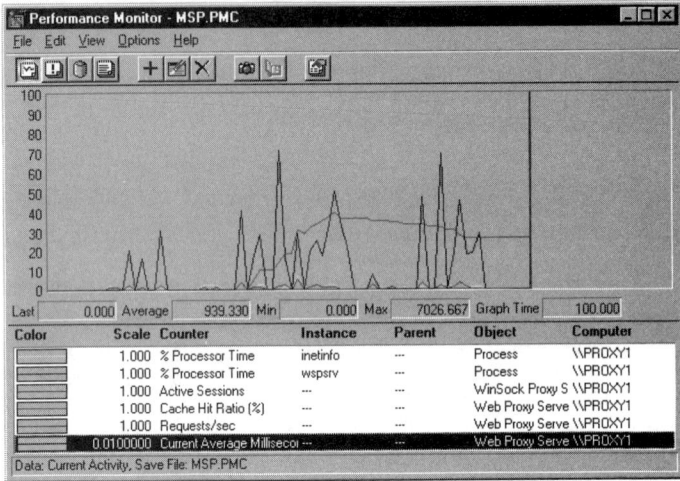

2. To add a new performance counter, click on the plus (+) sign in the toolbar, or click on the Edit menu and select Add To Chart to see the following screen:

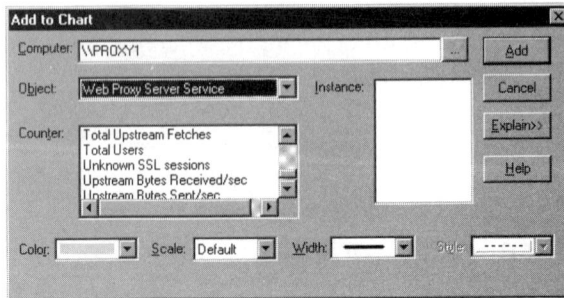

3. Select an object and a counter. For an explanation of the counter, click on Explain.

4. To add the counter, click on Add.

5. Click on Done.

Exam Essentials

Know how to use Performance Monitor to monitor various aspects of Proxy Server performance.   Performance Monitor can be used to monitor many different aspects of the WinSock Proxy service, the Web Proxy service, including caching operations, the Socks Proxy service, and packet filtering.

Key Terms and Concepts

Active caching: This is the process of downloading frequently requested sites in advance during periods of low network utilization.

Cache filtering: You can specify sites to be either always cached or never cached.

Cache hit: This refers to the process of a client request being served from cache rather than from the remote system.

Domain Naming System (DNS):   This is used to map domain names to IP addresses.

Performance Monitor counter: This is an analyzable element of an object that can be used for statistical analysis.

Performance Monitor object: This is a standard mechanism for identifying and using a system resource.

Sample Questions

1. You administer a corporate network that accesses the Internet using Microsoft Proxy Server. You need to submit a report to your boss including the highest number of users who have used the proxy server at one time. What tool should you use to accomplish this?

   A. Network Monitor.

   B. Performance Monitor.

C. Proxy Server Monitor.

D. Examine the proxy server log files.

Answer: B. Network Monitor would not give this type of information. There is no such thing as a Proxy Server Monitor. The log files also would not give you this information. This information can only be obtained using Performance Monitor.

2. Your corporate network uses Proxy Server for Internet access. Which of the following would increase the cache hit ratio?

A. Enable active caching.

B. Monitor the Total Actively Refreshed URLs counter in Performance Monitor.

C. Implement cache filters.

D. Move the cache location to a FAT volume.

Answer: A and C. Enabling active caching would mean that popular sites would be downloaded in advance, thereby increasing the number of times those sites would be served from cache. Creating cache filters set to always download specific sites again would increase the frequency of the site being served from cache. Monitoring the Total Actively Refreshed URLs might assist you in collecting information to raise the cache hit ratio but by itself would not accomplish that. The cache cannot be located on a FAT volume.

3. What does the Cache Hit Ratio counter represent?

A. The percentage of requests served from the remote server out of all requests

B. The percentage of cache objects refreshed by active caching

C. The percentage of requests served from cache out of all requests

D. The ratio of objects in cache whose TTL has expired out of all cache objects

Answer: C. The Cache Hit Ratio counter represents the percentage of requests served from cache out of all requests.

Analyze performance issues. Performance issues include:

- Identifying bottlenecks
- Identifying network-related performance issues
- Identifying disk-related performance issues
- Identifying CPU-related performance issues
- Identifying memory-related performance issues

The performance of your Windows NT server will also affect the performance of your proxy server. Identifying and then eliminating bottlenecks related to network, disk, CPU, and memory usage will serve to increase Proxy Server performance. A bottleneck is the part of the system that restricts workflow. There is a saying in the computer industry that you never get rid of bottlenecks completely; you just exchange one for another. This means that even though you may get rid of one bottleneck by, say, replacing a slow disk drive, you may have another bottleneck related to memory usage that was not obvious before. Fixing the memory bottleneck will reveal yet another bottleneck, and so on. It comes down to the fact that this will be an ongoing process as the network evolves, user needs change, and new software is implemented.

Critical Information

There are four main Windows NT subsystems that can be the cause of bottlenecks: network, disk, CPU, and memory functions. Performance Monitor is a very powerful tool that can be used to help identify bottlenecks in these areas.

Identifying Network-Related Performance Issues

The complexity of many of today's networks can make identifying performance bottlenecks somewhat difficult. However, there are some common counters in Performance Monitor that can give you a general idea of network performance and assist in uncovering bottlenecks:

Server: Bytes Total/Sec: This is the number of bytes the server has sent and received over the network. The desired value for this counter depends on the number of network cards and protocols being used, but it should be high.

Server: Logon/Sec: This is the number of authentication requests being handled by the server. Assuming it is a domain controller, this value should be high.

Server: Logon Total: This is the total number of authentication requests handled by the server since the last restart. Again, assuming that it is a domain controller, this value should be high.

Network Segment: % Network Utilization: This is the percentage of bandwidth in use on the network. This counter value will generally be lower than 30%, although on switched networks it can be higher.

NOTE Network Segment counters are added to Performance Monitor when the Network Monitor Agent service is added. When Performance Monitor is used to actively monitor these counters, it places the network adapter card into promiscuous mode, which means that the card will accept and process all network traffic, not just its own traffic. This will affect network performance and should not be used for long periods of time.

Network Interface: Bytes Sent/Sec: The number of bytes sent using this network adapter card. The optimum value for this counter will depend on the network adapter cards and the protocols being used, but it should be high.

Network Interface: Bytes Total/Sec: The number of bytes sent and received using this network adapter card. The optimum value for this counter will depend on the network adapter cards and the protocols being used, but it should be high.

NetBEUI- and NWLink-Related Counters

There are also Performance Monitor counters associated with specific protocols. NetBEUI and NWLink have similar counters:

Bytes Total/Sec: The number of bytes sent in frames and datagrams. The acceptable value for this counter depends on the number of network cards and the amount of protocol activity, but it should be a high value.

Datagrams/Sec: The number of non-guaranteed datagrams sent and received on the network. The acceptable value depends on the amount of protocol activity, but it should be high.

Frames/Sec: The number of data packets that have been sent and received on the network. The acceptable value depends on the amount of protocol activity, but it should be high.

Monitoring TCP/IP

When monitoring TCP/IP, you should pay attention to the following counters:

NOTE   TCP/IP counters are installed when the TCP/IP protocol is installed and the SNMP service has been installed.

TCP Segments/Sec: The number of TCP segments that are sent and received. The acceptable value for this counter depends on the amount of TCP/IP activity, but it should be high.

TCP Segments Retranslated/Sec: The number of frames that are retranslated. A low value is desirable.

UDP Datagrams/Sec: The number of UDP datagrams that are sent and received. The acceptable value depends on the amount of activity, but it should be low.

Network Interface: Output Queue Length: The length of the output packet queue. Generally, a queue longer than two indicates congestion, and further analysis is necessary.

Identifying Disk-Related Performance Issues

Bottlenecks are frequently caused by poor disk performance. Performance Monitor's counters can be used either with the LogicalDisk object, for logical partitions of physical drives, or with the PhysicalDisk object, which monitors individual hard disk drives. The following counters are a good place to start when trying to identify a bottleneck in the disk subsystem:

NOTE Performance Monitor disk counters are not enabled by default. They can be enabled by entering **diskperf –y** at a Command Prompt or **diskperf –ye** for systems with Windows NT RAID enabled. The computer must then be restarted. Enabling disk performance counters may adversely affect disk performance.

% Disk Time: The percentage of time that the disk drive is busy with read and write requests. If this is consistently close to 100%, the disk is experiencing very heavy usage. Ideally, this number should be under 50%.

Disk Queue Length: This is the number of disk I/O requests waiting for the disk drive. A consistent value over two indicates congestion.

Avg. Disk Bytes/Transfer: The average number of bytes transferred to or from the disk during write or read operations. A high value indicates efficiency.

Disk Bytes/Sec: The speed that bytes are transferred to or from the disk during write or read operations. A high value indicates efficiency.

Identifying CPU-Related Performance Issues

Virtually all operations that take place on a computer involve the CPU in some way. It follows that any type of CPU-related bottleneck can greatly affect all areas of performance. CPU-bound applications and drivers and excessive interrupts are two of the most common causes of bottlenecks in this area. To uncover CPU-related bottlenecks, the following counters should be monitored:

% Processor Time: The amount of time the processor is busy. A consistent value over 75% indicates a system bottleneck. Individual processes can be monitored to determine the cause of the processor activity.

% Privileged Time: The time the processor spends performing operating system services. This value should also be less than 75%.

% User Time: The time the processor spends performing user services. This value should also be less than 75%.

Interrupts/Sec: The number of interrupts the processor is servicing from applications or from hardware devices. On a 80486/66-based system, this should not consistently exceed 1000. On a Pentium 90 PCI bus system, it should not consistently exceed 3500.

System: Processor Queue Length: The number of requests in the processor's queue. A consistent value of more than two indicates a bottleneck.

Server Work Queues: Queue Length: The number of requests in the queue for the selected processor. A consistent value of more than two indicates a bottleneck.

Identifying Memory-Related Performance Issues

Windows NT uses two types of memory: paged and non-paged. The process of paging allows disk storage space to be used as RAM. As memory usage becomes more intensive, read and write accesses to paged memory on disk become more frequent and can become a performance issue. The following counters should be monitored to determine if memory is a bottleneck:

Pages/Sec: The number of requested pages that were not available in RAM and had to be accessed from the disk, or that had to be written to the disk to make room in RAM for other pages. A sustained value of more than 20 may indicate a bottleneck.

Available Bytes: The amount of physical memory available. A value consistently below 4MB may indicate excessive paging.

Committed Bytes: The amount of virtual memory committed to either physical RAM for storage or to pagefile space. The amount of committed bytes should be less than the amount of physical memory.

Pool Non-paged Bytes: The amount of RAM in the non-paged pool system memory area. This is where space is acquired by operating system components as they accomplish their tasks. If this value increases steadily when activity on the server is not increasing, there may be a process with a memory leak.

Necessary Procedures

Necessary procedures for this objective include installing the Network Monitor Agent and enabling disk performance counters.

Installing the Network Monitor Agent

1. Start Network in Control Panel and click on the Services tab.

2. Click on Add.

3. Select Network Monitor Agent and click OK. Insert the Windows NT Server CD-ROM when prompted and click Continue.

4. Click Close and restart the server when prompted.

Enabling Performance Monitor Disk Counters

1. From a command prompt, type **diskperf /?** to see the following syntax:

```
DISKPERF [-Y[E] | -N] [\\computername]

      -Y[E] Sets the system to start disk performance
            counters when the system is restarted.

      E     Enables the disk performance counters used
            for measuring performance of the physical
            drives in striped disk set when the system
            is restarted. Specify -Y without the E to
            restore the normal disk performance
            counters.

      -N    Sets the system disable disk performance
            counters when the system is restarted.
```

> \\computername Is the name of the computer you want to see or set disk performance counter use.

2. Enter **diskperf –y** to enable disk counters, or **diskperf –ye** if you are using a Windows NT RAID-enabled system. Entering **diskperf –n** will disable the disk counters.

The disk counters will be enabled the next time the system is restarted.

Exam Essentials

Know which Performance Monitor counters are used to identify network-, disk-, CPU-, and memory-related bottlenecks. You should be familiar with the acceptable values for each of the common counters used to identify bottlenecks. You should also understand what an unacceptable value indicates.

Key Terms and Concepts

Bottleneck: This is the part of the system that restricts workflow.

Interrupt: This is a temporary suspension of a process, which gives temporary control of the CPU to an interrupt handling routine.

NetBEUI: This is a small, very fast, non-routable protocol suitable for use in small networks.

NWLink: This is Microsoft's implementation of IPX/SPX (Internetwork Packet Exchange/Sequenced Package Exchange), a routable network protocol used primarily in NetWare-based networks.

Paging: In a virtual memory system, the process of transferring pages between disk storage and physical RAM is called paging.

TCP/IP: Transmission Control Protocol/Internet Protocol is a suite of protocols used on the Internet that enables cross-communication between diverse hardware configurations and operating systems.

Sample Questions

1. What is an acceptable value for the Committed Bytes counter?

 A. 4MB or more.

 B. Less than the amount of physical RAM in the computer.

 C. It depends on the amount of protocol activity, but a high value is desirable.

 D. A sustained value of less than five.

 Answer: B. The Committed Bytes value should be less than the amount of physical RAM in the computer.

2. What does a sustained value of more than 75% indicate in the %Processor Time counter?

 A. More RAM should be added to the computer.

 B. The paging file should be distributed across multiple disks.

 C. The CPU may need to be upgraded.

 D. The network adapter should be upgraded.

 Answer: C. A sustained value of more than 75% in the %Processor Time counter indicates that the CPU is overworked and may need to be upgraded.

3. Jill monitors various Performance Monitor counters on her NT server. Pages/Sec is consistently more than 20, System: Processor Queue Length is usually less than two, Interrupts/Sec averages around 700, and Disk Queue Length averages between four and five. Which are possible bottlenecks?

 A. CPU

 B. Memory

 C. Hard disk

 D. Network adapter

 Answer: B and C. A sustained value of more than 20 pages per second may indicate a memory bottleneck. The Disk Queue Length should not have a sustained value of more than two. An Interrupts/ Sec value of 700 is acceptable, as is a System: Processor Queue Length value of less than two.

Optimize performance for various purposes. Purposes include:

- Increasing throughput
- Optimizing routing

Up to this point we have discussed ways to optimize various subsystems of the proxy server machine itself, such as the disk system, the CPU, memory, or network hardware. But what if your proxy server is not the cause of the slow network? There are external network factors that can cause poor network performance. Fortunately, Microsoft has provided a tool called Network Monitor that can be used in conjunction with Performance Monitor to analyze your network.

Critical Information

In order to use Network Monitor, you need to install the Network Monitor Tools and Agent from the Services icon in Control Panel.

TIP If you have already installed the Network Monitor Agent, you will have to remove it and restart the server before installing Network Monitor Tools and Agent.

After installation, there will be a new object called Network Segment in Performance Monitor. The following counters should be monitored when attempting to identify network-related problems:

% Broadcast Frames: This is the percentage of frames that are broadcast traffic. This is an important counter because each broadcast causes every card on the network to generate an interrupt. If the percentage of broadcast frames is too high, CPU utilization on all computers on the network can be adversely affected. If this alone or combined with the %Multicast Frames counter reaches anywhere near 100% during a period of a second, the source of the traffic should be identified immediately.

% Multicast Frames: This is the percentage of network traffic made up of multicast frames. Multicast is often used to stream video content from one server to multiple clients. Like broadcast frames, each multicast causes every card on the network to generate an interrupt.

% Network Utilization: This is the amount of network bandwidth that is in use. This counter should be considered when network speed becomes unacceptable or when it reaches 40% or 50%. At this point, the network is the bottleneck.

Broadcast Frames Received/Second: This is the number of broadcast frames received per second. A rate over 100 indicates a problem.

Multicast Frames Received/Second: This is the number of multicast frames received per second. A rate over 100 indicates a problem.

Total Bytes Received/Second: This is the total number of bytes received. If this number is approaching the maximum speed for the medium used, e.g., 10Mbps for Ethernet, 100Mbps for Fast Ethernet, a problem is indicated.

This information can also be monitored by using Network Monitor to capture data from the network.

Another important factor to consider when examining an Ethernet network is the number of collisions. Collisions occur when two computers on the network attempt to send data simultaneously. Collisions are a normal part of an Ethernet network. However, if the rate of collisions becomes too high, you may need to take steps to lower the network load. Unfortunately, Network Monitor does not provide a method of measuring the number of collisions. In order to monitor this you will need to obtain a third party network sniffing tool. For all of these problems, solutions you may want to consider include segmenting your network, using bridges, or using switches.

The choice of routing protocols in your network can also affect network performance. Routing tables store routing information. Routing algorithms initialize and maintain these routing tables. Initially, a router only knows how to reach networks or subnets that are directly connected to it.

When configuring routing, you can either use static routing or choose a routing protocol that updates routes dynamically:

Static Routing: Static routers require that routing tables be built and updated manually. If a route changes, static routers don't automatically share this information to inform each other of the event. An administrator must manually update the static route entry whenever an internetwork topology change requires it. A benefit to creating static routes is that bandwidth is conserved. Why? Because broadcasts for updating routes aren't being continually sent over the network.

Dynamic Routing: Dynamic routing, on the other hand, does not require that an administrator manually update each new route or routing change. However, there is a price to be paid. Routing updates must be passed between routers as often as every 30 seconds, depending on the routing protocol used. This has the potential to cause network congestion.

Necessary Procedures

Installing the Network Monitor Tools and Agent is the only necessary procedure for this objective.

Installing the Network Monitor Tools and Agent

1. Start Network in Control Panel and click on Services.

2. Click on Add.

3. Select Network Monitor Tools And Agent and click OK.

4. Insert the NT Server CD-ROM when prompted and click Continue.

5. After file copying is finished, click Close.

6. Restart the server when prompted.

Exam Essentials

Know which Performance Monitor counters are used to identify possible network problems. Review the Network Segment counters and be sure and memorize the acceptable values for each.

Know in general terms what types of solutions can be implemented to solve network problems. Problems related to broadcasts, multicasts, and network load can often be solved by segmenting networks using bridges or switches. The use of static routing can eliminate overhead caused by routing updates used by dynamic routing protocols.

Key Terms and Concepts

Broadcast: This is when a packet is sent to all hosts on a network.

Collisions: These occur in an Ethernet network when multiple computers attempt to transmit data simultaneously.

Multicast: This is a communication that is sent from one site to a group of selected receivers.

Sample Questions

1. You are monitoring the Broadcast Frames Received/Second counter. Which of the following values could possibly indicate a problem?

A. 25

B. 75

C. 100

D. 125

Answer: C and D. Any value of 100 or more can indicate a problem with the network.

2. High numbers of broadcast and multicast frames can become a problem on your network because. What is the cause of this?

   A. These frames are larger than other typical frames on an Ethernet network and so can cause congestion.

   B. Each broadcast and multicast causes every network card on the network to generate an interrupt.

   C. Broadcast and multicast frames create collisions.

   D. Broadcast frames and multicast frames conflict with each other.

   Answer: B

Use Performance Monitor logs to identify the appropriate configuration.

Performance Monitor has the ability to log information over extended periods of time. These logs are saved and can be reviewed after the fact. In this manner, long term performance trends can be analyzed. This will bring to light changing conditions that otherwise might not be apparent. This data can also be exported to graphics programs or spreadsheet programs to create cool-looking tables and graphs to impress your supervisor.

Critical Information

In order to take advantage of Performance Monitor logging, select the View menu and choose Log. Now you can add Performance Monitor counters in much the same manner as in the Chart view, except that they can only be added by object. In other words, if you want to log the data for the Cache Hit Ratio (%), you must select the Web Proxy service object and log all of the performance counters associated with that object. Once you have selected the objects you need to log, click on the Options menu and select Log. Here you will need to choose a directory, a name for the log file, and whether to have periodic updates (measured in seconds) or manual updates. When you are ready to begin logging, click on Start Log.

After you have logged the data for a period of time, stop the log and play it back. This is accomplished by selecting the Options menu and selecting Data From. Enter the name of the log you just created. You can then change to the Chart view or the Report view and add counters from the objects you have logged. Realize, when you do this, that it is not real-time data—it is data being played back from logged information.

Logged data can also be exported in the form of TSV (tab delimited) files or CSV (comma delimited) files. These files can then be imported into a program such as Excel where the data can be manipulated.

TIP   Before you export the log, you must add the counters for which you want to export data to the chart or report view. Otherwise you will not export any data.

Necessary Procedures

For this objective, you will need to know how to start logging data with Performance Monitor and how to export logged data so you can use it with other programs, such as Excel.

Logging with Performance Monitor

1. Start Performance Monitor by selecting Start ➤ Programs ➤ Administrative Tools (Common) ➤ Performance Monitor.

2. Click on View and select Log.

3. Click on the plus sign in the tool bar to see the screen labeled Add To Log.

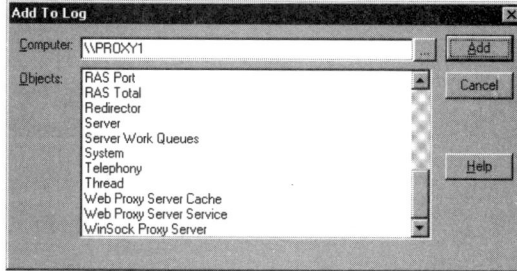

4. Add the objects you need to monitor, then click Done.

5. Click on Options and select Log to see the screen labeled Log Options.

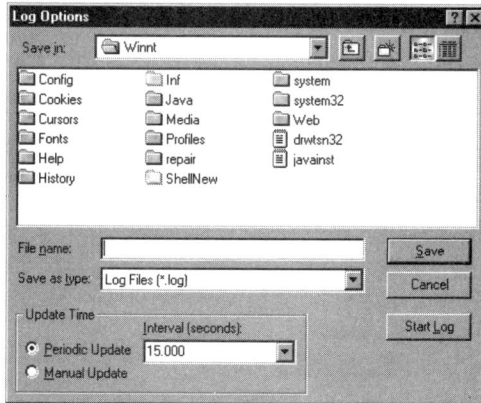

6. Browse to the directory you wish to store the log file in.

7. Type in the desired log file name.

8. Select an Interval for Periodic Update, or select Manual Update.

9. Click on Start Log.

Viewing Charts of Logged Data

1. Load Performance Monitor by selecting Start ➤ Programs ➤ Administrative Tools (Common) ➤ Performance Monitor.

2. Add the counters you wish to see from the object you have logged.

3. Click on the Options menu and select Data From to see the following screen:

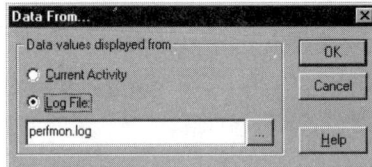

4. Select Log File and browse to the correct file.

5. Click OK.

Exporting Logged Data to Other Programs

1. In Performance Monitor, click on the File menu and select Export Chart to see the screen labeled Performance Monitor—Export As.

2. Choose a directory and a filename.

3. Next to "Save As Type," select either TSV for a tab delimited file, or CSV for a comma delimited file.

4. Click Save.

Exam Essentials

Know how to log Performance Monitor data. Review the steps required to log data. Performance Monitor can log data over extended periods of time.

Know how to view logged Performance Monitor data. Logged data can be viewed in either chart or report form by changing the source data for Performance Monitor from current to logged data.

Know how to export logged data to other programs such as Excel. Logged data can be exported either as TSV (tab delimited) files or CSV (comma delimited) files.

Key Terms and Concepts

CSV file: This is a file in which fields of information are separated by commas.

TSV file: This is a file in which fields of information are separated by tabs.

Sample Questions

1. What must you do in order to view charts of logged data in Performance Monitor?

    A. Change Performance Monitor options to view data from a log file instead of current data.

    B. Enable logging for the proxy service for which you want to view data.

    C. Add Performance Monitor counters to the chart you wish to view from logged data.

    D. Enable packet filter logging.

Answer: A and C. You must select to view data from a log file and you must add the specific counters you wish to see to the chart view. Proxy service logging and packet filter logging do not use Performance Monitor.

2. When exporting logged data from Performance Monitor, what file types can you choose from?

   A. SSV

   B. TSV

   C. DSV

   D. CSV

   Answer: B and D. TSV files are tab delimited, CSV files are comma delimited.

Perform Internet traffic analysis by using Windows NT Server tools.

Previously you were introduced briefly to the Network Monitor. This is a valuable tool that can be used to monitor and analyze network traffic. Many of the same types of information available from the network-related counters in Performance Monitor are also available in Network Monitor. The difference is that, with Network Monitor, you can examine network traffic down to the packet level and even examine the contents of individual frames.

Critical Information

Network Monitor is useful when you need to examine the network for certain types of traffic and it can be used to examine the traffic of any network interface. Figure 5.1 shows the Network Monitor interface.

FIGURE 5.1: The Network Monitor interface

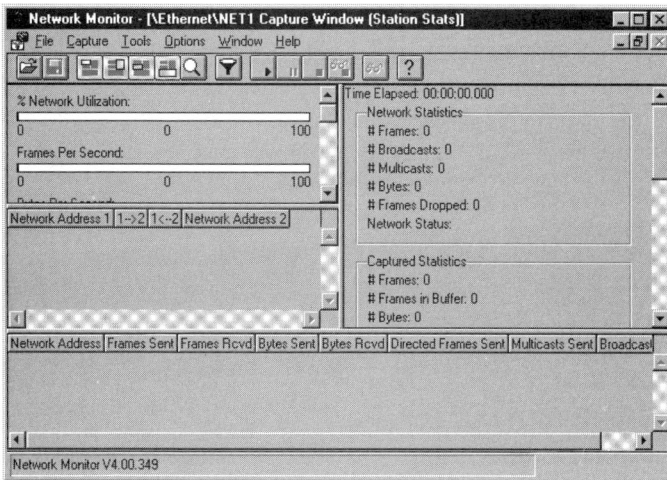

NOTE The version of Network Monitor shipped with Windows NT 4.0 is disabled so that it will only capture packets either destined for or sent from the server on which it is run. The full version of Network Monitor is shipped with Systems Management Server (SMS).

The Network Monitor interface is divided into four panes:

Graph: This displays current activity as a set of bar graphs. Information displayed includes network utilization, frames per second, bytes per second, broadcasts per second, and multicasts per second.

Session Statistics: This displays a summary of a conversation between two hosts. It also displays which host is initiating broadcasts and multicasts.

Total Statistics: This displays traffic detected on the network as a whole. Included are statistics for frame capture, utilization statistics, and network adapter card statistics.

Station Statistics: This displays a summary of the total number of frames initiated by the host. Included are the number of frames and bytes sent and received. The number of broadcast and multicast frames initiated is also displayed.

Figure 5.2 shows the types of information that can be reviewed from captured data. To capture data in Network Monitor, click on the Capture menu and select Start. To view the captured data, click on the Capture menu and select Stop And View.

F I G U R E 5.2: Information that can be reviewed from captured data

As mentioned previously, if you wish to run Network Monitor, you must install the Network Monitor Tools and Agent from the Services icon in Control Panel.

Necessary Procedures

For this objective you should know how to capture data in Network Monitor and then be able to examine that data.

Capturing and Examining Data with Network Monitor

1. Start Network Monitor by selecting Start ➤ Programs ➤ Administrative Tools (Common) ➤ Network Monitor.

2. Click on Capture in the menu and select Start.

3. When you have captured sufficient data, click on Capture in the menu and select Stop And View.

4. To examine a particular frame, double click on it.

Exam Essentials

Know what types of information can be monitored using Network Monitor. Network monitor can be used to monitor information about broadcast and multicast frames and to view network statistics. It can also be used to examine the contents of individual packets.

Key Terms and Concepts

No new terms or concepts are introduced in this objective.

Sample Questions

1. Sue wants to monitor in real time the amount of broadcast traffic received by the external interface on her proxy server computer. What tool must she use?

   A. Network Monitor

   B. Performance Monitor

   C. Internet Service Manager

   D. Packet filter logging

   Answer: A. Network Monitor is the only tool available that can accomplish this task.

2. What must you do before you can run Network Monitor?

A. Install Performance Monitor.

B. Install Microsoft Proxy Server.

C. Install Network Monitor Tools and Agent.

D. Install Network Monitor Agent.

Answer: C. Performance Monitor is installed with Windows NT. Microsoft Proxy Server is not necessary to run Network Monitor. Installing the Network Monitor Agent will allow remote monitoring of that computer. In order to run Network Monitor, you must install the Network Monitor Tools and Agent from the Services icon in Control Panel.

Monitor current sessions.

Another aspect of monitoring your proxy server is keeping track of current users. This can be accomplished by accessing the properties of any of the three proxy services and clicking on Current Sessions.

Critical Information

Figure 5.3 shows the interface for Microsoft Proxy Server User Sessions. From here you can monitor current users for the Web Proxy service, the WinSock Proxy service, and the Socks Proxy service. Clicking Refresh updates the data. Information displayed includes the connected user's name, the time they connected to the service, and the duration of their connection.

NOTE This screen allows you only to view this information. You cannot control connections from here.

FIGURE 5.3: The interface for Microsoft Proxy Server User Sessions

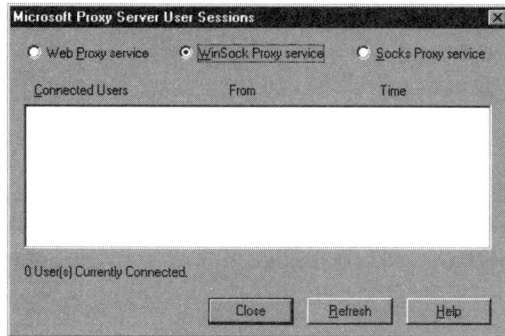

Necessary Procedures

For this objective, you need to be able to monitor current sessions using Internet Service Manager.

Monitoring Current Sessions Using Internet Service Manager

1. Start Internet Service Manager by selecting Start ➤ Programs ➤ Microsoft Proxy Server ➤ Internet Service Manager.

2. Select Properties for any of the three proxy services.

3. Click on Current Sessions.

4. Click on the radio button next to the service you need to monitor. You can click Refresh when you need to update the data displayed.

Exam Essentials

Know how to monitor current sessions using Internet Service Manager. Current sessions can be monitored by accessing the properties pages of any of the three proxy services and clicking on Current Sessions.

Key Terms and Concepts

No new terms or concepts are introduced in this objective.

Sample Questions

1. Lee needs to see how long a particular user has been connected to the Internet. What tool should he use to accomplish this?

   A. Internet Service Manager

   B. Performance Monitor

   C. Network Monitor

   D. Server Manager

   Answer: A. Current sessions can be monitored from Internet Service Manager by selecting the properties pages for any of the three proxy services and clicking on Current Sessions.

CHAPTER

6

Troubleshooting

Microsoft Exam Objectives Covered in This Chapter:

▶ **Resolve Proxy Server and Proxy Server client installation problems.** *(pages 275 – 280)*

▶ **Resolve Proxy Server and Proxy Server client access problems.** *(pages 281 – 291)*

▶ **Resolve Proxy Server client computer problems.** *(pages 291 – 295)*

▶ **Resolve security problems.** *(pages 295 – 301)*

▶ **Resolve caching problems.** *(pages 301 – 306)*

▶ **Troubleshoot a WINS server to provide client access to Proxy Servers.** *(pages 306 – 308)*

▶ **Troubleshoot hardware-related problems such as network interfaces and disk drives.** *(pages 308 – 312)*

▶ **Troubleshoot Internet/intranet routing hardware and software. Software includes Microsoft Routing and Remote Access Service (RRAS).** *(pages 313 – 314)*

N ow that you've planned your Proxy Server installation, installed Proxy Server, configured Proxy Server and the Proxy Server clients, and learned how to monitor and optimize various aspects of Proxy Server, you should be finished, right? Well, not quite. Any network administrator can tell you that the bulk of their time is spent troubleshooting problems that arise during day-to-day use of the network. In this chapter you will review troubleshooting tactics for your Proxy Server network.

Resolve Proxy Server and Proxy Server client installation problems.

Proxy Server installation is typically trouble free. However, certain conditions may exist in your particular configuration that will cause errors. These can either cause Setup to configure Proxy Server incorrectly or they can cause Setup to fail completely. These errors are event messages. They are either displayed as pop-up messages during installation or recorded in the Windows NT System Event log, which can be viewed with Event Viewer.

Critical Information

Error messages may be generated when there is an error in Proxy Server installation or in Proxy Server client installation.

Proxy Server Installation Errors

The following is a list of some of the more common errors that may be encountered during Proxy Server installation:

Could not identify disk drive configuration. This means that the Setup program could not recognize the current drive configuration. The Disk Administrator can be used to examine the drive configuration.

Either the logged account is not permitted to modify the system file *filename,* **or the file is locked by another application.** This means either that another Internet service is currently active on the server, or that you are using an account without administrative privileges to install Proxy Server. Try using Internet Service Manager to stop all other Internet services and verify that you are using an account with administrative privileges.

Proxy Server Setup requires administrator privileges. The account you are using to install Proxy Server does not have administrative privileges. Log on as an administrator and run the Setup program again.

Out of memory. There are not enough available resources to run the Setup program. Close all applications and restart the computer, then run Setup again.

Setup cannot delete the Registry entry *entryname.* The Registry could not be updated by the Setup program, probably for one of the following reasons:

- You are not logged on as an administrator.

- Microsoft Proxy Server has already been installed on the computer.

- There are problems with the Registry.

Run the Setup program again and select Remove All. Try installing again.

Setup cannot load protocols to the Registry. Error= *errornumber.* If you are running the Setup program from a network share path created by copying the files from the Proxy Server CD, the file PROTO.BIN may not be in the share path. Copy the PROTO.BIN file from the CD to the network share path.

Setup could not create the directory *directoryname.*
Error= *errornumber.* The named directory could not be created, probably because the disk drive was full.

Setup could not find the IIS virtual root Scripts directory. Make sure that there are no problems with the default Scripts directory that is set up by Internet Information Server (IIS).

This software can only be installed on a computer with an Internet Information Server installation that includes the WWW service. Proxy Server requires that the WWW service for IIS 3 or later already be installed.

WSAStartup failed. Error=*errornumber*. This indicates that there is some type of problem with TCP/IP configuration. Double check TCP/IP settings to ensure that they are correct.

Client Setup Program Errors

The following is a list of common errors that might be encountered while running the client Setup program:

Instances of WinSock DLLs appear in both the System and Windows directories. Setup cannot proceed until there is only one TCP/IP installation. There are multiples copies of WINSOCK.DLL on your system. Make sure there is only one copy located within the Windows or System directory.

Please set a description of the internal network. There is not a Local Address Table (LAT) present on the computer. This is contained in the file named MSPLAT.TXT. The default location for this file is C:\WSPCLNT. Check to see if the logon account you are using has permission to write to this directory and that there is enough available disk space. Also, this file must have at least one valid range of address pairs that identify internal IP clients.

Setup cannot locate the Microsoft Internet Explorer 2.0 location. The installation path to the browser application cannot be determined. Setup will complete, but you will need to configure your Web browser manually.

Setup cannot locate the Netscape Navigator location. The installation path to the browser application cannot be determined. Setup will complete, but you will need to configure your Web browser manually.

Setup could not find the file WSOCK32.DLL on your system. Please consult the documentation for your system. For Windows NT operating systems, make sure the WSOCK32.DLL file is located in C:\WINNT\SYSTEM32.

Setup could not rename the file *filename1* back to *filename2*. A system file update cannot be completed, possibly because critical system files are missing or incorrectly named. Try running Setup again and choosing the Remove All option. If Setup still gives the same error, try one of the following:

- For Windows 95 or Windows NT, rename _MSRWS32.DLL to WSOCK32.DLL.

- For Windows 3.1, rename _MSRWS16.DLL to WINSOCK.DLL.

Then try running the Setup program again.

Setup could not save the Local Address Table. The LAT file, named MSPLAT.TXT and installed in C:\WSPCLNT, cannot be saved to disk. Verify that you have enough disk space and permissions to write the file, and that the file is not already installed and in use by another application.

Your system may be in an inconsistent state. Please run Setup again. Setup cannot finish the file updating needed to continue installation, possibly because critical system files are missing or incorrectly named. Run Setup again and select the Remove All option, then try the installation again. If Setup still gives the same error, try one of the following:

- For Windows 95 or Windows NT, rename _MSRWS32.DLL to WSOCK32.DLL.

- For Windows 3.1, rename _MSRWS16.DLL to WINSOCK.DLL.

Then try running the Setup program again.

Necessary Procedures

For this objective and other objectives in this chapter, you need to know how to view Proxy Server errors or client errors in Event Viewer.

Using Event Viewer

1. Start Event Viewer by selecting Start ➤ Programs ➤ Administrative Tools (Common) ➤ Event Viewer to see the screen labeled Event Viewer – System Log On *servername*.

Date	Time	Source	Category	Event	User	Co
9/8/98	8:41:17 PM	BROWSER	None	8015	N/A	
9/8/98	8:41:17 PM	BROWSER	None	8015	N/A	
9/8/98	8:41:17 PM	BROWSER	None	8015	N/A	
9/8/98	8:40:45 PM	WebProxyServer	None	118	N/A	
9/8/98	8:40:39 PM	SNMP	None	1001	N/A	
9/8/98	8:40:39 PM	SNMP	None	1106	N/A	
9/8/98	8:40:39 PM	WinSockProxy	None	32	N/A	
9/8/98	8:40:39 PM	SNMP	None	1106	N/A	
9/8/98	8:39:38 PM	EventLog	None	6005	N/A	
9/7/98	4:18:04 PM	BROWSER	None	8015	N/A	
9/7/98	4:18:03 PM	BROWSER	None	8015	N/A	
9/7/98	4:17:25 PM	SNMP	None	1001	N/A	
9/7/98	4:17:24 PM	SNMP	None	1106	N/A	
9/7/98	4:16:24 PM	EventLog	None	6005	N/A	
9/7/98	4:14:29 PM	BROWSER	None	8033	N/A	
9/7/98	4:14:29 PM	BROWSER	None	8033	N/A	
9/7/98	4:14:29 PM	BROWSER	None	8033	N/A	
9/7/98	10:44:02 AM	BROWSER	None	8015	N/A	
9/7/98	10:44:02 AM	BROWSER	None	8015	N/A	
9/7/98	10:44:02 AM	BROWSER	None	8015	N/A	
9/7/98	10:43:23 AM	SNMP	None	1001	N/A	

2. Double click on any event to see details.

Exam Essentials

Know common installation problems that may be encountered and how to resolve those problems. Installation problems are either reported in a pop-up message during installation or recorded in the Windows NT System Event log, which may be viewed with Event Viewer.

Key Terms and Concepts

Local Address Table (LAT): This is a Proxy Server configuration file defining the IP address ranges that are internal to the network.

All addresses external to the network should be excluded from this file.

Registry: The registry is a database used by Windows NT and Windows 95 to store information about configuration.

Sample Questions

1. You are installing Proxy Server 2 on a new server. No errors are reported during the installation. However, after rebooting your server, the proxy server does not function properly. Which tool would you use to display errors that occurred during your installation?

   A. Performance Monitor

   B. Diskperf

   C. Event Viewer

   D. Control Panel

   Answer: C. Setup errors are recorded in the Windows NT System Event log, which can be viewed using the Event Viewer.

2. During client setup, you receive the following error: **Setup cannot locate the Microsoft Internet Explorer 2.0 location.** Which of the following steps would you take?

   A. Reinstall the client software.

   B. Manually configure the browser.

   C. Reinstall the browser.

   D. Modify the client Setup configuration.

   Answer: B. The browser will have to be modified manually to function properly. No reinstallation is required.

Resolve Proxy Server and Proxy Server client access problems.

Microsoft provides several utilities that can be used to troubleshoot both server and client access. Typically, in-depth troubleshooting is not necessary on access-related issues. However, some issues can only be resolved using the tools and techniques discussed in this objective.

Critical Information

In this objective, there are three areas of Proxy Server operations for which you need to understand problem-solving techniques. These are: Proxy Server access problems, Web Proxy client access problems, and WinSock Proxy client access problems.

Troubleshooting Proxy Server Access Problems

Once you have successfully completed the proxy server installation, you can investigate simple configuration problems with a tool provided by Microsoft called MSPDIAG.EXE, located in the C:\MSP directory. When executed, this program will verify the following:

- The version of Proxy Server installed.
- Windows NT 4.0 or later is installed.
- Internet Information Server (IIS) 3 or later is installed.
- The SAP Agent is installed when IPX is configured.
- Valid IP addresses are listed in the Local Address Table (LAT).
- The status of the IIS WWW service.
- The status of the proxy services.
- Administrative privileges of the Windows NT logon account that is being used.

- IP forwarding is disabled.

- Only one default gateway is defined.

- The settings in the MSPCLNT.INI agree with the proxy server's configuration settings.

Once you have used MSPDIAG.EXE to eliminate basic configuration problems, you can examine Proxy Server event messages using Event Viewer to diagnose less obvious problems. Event messages for Proxy Server regarding access problems are divided into the following groups: Web Proxy service, Web Proxy array and chain, WinSock Proxy service, and Socks Proxy service.

Web Proxy Service Event Messages

Web Proxy service events are recorded in the Windows NT System Event log under the source names WebProxyServer and WebProxyLog. The following is a list of the more common Web Proxy service event messages:

HTTP/1.0 500 server error (An attempt has been made to operate on an impersonation token by a thread that is not currently impersonating a client.) This happens when the properties for the home directory of the WWW service are changed when the Web Proxy service is also in use. For instance, if the home directory setting is changed to use a remote UNC path name, e.g., *servername*\ *sharename*, instead of a currently mapped local drive, Web Proxy service requests will fail. Stopping and restarting the WWW service and Web Proxy service will correct the problem.

HTTP/1.0 500 server error (-*number*) This error is sometimes encountered when Windows NT Challenge/Response authentication is used to validate Web Proxy clients. The authentication method is specified in the WWW service properties. Make sure that clients are using Internet Explorer. Basic (Clear text) authentication may be selected as a temporary alternative.

HTTP/1.0 500 server error (The specified module could not be found.) This error will be encountered when necessary Proxy Server binaries are not in the Proxy Server scripts directory. Verify the location of the IIS scripts directory and make sure that it contains a proxy subdirectory. Create this directory if it does not exist.

115—W3Proxy failed to start because the system time is incorrect. The date and time on the server are not correct. Reset the date and time and restart the service.

Web Proxy Array and Chain Event Messages

Web Proxy array and chain events are recorded in the Windows NT System Event log, also under the source names WebProxyServer and WebProxyLog. The following is a list of the more common events in numerical order:

130—The Web Proxy service detected that the upstream proxy *servername* is down. The upstream proxy server is not available. Troubleshoot that server.

132—The Web Proxy service detected that the array member *servername* is down. A proxy server array member has gone down. Troubleshoot the proxy server indicated.

139—Proxy Server *servername* requires proxy-to-proxy authentication. Proxy Server *servername* is not configured with this type of authentication. Proxy server computers in an array or chained configuration must authenticate between servers. Configure the proxy server computer named for proper authentication.

WinSock Proxy Service Event Messages

WinSock Proxy service events are recorded in the Windows NT System Event log, under the source names WinSockProxy and WinSockProxy-Log. The following is a list of common events in numerical order:

1—The WinSock Proxy service failed to initialize. The data is the internal error code. A client request failed, possibly due to missing system files or configuration settings. Restart the WinSock Proxy service. If the problem recurs, run the Proxy Server Setup program and reinstall.

2—The WinSock Proxy service failed to initialize the network. The data is the error. A client request failed, possibly due to missing or corrupted network settings. Stop and restart the network and all Internet services on the proxy server computer. Recurrence of the problem may indicate a physical problem with the network.

4—The WinSock Proxy service cannot initialize due to a shortage of available memory. The data is the error. The service cannot initialize because there is not enough available memory on the server. Close any applications that are not needed on the server. If the problem persists, consider adding more memory to the server.

7—The WinSock Proxy service has failed due to a shortage of available memory. The data is the number of connections. Additional connections cannot be supported because of a lack of available resources. Monitor the current connections in use and memory usage on the proxy server computer.

10—The WinSock Proxy service failed to initialize because of missing or corrupted Registry settings. The data is the error. A client request failed, possibly due to missing or corrupted Registry settings. Restart the WinSock Proxy service. If the error occurs again, run the Proxy Server Setup program and reinstall.

15—The WinSock Proxy service failed to load security DLL. A required file, SECURITY.DLL, cannot be found. Without this DLL, client requests cannot be processed. Check to make sure that this file is in *drive*:*root*\SYSTEM32 and restart the service.

16—The WinSock Proxy service failed to determine network addresses. The proxy server does not know if the IP addresses used to establish a connection are on the internal or external network. Verify that the Local Address Table (LAT) is correct and that the client copy of the LAT contains the same information. Also, verify the TCP/IP configuration on the client.

17—Incorrect network configuration. None of the server's addresses are internal. At least one IP address for the internal network adapter of the server must be included in the LAT. Use Internet Service Manager to correct the LAT.

18—The WinSock Proxy service failed to start because the system time is incorrect. The proxy server's date and time are incorrect. Correct the date and time and then start the service.

Another problem that can occur with the Web Proxy service involves IIS settings. Web Proxy clients will receive either a 500 Server Error (The system cannot find the path specified.) or a 404 Object Not Found error. This happens when all of the servers specified in the Directories tab of the

WWW service properties pages are virtual servers. Make sure that at least one of the WWW service home directories is not a virtual server.

The following is a list of common problems associated with the Win-Sock Proxy service that are not recorded as system events:

Users cannot access or administer different protocols: By default, only an account with administrative rights can access any port. If you want to allow other users to access and administer protocols or assigned ports, you must take the following steps:

- Make sure the IP address of the user's computer is included in the LAT.

- Make sure that the protocol has been added.

- Grant access permission for the protocol to the user or to a group the user belongs to.

Ping and Tracert do not perform reliably: Ping and Tracert use Internet Control Message Protocol (ICMP). ICMP does not use Windows Sockets, and the proxy server computer cannot redirect applications using it.

Problems occur with third-party TCP/IP stacks: Proxy Server has not been tested with third-party TCP/IP stacks and may produce unpredictable results.

Domain name lookups fail on the local network: If you have a DNS server on your internal network, make sure that its IP address is in the LAT.

Socks Proxy Service Event Messages

Socks Proxy service events are recorded in the Windows NT System Event log under the source names SocksProxy and SocksProxyLog. An event is recorded when a connection is established and when a connection is terminated. Abortive connection terminations have a different result code. Typically, Socks Proxy service operation is trouble free. There are a few points you should keep in mind to ensure correct operation:

- If you are using manual packet filtering, all used ports must be defined. In case you don't know which ports to define, use dynamic filtering.

- The standard 4.3a version of Socks should be used.

Troubleshooting Web Proxy Client Access Problems

Web Proxy service errors can be encountered by any CERN-compliant Web browser on any platform. Common problems encountered include the following:

Clients cannot browse external Web sites: The first possible cause of this problem is a connectivity issue between the proxy server and the external network. Verify connectivity by Pinging the external Web server in question from the proxy server. If you can Ping the server using its IP address but not its DNS name, then you should check your DNS server. The problem could also be caused by incorrect permissions. If you have enabled access control, check to make sure you have assigned the correct permissions for the associated protocols.

Clients cannot browse internal Web sites: The first possible cause is that the internal servers' IP addresses have not been included in the LAT. It could also be because the client browsers are not configured to bypass the proxy server for local servers. You should try to Ping the internal servers from a workstation by computer name to verify that name resolution is taking place.

When using older versions of Netscape Navigator, files requested from FTP sites appear as plain text rather than being downloaded: Older versions of Netscape Navigator may not see the HTTP document-type header and may display the file as text. This can be overcome by holding the shift key down while clicking on the link to download the file.

HTTP Browser Messages

Problems can also be identified by event messages returned to Web Proxy client Web browsers. HTTP browser messages are delivered in the following format: **The Proxy Server has encountered an error.** *Error message.* Some of the more common errors are as follows:

Access is denied. HTTP Error 5. This means that access has been denied to that particular site due to a permissions or security violation.

A connection with the server could not be established. The server requested is not responding.

HTTP error 5 occurred. The client browser connection was refused. Verify that the IUSR_*computername* account has permission to use the protocol.

HTTP error 12 occurred. Check to make sure that the internal address of the proxy server is included in the LAT.

HTTP error 10060 occurred. A time-out occurred while trying to access the site. This could be because the remote server is too busy, the remote server is down, or there is a connection problem between the proxy server and the remote network.

The connection with the server was reset. Either the remote server was shut down or the connection was cleared by the remote server.

The server returned an invalid or unrecognized response. The request may have encountered transmission errors that caused it to be corrupted.

Troubleshooting WinSock Proxy Client Access Problems

WinSock Proxy clients are typically trouble free. However, you may encounter the following problems with client access:

WinSock applications that are proxy server aware, such as RealAudio, do not work when configured to access the proxy server: When the Proxy Server client is installed, redirection of WinSock requests is transparent. No further application configuration is required.

An IPX client Web browser configured to use the Web Proxy service cannot browse Web sites: The Web browser must be configured using the IP address of the proxy server.

Users cannot connect to ISPs after installing WinSock Proxy client: Since the WinSock Proxy client redirects all WinSock traffic, the ISP will not receive that traffic. This will typically happen with users dialing into the network using RAS. This can be resolved by disabling the WinSock Proxy client.

WinSock Proxy clients cannot reach all internal networks: This is caused by new subnets being added into the network that are not updated in the LAT to include those address ranges.

The WinSock Proxy service does not work properly with third party TCP/IP stacks: Proxy Server has not been tested with third party TCP/IP stacks. Using these stacks may cause problems.

Windows for Workgroups clients using IPX cannot access the WinSock Proxy service: Proxy Server only supports 32-bit IPX clients.

Connections to internal servers are slow: Make sure the IP addresses of the local servers are included in the LAT.

Necessary Procedures

For this objective you should know how to use the MSPDIAG.EXE utility. You should also review the use of Event Viewer, covered in the previous objective.

Using MSPDIAG.EXE to Troubleshoot Proxy Server Performance

1. From a Command Prompt, change to the C:\MSP directory.

2. Type **MSPDIAG.EXE** and press Enter.

3. You will see something similar to the following:

    ```
    Security warning: The IP forwarding option is
    enabled on this machine!
    Proxy version 2.0.372.2 detected.
    The client configuration file is configured only for
    TCP/IP. IPX/SPX clients cannot connect because the
    [Servers Ipx Addresses] section in mspclnt.ini is
    missing.
    Could open registry value AutoDialFlags.
    ```

Exam Essentials

Know how to troubleshoot basic Web Proxy service problems.
Review the procedure for using such tools as MSPDIAG.EXE to identify basic configuration problems. Understand what problems are being
indicated by common event messages and how they can be resolved. Be
familiar with common problems encountered with proxy server configurations and how they can be resolved.

Know how to troubleshoot basic WinSock Proxy service problems.
Be familiar with common problems encountered with WinSock Proxy
service configuration problems and how to resolve them. Be familiar with
common event messages generated by WinSock Proxy service errors.

**Know how to troubleshoot basic Web Proxy and WinSock proxy
client access problems.** Review the meanings of common error
messages and understand how to resolve those errors.

Key Terms and Concepts

Basic (Clear text) authentication: This authentication method
transmits clear-text–encoded user credentials across the network.
It is supported by a wide variety of browsers and platforms.

Hypertext Transfer Protocol (HTTP): This is an Internet standard protocol used on the World Wide Web.

Internet Control Message Protocol (ICMP): This is part of the
TCP/IP protocol suite that handles control and error messages.

MSPDIAG.EXE: This is a troubleshooting tool provided by Microsoft to search for basic Proxy Server configuration problems.

Ping: This stands for Packet Internet Groper. Ping sends a packet
to a specified destination and requests a response.

Proxy array: Multiple proxy servers configured to work together
provide load balancing, fault tolerance, and distributed caching.

Windows NT Challenge/Response authentication: This authentication method does not transmit user credentials across the network, using instead a series of complex calculations on both the client and server to authenticate the user. It is available only to Internet Explorer clients using Windows.

Sample Questions

1. While troubleshooting a proxy server problem, you find the following event message: **Incorrect network configuration. None of the server's addresses are internal.** What causes this?

   A. You are using IPX as an internal protocol and you have TCP/IP enabled on the proxy server's internal interface.

   B. The IP addresses assigned to the proxy server's internal interfaces are not included in the LAT.

   C. You have manually configured packet filtering incorrectly.

   D. The IP addresses assigned to the proxy server's external interfaces are not included in the LAT.

   Answer: B. At least one address assigned to an internal interface must be included in the LAT.

2. You administer a corporate network that uses Proxy Server to regulate Internet access. You use IPX as your internal network protocol. Windows for Workgroups clients cannot access the Internet. What must you do to resolve this problem?

   A. Install the WinSock Proxy client application.

   B. Start a WinSock application at logon to supply user credentials.

   C. Manually edit the MSPCLNT.INI file to include the proxy server's IPX address.

   D. Upgrade the Windows for Workgroups clients to a 32-bit operating system, such as Windows 95 or Windows NT.

   Answer: D. Proxy server does not support using IPX with 16-bit operating systems.

3. You administer a corporate network. Users complain that, while they can access external Web sites, they cannot access internal Web sites. Which of the following is a possible cause of this?

    A. The addresses of the internal Web servers are not included in the LAT.

    B. Client browsers are not configured to bypass the proxy server for local servers.

    C. Protocol permissions are not configured correctly.

    D. Packet filtering permissions are not configured correctly.

Answer: A and B. C and D are wrong because these permissions apply to traffic to and from the external network.

Resolve Proxy Server client computer problems.

P roxy Server client computer problems are typically caused by improper configuration settings. Microsoft provides tools to trouble-shoot client problems, along with pop-up error messages and events that are reported to the Windows NT System Event log. These events can be viewed using the Event Viewer. These troubleshooting tools combine to provide comprehensive support for resolution of Proxy Server client computer problems.

Critical Information

To aid in troubleshooting WinSock Proxy client problems, a diagnostic utility is provided with the client installation. For 32-bit systems, the file is called CHKWSP32.EXE. For 16-bit systems, the file is called CHKWSP16.EXE. These files are located in the MSPCLNT directory. This utility will check for connectivity with the proxy server. A successful connection will result in the following response:

```
*********************************************************
****     Winsock Proxy Diagnostic Information     ****
*********************************************************


WAIT...
WAIT...


------------------------------------------------


Client control protocol version MATCHES the server
control protocol
```

If a message is returned stating that the client is not installed properly, check the following:

- Make sure configuration information is not missing in the SYSTEM .INI file under the [Microsoft Proxy Service] section, Configuration Location key.

- Make sure there is only one copy of the WINSOCK.DLL file and that it is the one installed by the client Setup program and not the one originally supplied with the operating system.

Common Proxy Server Client Problems

The following is a list of common problems encountered with Proxy Server clients:

Changes made to the MSPLAT.TXT file on the client computer are lost.   The MSPLAT.TXT file is refreshed periodically from the proxy server. If you need to make additions to the file and have them affect only that client computer, you should create a file called LOCALLAT.TXT and include the necessary information there.

You receive the following event message: The WinSock Proxy service has denied client authentication.   This means that either the username being used is invalid or that the account's password has expired.

You receive the following event message: The WinSock Proxy service client authentication has failed. This means that the client authentication has ended on the client side. This occurs with services or applications that use a local system account and run as WinSock Proxy client applications. This can be resolved by creating a section in the WSPCFG.INI file. Enable the ForceCredentials entry and use CREDTOOL.EXE to create alternative user authentication credentials.

A prompt to "Enter Domain Credentials" appears when new WinSock applications are launched on Windows for Workgroups Clients. Domain credentials must be supplied whenever a WinSock application is first launched. If at least one WinSock application remains running, subsequent applications launched will not require those credentials to be supplied again.

Configuration files are not refreshed or connections to the server fail. This can happen when the MSPCLNT share on the server is not available to clients. It can also happen with IPX clients when TCP/IP is installed on the client computer but is not enabled on the internal interface of the proxy server computer. This can be resolved by removing TCP/IP from the client computer or by forcing the use of IPX. Forcing the use of IPX can be accomplished by removing the [Servers Ip Addresses] section from the MSPCLNT.INI file.

Client computers using NetBEUI cannot connect to the proxy server. Proxy Server does not support the NetBEUI protocol. Only TCP/IP or IPX/SPX are supported.

IPX clients cannot communicate with the proxy server. This can happen if the [Server Ipx Address] section is not configured in the MSPCLNT.INI file. It happens if the frame type the proxy server is using does not match the frame type on the client computer.

After creating a WSPCFG.INI file for a specific application on a client computer, other applications in the same directory do not work. You should either create a unique section in the WSPCFG .INI file for each application or move the other applications to a different directory.

Necessary Procedures

For this objective you should know how to use the CHKWSP16.EXE diagnostic utility for 16-bit operating systems and CHKWSP32.EXE for 32-bit operating systems to check WinSock Proxy client configuration.

Using CHKWSP16.EXE or CHKWSP32.EXE

1. From a Command Prompt, change to the MSPCLNT directory.

2. Type either **CHKWSP16** or **CHKWSP32** and press Enter.

Exam Essentials

Know common client problems and how they can be resolved. The basic configuration of WinSock Proxy clients can be checked using either the CHKWSP16.EXE or CHKWSP32.EXE utilities. The Event Viewer and configuration settings can be used to troubleshoot more difficult problems.

Key Terms and Concepts

CHKWSP16: This is a utility used to troubleshoot 16-bit WinSock Proxy clients.

CHKWSP32: This is a utility used to troubleshoot 32-bit WinSock Proxy clients.

Sample Questions

1. You administer a proxy server network. Windows for Workgroups users complain that each time they load a WinSock application, they must enter domain credentials. What is causing this?

   A. Protocol permissions are set incorrectly.

   B. A WinSock application is not running continuously.

C. The WinSock Proxy service does not support 16-bit clients.

D. The WSPCFG.INI file needs to be modified to force the use of alternate user credentials.

Answer: B. The first time a WinSock application is loaded, domain credentials must be supplied. Subsequent applications launched will not require that the domain credentials be entered again as long as at least one WinSock application remains running.

2. You administer a corporate network. You install Proxy Server on your network, which uses only NetBEUI as its internal protocol. You find that none of your client computers are able to access the proxy server. How can this problem be resolved?

A. You must configure a WINS server so that client computers can resolve the computer name of the proxy server.

B. Proxy Server does not support using the NetBEUI protocol. Use either TCP/IP or IPX/SPX on the client computers.

C. You must configure the LMHOSTS file so that the client computers can resolve the computer name of the proxy server.

D. You must install a DHCP relay agent on the client computer network.

Answer: B. Proxy Server only supports TCP/IP or IPX/SPX.

▶ Resolve security problems.

Proxy Server does a relatively good job of making security administration very easy. However, there are a few issues that can arise. Security problems are not generally caused by hardware problems or corrupted configurations. Rather, they are caused by incorrectly set Proxy Server configuration parameters.

Critical Information

The following is a list of common security issues encountered with Proxy Server:

A domain filter has been configured for a particular site, but users can still access it: If IP forwarding is enabled, this can be accomplished by configuring the Web browser not to use the proxy server and by configuring the default gateway to be the IP address of the internal interface of the proxy server. Disabling IP forwarding will prevent this. Running the MSPDIAG.EXE program will inform you if IP forwarding is enabled.

External users can bypass proxy server security and access internal resources: This can happen if external addresses are included in the LAT since security features, such as packet filtering, will not be applied.

External users have access to NetBIOS naming information on the internal network: This can be resolved either by enabling packet filtering or by unbinding the WINS client from the external interface of the proxy server.

Disabling client refreshing of configuration information: In some situations, security conditions may necessitate that client refreshing not take place. This can be accomplished by editing Configuration Refresh Time in the Common section of the MSPCLNT.INI file to read as follows:

```
[Common]
Configuration Refresh Time (Hours)=1000000000
```

Necessary Procedures

For this objective you need to know how to disable IP forwarding, to unbind the WINS client from the external interface of the proxy server, and to enable either static packet filtering using predefined or custom filters or dynamic packet filtering.

Disabling IP Forwarding

1. Start Network in Control Panel.

2. Select the Protocols tab and then select Properties for TCP/IP Protocol.

3. Select the Routing tab.

4. Clear the Enable IP Forwarding checkbox and click OK.

5. Click Close.

6. Restart the server.

Unbinding the WINS Client from the External Network Adapter

1. Start Network in Control Panel.

2. Click on the Bindings tab.

3. From the Show Bindings For pull-down menu, select Adapters.

4. Click on the plus sign next to the external adapter.

5. Highlight the WINS client and click on Disable.

6. Click OK.

Enabling Dynamic Packet Filtering

1. Start the Internet Service Manager and select Properties for any of the three proxy services.

2. In the Shared Services section, click on Security. Ensure that Enable Packet Filtering on External Interface is checked.

3. Click on the checkbox labeled Enable Dynamic Packet Filtering Of Microsoft Proxy Server Packets.

4. Click OK.

5. Click OK or Apply.

Using Predefined Packet Filters

1. Start the Internet Service Manager and select Properties for any of the three proxy services.

2. In the Shared Services section, click on Security. You will see the following screen:

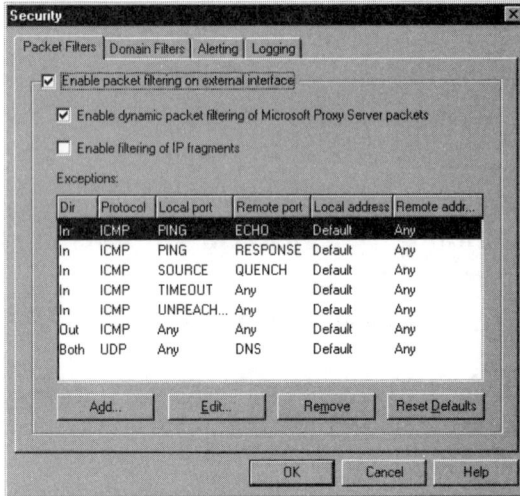

3. Ensure that "Enable Packet Filtering on External Interface" is checked.

4. Click Add.

5. Select Predefined filter.

6. From the pull-down menu, choose the protocol you wish to add to the packet-filtering list. Some of the filters are already in place by default. Choose one that is not, such as Identd.

7. Select local and remote port options.

8. Click OK.

Defining Custom Packet Filters

1. Start the Internet Service Manager and select Properties for any of the three proxy services.

2. In the Shared Services section, click on Security. Ensure that "Enable Packet Filtering on External Interface" is checked.

3. Click Add. You will see the following screen:

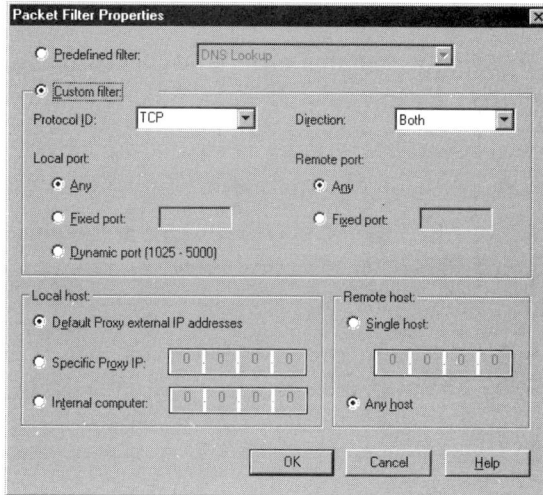

4. Select Custom Filter. Then select a protocol from the Protocol ID pull-down menu.

5. Using the Direction pull-down menu, define the direction from which you wish to apply the filter: Both, In, or Out.

6. Define the local port: Any, Fixed, or Dynamic.

7. Define the remote port: Any or Fixed.

8. Define the local host: the default external adapter, a specific proxy server IP address, or an internal computer.

9. Define the remote host: a Single Host or Any Host.

10. Click OK twice.

Exam Essentials

Know how to troubleshoot basic security problems with Proxy Server. Understand the implications of enabling IP forwarding, of configuring the LAT incorrectly, and of having WINS client services bound to the external interface of the proxy server.

Key Terms and Concepts

Dynamic packet filtering: When this is enabled, the proxy server opens and closes TCP/IP ports as needed for transmission.

NetBIOS: Network Basic Input/Output System (NetBIOS) is an API used by applications on a local area network.

Packet filtering: This is the process of allowing or denying packets based on protocol, local or remote port, direction, and source or destination address.

Static packet filtering: TCP/IP ports are manually enabled or disabled by the administrator.

Sample Questions

1. You have implemented a domain filter for denying access to a particular site. While examining proxy server log files, you discover that some users on your network have been able to access that site. Which of the following is a possible cause of this?

   A. Packet filtering is disabled.

   B. The WINS client is bound to the external interface of the proxy server.

   C. IP forwarding is enabled on the proxy server.

   D. Web Proxy logging is configured incorrectly.

   Answer: C. When IP forwarding is enabled, clients can configure the Web browser not to use the proxy server, and they can configure the default gateway to be the IP address of the internal interface of the proxy server.

2. You administer a network using Microsoft Proxy Server. You are concerned that external clients may be able to gain access to internal NetBIOS naming information. What should you do to prevent this?

   A. Unbind the WINS client from the internal interface of the proxy server.

B. Create a NetBIOS packet filter.

C. Unbind the WINS client from the external interface of the proxy server.

D. Enable packet filtering.

Answer: C and D. The WINS client should be disabled on the external interface of the proxy server, not on the internal interface. Creating a NetBIOS packet filter would allow NetBIOS packet filters, not deny them. Enabling packet filtering will accomplish this.

Resolve caching problems.

As with Proxy Server security, caching is usually trouble free and automatic. However, there are some problems that can arise. Either a physical disk problem or an incorrect configuration is typically the cause of caching problems. An understanding of the caching process will help you to understand why problems occur and how they can be resolved.

Critical Information

If caching does not occur, you should first verify that there is enough disk space on the partition storing the cache and that the disk drive used for caching is not full. Increasing the disk cache space may solve the problem. There are also a number of Web Proxy service cache event messages in the System Event log, under the source name Web-ProxyCache, which are helpful in troubleshooting caching problems.

WebProxyCache Event Messages

The following is a list of common caching problems that are reported as system events:

111—Web Proxy cache initialization failed due to an incorrect configuration. Please use the administration utility or manually edit the Registry to correct the error and restart the service. This indicates that there is something about the way you have configured caching that is causing a problem. Use Internet Service Manager to stop the WWW service. This will also stop the Web Proxy service. Go to the properties pages for the Web Proxy service and click on the Caching tab. Click Advanced and then click Reset Defaults. If, after restarting the WWW service, initialization still fails, run Setup and reinstall. If initialization still fails, then delete the cache directories and reinstall.

TIP   Remember that you must have at least one NTFS partition, at least 5MB in size, on your computer in order to install Proxy Server with caching.

112—Web Proxy cache corrected a corrupted or old format URL cache by removing all or part of the cache's contents.   This means that there have been cached objects either removed or deleted from the cache. There is no further action required, although if the message recurs you can type **chkdsk /r** at a Command Prompt to locate disk errors.

113—Web Proxy cache failed to initialize the URL cache on disk.   Using Internet Service Manager, stop the WWW service. This will also stop the Web Proxy service. Go to the properties pages for the Web Proxy service and click on the Caching tab. Click Advanced and then click Reset Defaults. If, after restarting the WWW service, initialization still fails, run Setup and reinstall. If initialization still fails, delete the cache directories and reinstall, or type **chkdsk /r** at the Command Prompt to recover readable information.

TIP   The WWW service must be stopped before the Web Proxy cache directories can be deleted.

114—The hard disk used by the Web Proxy server to cache popular URLs is full. Space needs to be freed, or the Web Proxy cache needs to be reconfigured to resume normal operation.   You need to delete cached objects from the hard disk.

Other Caching Problems

The following is a list of common caching problems that are not reported as system events:

Requested Web pages contain data that is out of date: This can be caused by incorrectly set TTL values from the site and can be resolved by creating a cache filter specifying that the site never be cached.

When IP addresses of servers change, Proxy Server uses the old addresses: Proxy Server caches DNS entries. When changes are made in DNS, Proxy Server will not use the new entries until the old entries are flushed. This activity can be monitored using Performance Monitor.

Web Proxy logging does not always record the client IP address: Although this is a concern about logging, it is caused by active caching. Because the active caching process is causing sites to be downloaded in advance, there is not a client IP address associated with that connection.

TIP If the size of caching is decreased, the change takes effect when the Web Proxy service is restarted. If the cache was full before its size was reduced, cache objects are deleted.

Necessary Procedures

Necessary procedures for this objective include configuring cache filters and resetting advanced caching configuration settings to the default settings.

Configuring a Cache Filter

1. Start Internet Service Manager by selecting Start ➤ Programs ➤ Microsoft Proxy Server ➤ Internet Service Manager.

2. Select Properties for the Web Proxy service.

3. Click on the Caching tab.

4. Click on the Advanced button.

5. Click on the Cache Filters button. You will see the screen labeled Cache Filters.

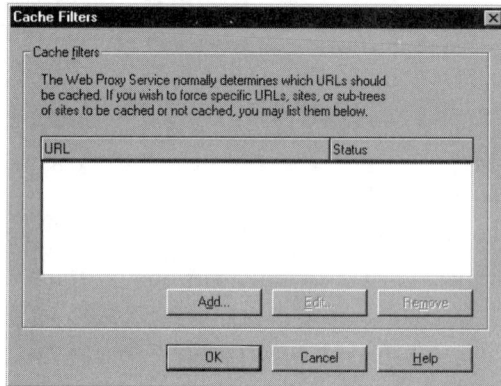

6. Click Add.

7. Type the URL you wish to block. Asterisks may be used as wild cards, e.g., *.adomain.com/ or www.adomain.com/somepath/*.

8. Under Filtering Status, select Always Cache or Never Cache.

9. Click OK twice.

Resetting Cache Configuration to Default Settings

1. Start Internet Service Manager by selecting Start ➤ Programs ➤ Microsoft Proxy Server ➤ Internet Service Manager.

2. Select Properties for the Web Proxy service.

3. Click on the Caching tab.

4. Click on the Advanced button.

5. Click on Reset Defaults.

6. Click on OK or Apply.

Exam Essentials

Know how to troubleshoot basic caching problems.   If problems with caching occur, verify that there is enough space on the partition where the cache is stored. Increase the cache size if necessary. Reset the advanced caching configuration settings if necessary, and then delete the cache and reinstall if necessary.

Key Terms and Concepts

Active caching: This is the process of downloading frequently requested sites in advance during periods of low network utilization.

Cache filtering: This is the process of specifying sites to always be cached or to never be cached.

Sample Questions

1. You administer a corporate network using Proxy Server. While examining your Web Proxy service log files, you discover that many of the requests processed to the Internet do not have client IP addresses associated with them. Which of the following would cause this?

   A. There is a problem with the LAT.

   B. Active caching is enabled.

   C. Active caching is not enabled.

   D. Web Proxy service logging is not configured to log in the verbose format.

   Answer: B. When active caching is enabled, sites that are downloaded in advance will not have a client IP address associated with the connection. The information in the LAT would not affect this. The client IP address is included in the regular logging format.

2. Using Internet Service Manager, you have decreased the size of cache. Which of the following will cause that disk space to immediately be recovered?

A. Restarting the Web Proxy service

B. Restarting the WinSock Proxy service

C. The disk space is recovered as soon as the change is made in Internet Service Manager.

D. Restarting the Caching service

Answer: A. Restarting the Web Proxy service will cause the newly configured size of cache to take effect immediately.

▶ Troubleshoot a WINS server to provide client access to Proxy Servers.

Windows Internet Name Service (WINS) is a name resolution service run on Windows NT Server that maps NetBIOS names to IP addresses. WINS can be used together with DNS and Proxy Server to increase network efficiency.

Critical Information

An understanding of the way name resolution works is essential when trying to resolve problems with WINS. With Windows NT, if a machine is configured to use both DNS and WINS, when a WinSock application initiates the name resolution process, the DNS server is queried first, the WINS server next. Why is this important? Because WINS contains a dynamic database of local machines, so its information is typically correct. DNS, on the other hand, contains a static database that must be manually entered by a network administrator. So what happens if an IP address belonging to a local server is entered incorrectly in DNS but correctly mapped in WINS? The request will go to the incorrectly mapped IP address returned by the DNS server.

When troubleshooting problems with WINS, make sure that you can Ping the server in question using its computer name. If you cannot, it may be necessary to add a static mapping to the WINS database for that server.

Necessary Procedures

There are no necessary procedures associated with this objective.

Exam Essentials

Know how to troubleshoot basic WINS problems.   Ping servers that you are having trouble with, using both the computer name and the DNS name. If necessary, add a static mapping to the WINS database.

Key Terms and Concepts

Domain Naming System (DNS):   This is a name resolution service used to map domain names to IP addresses.

Windows Internet Name Service (WINS):   This is a name resolution service run on Windows NT Server that maps NetBIOS names to IP addresses.

Sample Questions

1. You administer a corporate network using Proxy Server and a WINS server. Users complain that they cannot access an internal server. While troubleshooting, you discover that you can Ping the server by its IP address, but you cannot Ping it by its computer name. What should you do to resolve the problem?

   A. Create a static mapping in DNS.

   B. Create a static mapping in WINS.

   C. Create a static packet filter.

   D. Create a domain filter.

Answer: B. Creating a static mapping in the WINS database should solve the problem. Because you are using a computer name, not a DNS name, creating a DNS entry would not help. Neither a packet filter nor a domain filter would help with this problem.

2. You administer a corporate network using Proxy Server, WINS, and DNS. Users complain that they cannot access a particular server. While troubleshooting, you discover that you can Ping the server by its computer name but you cannot Ping it by its DNS name. Which of the following is a possible cause?

   A. The DNS name is mapped to the wrong address.

   B. A static mapping in the WINS database is entered incorrectly.

   C. The server is down.

   D. The server is on a remote subnet.

Answer: A. Because you can Ping the server by its computer name, you know that there is not a problem with connectivity. You also know that the server is up and that WINS is functioning correctly. If you can't Ping the server by its DNS name, it must be that the IP address is mapped incorrectly.

Troubleshoot hardware-related problems such as network interfaces and disk drives.

While it may seem obvious that hardware failures will adversely affect (or even kill) the performance of your proxy server, it is important to recognize common hardware failures and be able to distinguish them from software-related problems. The two most critical hardware failures for Proxy Server are network card and disk drive failures.

Critical Information

For this objective you need to know how to troubleshoot network card problems and disk problems.

Troubleshooting Network Card Problems

When troubleshooting an unresponsive network card, it is usually worthwhile to try these simple steps first before tearing the card out of the server:

- Check the connections both at the server and at the attachment to the network.

- If you are using Ethernet, check the link status light on both the server and hub.

- Try swapping the cable with a known good cable.

- Try switching the port you are using to attach to the network.

- If you have modified your hardware configuration, check for interrupt or I/O conflicts.

One useful tool in diagnosing hardware problems is the Windows NT Diagnostics utility. Figure 6.1 shows this utility displaying current IRQ configurations.

FIGURE 6.1: Windows NT Diagnostics utility

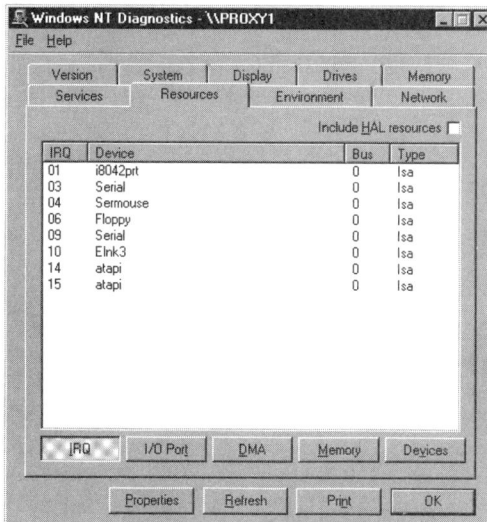

The resources tab in the Windows NT Diagnostics utility will also display I/O, DMA, and memory information.

Should none of the above steps fix the problem, you may be forced to swap out the network card. If you are able to replace the failed card with an identical card, you will be saved the trouble of installing drivers for the new card.

Troubleshooting Disk Problems

In Chapter 5 you were introduced to the Performance Monitor tool. There are several disk indicators you can monitor that indicate that a disk may be in the process of failing. They include:

PhysicalDisk: % Disk Time   This counter reports the percentage of time that the disk is servicing I/O requests. Values in excess of 66% or any sudden, unexplained increase, may indicate that a disk is in the process of failing.

PhysicalDisk: Current Disk Queue Length   This counter indicates the number of I/O requests waiting to be serviced by the disk. Values above two may indicate a problem with the disk itself or the disk controller.

Realize that excessive paging may cause a disk to appear abnormally busy. The following formula can be used to calculate the percentage of time that paging requests are occupying the disk:

```
100 * (Memory:Pages/Sec * PhysicalDisk:Avg Disk Sec/
Transfer)
```

The variables in this formula have the following definitions:

- **Memory:Pages/Sec** is the value of the counter in Performance Monitor that gives the number of pages read from or written to disk.

- **PhysicalDisk:Avg. Disk Sec/Transfer** is the value of the counter in Performance Monitor that gives the time in seconds of the average disk transfer.

Normally, paging activity should not exceed 10%. Excessive paging can be corrected by adding RAM or sometimes by distributing the pagefile across multiple disks.

Necessary Procedures

The only procedure for this objective is running the Windows NT Diagnostics utility to examine system configuration. Using Performance Monitor was covered in Chapter 5.

Using the Windows NT Diagnostics Utility

1. Start the Windows NT Diagnostics utility by selecting Run from the Start menu, typing in **WinMSD**, and pressing Enter.

2. Click on the Resources tab.

3. View IRQ information displayed.

4. Explore the additional dialog boxes for memory, I/O, and DMA information.

5. Explore the additional tabs such as Services, Environment, or Network.

TIP   You can use the print option at the bottom of the Windows NT Diagnostics utility screen either to print or to save to a file any or all configuration information.

Exam Essentials

Know how to troubleshoot basic physical and disk-related problems.   Windows NT provides utilities that are useful when troubleshooting questionable hardware. Windows NT Diagnostics utility and Performance Monitor can both be used to isolate suspected system failures. Review the basic procedures for troubleshooting network connectivity.

Key Terms and Concepts

IRQ: This is the interrupt request used to contact the CPU.

Performance Monitor: This is a tool, provided with Windows NT, that can be used to monitor virtually every aspect of computer performance.

Sample Questions

1. You administer a corporate network using Proxy Server 2 to regulate access to the Internet. Your users report that they are no longer able to access the Internet. Upon investigation, you discover that the Ethernet card on the server does not have link status. Which of the following would be appropriate steps?

   A. Verify that the cable is securely attached to the server and hub.

   B. Swap the cable with one that you know works.

   C. Upgrade your Ethernet card to ArcNet.

   D. Switch ports on the hub.

   Answer: A, B, and D.

2. You administer a proxy server used to cache WWW pages. Lately, your users have reported that the system is slow to respond. You suspect that the disk system may be the problem. Which of the following Performance Monitor counters should you check?

   A. Memory:Pages/Sec

   B. Processor:%ProcessorTime

   C. PhysicalDisk:%DiskTime

   D. Objects:Mutexes

   E. PhysicalDisk:CurrentDiskQueueLength

   Answer: C and E. B and D are not relevant to disk performance. Memory:Pages/Sec can be used to demonstrate a memory problem that affects disk performance but is not useful in isolating a failing disk.

Troubleshoot Internet/intranet routing hardware and software. Software includes Microsoft Routing and Remote Access Service (RRAS).

Microsoft Proxy Server typically does not require routing. However, there are special situations where you may encounter both Microsoft Proxy Server and Microsoft Routing and Remote Access Service (RRAS) running on the same server.

Critical Information

Perhaps the most common problem has to do with the actual installation of RRAS and Proxy Server on the same computer. After installing RRAS, you must apply the RRAS hot fix, available from Microsoft's Web site. Proxy Server will not function properly until this is done.

There are a number of documented bugs in the RRAS interface. Most of these are addressed in the RRAS hot fix. One common complaint is that the graphical interface does not always update to reflect configuration changes. Quitting and restarting the Routing and RAS Admin utility usually corrects these discrepancies.

Necessary Procedures

There are no necessary procedures associated with this objective.

Exam Essentials

Know basic RRAS installation and administration troubleshooting. After installing RRAS on a server running Proxy Server, you must install the RRAS hot fix to ensure proper functionality.

Key Terms and Concepts

Routing and Remote Access Service (RRAS): This service enables a Windows NT server to act as a router.

RRAS hot fix: This is a patch used to fix problems with the current version of RRAS.

Sample Questions

1. You install RRAS on a server that already has Proxy Server running on it. When you reboot, an error message informs you that Proxy Server cannot load. Which of the following will correct this problem?

   A. Reinstall Proxy Server 2.

   B. Reinstall Windows NT Server.

   C. Install the RRAS hot fix.

   D. Enable IP forwarding.

   Answer: C. Without RRAS hot fix, RRAS and Proxy Server are incompatible.

Index

Note to the Reader: Throughout this index *italics* page numbers refer to figures; **boldfaced** pages refer to primary discussion of the topic.

MCSE ELECTIVE STUDY GUIDES FROM NETWORK PRESS®

Sybex's Network Press expands the definitive study guide series for MCSE candidates.

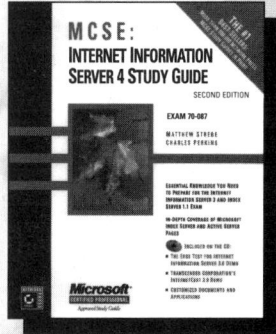

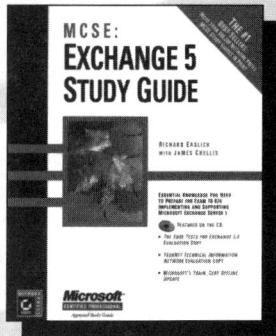

Microsoft® Certified
Professional
Approved Study Guide

NETWORK PRESS® SYBEX

STUDY GUIDES FOR THE MICROSOFT CERTIFIED SYSTEMS ENGINEER EXAMS